2017 Chicago Architecture Biennial Participants

0   51N4E
    6a architects
A   Ábalos + Sentkiewicz
        and Armin Linke
    Adamo-Faiden
    addenda architects
        with Joachim Brohm
        and Moritz Küng
    AGENdA - agencia de
        arquitectura
    Aires Mateus
    An Te Liu
    Andrew Kovacs
    Angela Deuber Architect
    Ania Jaworska
    Aranda\Lasch and
        Terrol Dew Johnson
    Archi-Union Architects
    architecten de vylder
        vinck taillieu
    Architecture of the VII Day
    Atelier Manferdini
    AWP office for territorial
        reconfiguration
B   Bak Gordon Arquitectos
    Barbas Lopes Arquitectos
    Barkow Leibinger
    Barozzi Veiga
    Baukuh and Stefano Graziani
    Besler & Sons LLC
    BLESS
    Brandlhuber+ and
        Christopher Roth
    BUREAU SPECTACULAR
C   Cameron Wu
    Caruso St John with Thomas
        Demand and Hélène Binet
    Charlap Hyman & Herrero
    Charles Waldheim with Office
        for Urbanization Harvard
        Graduate School of Design
        and Siena Scarff Design
    Christ & Gantenbein
    Christian Kerez
D   Daniel Everett
    David Schalliol
    Dellekamp Arquitectos
    Design With Company
    Diego Arraigada Arquitectos
    Dogma
    Dominique Perrault
        Architecture
    DRDH Architects
E   Ensamble Studio
    Éric Lapierre Architecture

F   Fake Industries Architec
        Agonisms and Aixoplu
    fala atelier
    Filip Dujardin
    Fiona Connor and Erin B
    First Office
    formlessfinder
    Fosbury Architecture
    Francois Perrin
    Frida Escobedo
G   Gerard & Kelly
    Go Hasegawa
H   HHF Architects
I   IIT College of Architecture +
        SANAA
    Iñigo Manglano-Ovalle
J   J. MAYER H. und Partner,
        Architekten and
        Philip Ursprung
    James Welling
    Jesús Vassallo
    Jorge Otero-Pailos
    June14 Meyer-Grohbrügge
        & Chermayeff
    junya ishigami+associates
K   Karamuk * Kuo Architects
    Katharina Gaenssler
    Keith Krumwiede
    Kéré Architecture
    Khoury Levit Fong
    Kuehn Malvezzi
L   LAN with Franck Boutté
        and project produced
        by Pavilion de l'Arsenal
    l'AUC as l'AUC
    Luca Galofaro
    Luisa Lambri
    Lütjens Padmanabhan
        Architekten
M   Machine Project
    Made in
    MAIO
    MALL
    Marianne Mueller
    Marshall Brown
    Matilde Cassani
    MG&Co.
    Michelle Chang
    Monadnock
    MOS
N   Norman Kelley
    Nuno Brandão Costa with
        André Cepeda
O   OFFICE Kersten Geers
        David Van Severen with
        Peter Wächtler and
        Michaël Van den Abeele
P   Pascal Flammer
    Paul Andersen and Paul Preissner

    Giovanna Silva
    Point Supreme
    PRODUCTORA
R   REAL Foundation
    Robert Somol
S   SADAR+VUGA
    Sam Jacob Studio
    SAMI-arquitectos and
        Paulo Catrica
    Sauter von Moos
    Scott Fortino
    Sergison Bates
    Serie Architects
    SHINGO MASUDA +
        KATSUHISA OTSUBO
        Architects
    SO-IL and Ana Prvački
    Stan Allen Architect
    Studio Anne Holtrop
    Studio Gang
    Studio Mumbai
    Sylvia Lavin with Erin Besler
        and Norman Kelley
T   T+E+A+M
    Tatiana Bilbao Estudio
    Tham & Videgård Arkitekter
    The Empire with Ilaria Forti,
        Joseph Swerdlin,
        and Barbara Modolo
    The Living
    The LADG
    Theaster Gates
    Thomas Baecker Bettina
        Kraus
    Tigerman McCurry
        Architects
    Toshiko Mori Architect
U   UrbanLab
    Urbanus
V   Veronika Kellndorfer
W   WELCOMEPROJECTS
    WORKac
Z   Zago Architecture
    ZAO/standardarchitecture

Edited by
Mark Lee
Sharon Johnston
Sarah Hearne
Letizia Garzoli

Published by
Lars Müller Publishers

Make New History
2017 Chicago Architecture Biennial

Edited by Mark Lee, Sharon Johnston, Sarah Hearne, Letizia Garzoli
Published by Lars Müller Publishers

2017 Chicago
Architecture Biennial
Make New History

Board of Directors
Jack Guthman, Chairman
Ambassador Louis Susman,
    Director Emeritus
Michelle T. Boone
Robert Clark
Valerie Corr Hanserd
Sarah Herda
Robin Loewenberg Tebbe
Lynn Lockwood Murphy
Kelly Semrau
Mark P. Sexton, FAIA LEED AP
RaMona Westbrook,
    AIA LEED AP

International Advisory Committee
Sir David Adjaye OBE, London
Wiel Arets, Chicago
Elizabeth Diller, New York
Jeanne Gang, FAIA, Chicago
Frank O. Gehry, FAIA, Los Angeles
Sylvia Lavin, Los Angeles
Hans-Ulrich Obrist, London
Lord (Peter) Palumbo, London
Zoë Ryan, Chicago
Stanley Tigerman, FAIA, Chicago
Joseph Grima, Genova
Martino Stierli, New York

Artistic Directors
Sharon Johnston and Mark Lee,
    Johnston Marklee &
    Associates

Associate Curators
Letizia Garzoli
Sarah Hearne

Publications Team

Project Manager
Stephanie Emerson

Copy Editor
Eli Pulsinelli
Christie Hayden

Biennial Staff and Team

Executive Director
Todd Palmer

Director of Marketing
Jan Kostner

Manager of Production
Rachel Kaplan

*Special Events and
    Engagement Manager*
Ashley Galloway

*Public Programs and
    Partnerships Coordinator*
Gibran Villalobos

Content Coordinator
Ryan Hageman

Project Coordinator
Devon Morris

Graphic Design and Art Direction
Zak Group

Digital Strategy
Consortia

Public Relations
Sutton PR
FleishmanHillard

Presenting Sponsor
SC Johnson

Founding Sponsor
BP

Principal Sponsors
Alphawood Foundation Chicago
The Chicago Community Trust
Clayco, The Art and Science
    of Design
Zell Family Foundation
MacArthur Foundation
Marriott

Contributing Sponsors
Shahid Khan
Richard H. Driehaus Foundation
Mansueto Foundation
Edlis-Neeson Foundation
Magellan Development Group
The American Institute of
    Architects
Comcast NBCUniversal

Signature Sponsors
National Endowment for the Arts
Robert R. McCormick Foundation
Samuel M. and Ann S. Mencoff
    Foundation
Taft, Stettinius & Hollister LLP
Thorton Tomasetti

Supporting Sponsors
Graham Foundation
AT&T
The Field Foundation of Illinois
Liz and Eric Lefkosky
Allstate

Investors
Golub CIM
Kenny Construction Co.
Onni Group
Tribune Tower West (Chicago)
    Owner, LLC

Friends
Kenny Construction
Powers and Sons Construction

Media Sponsors
ArchDaily
The Architect's Newspaper
Architectural Record
Architizer
Archinect
artnet News
Bustler
Cultured Magazine
Dezeen
designboom
Metropolis

Presenting Partner
City of Chicago, Department
    of Cultural Affairs and
    Special Events

Signature Education Partner
Chicago Architecture Foundation

Program Partners
6018North
Adaptive Operations
AIA Chicago
AIA National
AIA Practice Management
    Knowledge Community
AIGA Chicago
Archeworks
Architecture & Design Society
Arquitectos Inc
Art Institute of Chicago
Arts + Public Life
Arts Club of Chicago
Aspect/Ratio Gallery

Association of Architecture
    Organizations
Benjamin Marshall Society
Beverly Willis Architecture
    Foundation
California College of the Arts
Canadian Centre for Architecture
Chicago Architectural Club
Chicago Architecture Foundation
Chicago Cultural Alliance
Chicago Design Museum
Chicago History Museum
Chicago Ideas Week
Chicago Loop Alliance
Chicago Park District—Culture,
    Arts & Nature
Chicago Public Library
Chicago Public Library,
    Chinatown Branch
Chicago Women in Architecture
City of Chicago, DCASE,
    Year of Public Art
City of Chicago, Department
    of Cultural Affairs and Special
    Events
City of Chicago, Department
    of Planning and Development
Columbia Books on Architecture
    and the City
Columbia GSAPP (Graduate
    School of Architecture,
    Planning and Preservation)
Defibrillator Gallery
DePaul Art Museum
DePaul University Department
    of History of Art
    and Architecture
Design Evanston
DOCOMOMO_Chicago
DuSable Museum of African
    American History
Edgar Miller Legacy
Experimental Sound Studio
EXPO Chicago
Frank Lloyd Wright Foundation
Frank Lloyd Wright Trust
Friends of Historic Second Church
Gallery 400 at University
    of Illinois at Chicago
Garfield Park Conservatory
Glessner House Museum
Goethe-Institut
Graham Foundation for
    Advanced Studies in Fine Arts
Harvard Graduate
    School of Design
Hong Kong Design Center
Hyde Park Art Center
Illinois Humanities Council
Illinois Institute of Technology
Institute for Public Architecture
Lampo
Landmarks Illinois
Logan Center Exhibitions
Mana Contemporary
Mary and Leigh Block Museum
    of Art
MAS Context
Metropolitan Planning Council
Mies van der Rohe Society
Monique Meloche Gallery
Museum of Contemporary Art
    Chicago
National Museum of Mexican Art
National Museum of Puerto Rican
    Arts and Culture
National Public Housing Museum
Navy Pier, Inc.
Neubauer Collegium for Culture
    and Society
Northwestern University
    Department of Art History
Palais de Tokyo
Pleasant Home Foundation
Preservation Chicago
Rebuild Foundation
The Renaissance Society

Rhona Hoffman Gallery
Rootwork Gallery
Royal Institute of British
    Architects US Region
SC Johnson
Frank Lloyd Wright School
    of Architecture at Taliesin
School of the Art Institute
    of Chicago
Sixty Inches from Center
Smart Museum of Art
Society of Architectural
    Historians
The Cliff Dwellers
The Farnsworth House in Plano,
    Illinois
The National Trust for Historic
    Preservation Annual
    Conference, *PastForward*
The Obama Foundation
The Richard H. Driehaus
    Foundation
The Ruth Page Center for the
    Arts
Unity Temple Restoration
    Foundation
The University of Chicago
University of Illinois Chicago
    School of Architecture
University of Wisconsin-
    Milwaukee School of
    Architecture and Urban
    Planning (SARUP)
Van Alen Institute
Volume Gallery
Workshop 4200

Chicago Architecture Biennial
is a 501(c)(3) non-profit organization dedicated to creating an
international forum on architecture and urbanism through the
production of exhibitions and
public programs. The Chicago
Architectural Biennial seeks
to convene the world's leading
practitioners, theorists, and
commentators in the field
of architecture and urbanism to
explore, debate, and demonstrate
the significance of architecture
to contemporary society.

The inaugural 2015 Biennial
was a manifestation of Mayor
Rahm Emanuel's vision for a major
international architectural event
and an outcome of the comprehensive cultural plan developed
by Chicago's Department
of Cultural Affairs and Special
Events, under the leadership
of Michelle T. Boone. Entitled *The
State of the Art of Architecture*,
it was curated by Joseph Grima
and Sarah Herda, co-artistic
directors. Biennial sponsors and
partners listed as of 7/26/17.

Contents

Dear Friends,

As mayor, and on behalf of the City of Chicago, I am pleased to present the second edition of the Chicago Architecture Biennial—the largest survey of contemporary architecture in North America.

The Chicago Architecture Biennial is a key component of my commitment to further elevate Chicago as a global hub for arts, culture, and innovation. In the first edition, the international conversation about the state of architecture was brought to neighborhoods around the city through a variety of events and programming. In fact, the success of the 2015 Chicago Architecture Biennial exceeded our expectations, with more than 500,000 visitors from around the world. We expect 2017 to be even better.

Chicago's rich architectural legacy is a vital part of the character of our city, but it is also a foundation of architectural history around the world. We are home to the first skyscraper, pioneers of the industry, and innovative practices of the future. It is only fitting that Make New History is the theme of the 2017 Chicago Architecture Biennial. More than one hundred architects, designers and artists from around the globe have contributed their ideas, projects, and installations to demonstrate how the past has informed the future of architecture in Chicago's diverse neighborhoods and communities. New in 2017, the Chicago Architecture Biennial is drawing on the diversity and robust history of our neighborhoods to extend into more of the city. This is an opportunity for people around the world to experience the future of architecture and envision together how to live, build, and thrive in the twenty-first century. It is an opportunity to engage the next generation of architects, designers, and thinkers who will shape our future; this year we will be working with students across Chicago to introduce our youth to the illuminating world of architecture and design.

This catalogue offers a sample of all works represented at the 2017 Chicago Architecture Biennial. It is a window into the world of modern architecture, design, and what's on the horizon. I would like to extend a sincere thank you to the architects, photographers, and writers for your many contributions to this book, and to invite visitors of the Chicago Architecture Biennial to explore the pages within.

Sincerely,
Rahm Emanuel
Mayor of Chicago

Welcome to the 2017 Chicago Architecture Biennial.

We invite you to explore our exhibits and participate in our programs—all are intended to provoke thought, discussion, and debate about architecture and the built environment. In this iteration of the biennial, we urge you to reflect on how the past informs the future, hence our theme: Make New History.

Our guides, metaphorically speaking, are Sharon Johnston and Mark Lee, the talented 2017 Artistic Directors who have assembled a galaxy of architects from around the world to challenge you. Principals in the Los Angeles-based firm Johnston Marklee & Associates, they are exceedingly well suited to this task: respected practitioners and frequent contributors in academic settings and at professional gatherings.

Even as the biennial is the product of its capable artistic leadership and the quality of those from around the globe whose works give it substance, this endeavor would not be possible without a strong civic will. There would be no Chicago Architecture Biennial without the vision, commitment, and support of Mayor Rahm Emanuel. His leadership and the skilled guidance of the then-Commissioner of Cultural Affairs and Special Events Michelle T. Boone were the foundation of the first biennial in 2015. They continue to be our most ardent champions.

The biennial has diverse audiences. Of course, it must be recognized by the international architecture community as a critical platform for discourse about the profession. But its home is in Chicago, and Chicagoans must embrace it. To that end, we have expanded the biennial to include community-based museums which will feature architecture exhibitions within the context of their own mission and program during the run of the show at the Chicago Cultural Center. Additional biennial programming can be seen at the Chinatown branch of the Chicago Public Library, the Garfield Park Conservatory, and Navy Pier.

We thank those who are collaborating with us at these nine locales for facilitating our expansion into Chicago's neighborhoods. The Chicago Cultural Center continues to be our primary venue and the focal point of the biennial. We extend our special gratitude to Commissioner Mark Kelly and his dedicated staff for their skillful and wide-ranging assistance.

Many others are also owed thanks. My personal gratitude goes to the initial members of the 2017 Chicago Architecture Biennial Board of Directors: Robert Clark, Valerie Corr Hanserd, Sarah Herda, Lynn Lockwood Murphy, Kelly M. Semrau, director emeritus Ambassador Louis B. Susman, and to Executive Director Todd Palmer. They have been steadfast in their dedication to this effort.

The Chicago Architecture Biennial's alignment with EXPO CHICAGO, and the many contributions of its president and director, Tony Karman, has broadened the reach of both institutions and provided great synergy. Similarly, the Chicago Architecture Foundation has been invaluable in developing an extensive education program for Chicago students within the context of the exhibition.

The Biennial would not have become a reality without the financial support of numerous individuals, foundations, and businesses. Presenting sponsor SC Johnson and founding sponsor BP have led the way. A list of all those whose commitments have been received as of the date of this catalog going to press are found elsewhere in these pages.

Finally, our thanks to you, our visitors—enjoy the show!

Jack Guthman
Chairman
Chicago Architecture Biennial

Sharon Johnston and Mark Lee have begun a vital conversation that has been deepened by the esteemed authors contributing to this volume, and made visible to the public through the Chicago Architecture Biennial's remarkable participants in art and architecture. The Chicago Architecture Biennial's second edition theme, Make New History, resounds as a declaration and reminder: making an impact on the built environment is deeply connected to learning from what has come before.

The exchange of ideas around this sensitive notion of architectural impact, and related to that, of a biennial legacy, has only just begun. How will these illustrated pages reveal the way design visionaries have inherited legacies of building on the planet to inform collective thinking about future progress? How many young citizens' eyes will be opened by the surprising collection of reimagined skyscrapers in *Vertical City*? What communities will one day benefit from the structures they imagine?

Key to connecting such questions to Chicago and the world are the biennial staff and our extensive creative team's diligent efforts to organize the *Make New History* exhibition and connect it with more than 100 partners, including community anchors and special projects. Through allied talks, performances, workshops, exhibitions, and, most critically, by means of outreach to thousands of young people taking field trips, weekend studios, and curriculum in partnership with the Chicago Architecture Foundation, the biennial is prompting more than half a million minds to consider a rich mosaic of back stories belonging to an inclusive and diverse range of places and creative practices.

Together, these works comprise the biennial, and point to what is—for me as the Executive Director—a most promising legacy for our ambition to be a recurring platform for innovation in the built environment. It's about making space and time for the world to come together with, and in, Chicago—to define a common future designed and built around what we can learn from one another.

Todd Palmer
Executive Director
Chicago Architecture Biennial

This Year's History

Collectors, we know, have "tactical instincts" in their encounters with culture; in other words, they meticulously calculate their own takeaway from a grander set of objects, ideas, or experiences that have been historically established. In a nod to the contemporary nature of reference as a form of collecting and to the circulation of ideas that mark our creative moment, Johnston Marklee borrowed the title of Ed Ruscha's *Make New History* as their own for the 2017 Chicago Architecture Biennial.[2] Ruscha's book, a fixture in the office collection, is a thick volume deceptively filled with 600 empty white pages. This void of content is an invitation, but it is also an invocation of critiques on originality that suggest every blank page to be invisibly regulated and influenced by what has come before.

The biennial started from a similar premise— to examine the paradoxical resource and restriction that the horizon of historical material presents us with. The visibility of these types of collecting and referencing practices—shared by many contemporaries of Johnston Marklee—has seemingly increased as new platforms emerge around architecture and its discourse. Such emergence is a reminder that an important aspect of the so-called return to history is a question of access and format; how architects collect and reference publications, lectures, interviews, and exhibitions; and of the constellations of sites that are set up to record and distribute architectural ideas.

Make New History poses a seemingly simple mission—to understand the channels through which history moves and is shaped in architecture today. Over 100 participants were invited to consider how they saw their work in relation to notions of history and how that deliberation might be an indicator of the current state of the field. The diversity of responses, considered together, revealed some telling interests and tendencies. As with any collecting activity, one sorts through and searches for patterns and likenesses that suggest latent thematic groupings and foci. In this case, these commonalities were building histories, material histories, image histories, and civic histories. These topics became like thematic anchors and guided curatorial conversations. It makes sense, then, that they also anchor this book. You'll find these four concepts interspersed throughout the pages of this volume. They should be read as a guide by means of curatorial observation and, also, as a further application of tactical instinct.

Our curatorial conversations have been richly informed by our invited interlocutors: Giovanna Borasi, Edward Eigen, Sarah Herda, Robert Somol, Martino Stierli, Jesús Vassallo, and Sarah Whiting. Their writing, as a collection, informs and shapes the thematic preoccupations of the participants and demonstrates the vital work of making new history that occurs in the production of historical essays, texts, and conversations. Much like Ed Ruscha's invitation to the blank page, this book—interspersed with an unexpected combination of images and a myriad of voices—reflects a contemporary commentary that invites you to navigate the material in ways that recombine, sample, and generate new meanings.

Sarah Hearne
May 2017

1   Walter Benjamin, "Unpacking My Library," in *Illuminations*, ed. Hannah Arendt
     (New York: Schocken Books, 1969): 59.
2   Ed Ruscha, *Make New History* (Los Angeles: The Museum of Contemporary Art, 2009).

From the First Biennial to the Second and Back Again

In 2017, Sarah Herda, co-artistic director of the inaugural 2015 Chicago Architecture Biennial, and current directors Sharon Johnston and Mark Lee met in New York and reflected on both shows and the biennial format.

Sarah   Why history?

Sharon   Although there have been episodes of unprecedented architecture, in which architects were reluctant to consider their work as being part of the continuum of architectural history, we feel that the act of looking to the past to inform the present has always been central to architecture. The biennial presents the chance to consider anew the role history plays in the field today and to try to rethink this collective project of architecture.

Sarah   Are you suggesting history as a reactionary stance?

Mark   Using the term "history" is not meant to invoke the burden of modernism's discarded past or symbolize a reactionary response to progress. To state the problem differently, you might say that today's endless information is transforming our access and attention to things of the past. We started to think about how we might consider this "eternal present" and through the biennial reveal the means by which historical knowledge and materials are shaping and being shaped by architects.

Recently, we've seen a renewal of interest in historical precedents among a generation of architects perhaps less encumbered by the past 30 years. This interest has often been described as a return to Postmodernism. When we first presented our theme, the typical reaction we received was along those lines.

Sharon   Postmodernism represents one of the more visible recent episodes of this interest in historical precedent, perhaps because it was tied to exhibition culture. We anticipate that issues pertaining to communication that predominated during this period of the 1970s, from the study of signage and kitsch to the disciplinary conversations of classical elements, could be a part of the dialogue from some of the participants in the biennial. But the abundance and accessibility of images and information today has flattened the former distinctions between "high" and "low" culture that Postmodernism sought to undermine. And as individual images are less charged and perhaps less significant than in the past, architectural history may become less hierarchical and much more free within the cultural landscape.

Sarah   Yes, I'm increasingly thinking about history as an active set of ideas that are available to us. That's how I see history being used, but maybe not literally. There's a return to different points in history, not solely to one period, like a return to the classical signs in architecture.

I was speaking with a supporter of architecture who was only interested in historical or classical architecture. I responded, "Well, we've just supported a project by contemporary architects working on Bramante." That willingness, I think, upsets the idea that returning to history is just a surface move or that Postmodernism wasn't architecture. It upsets the notion of the relationship between the contemporary and the historical.

Sharon   And the relationship between architects and historians, perhaps?

Sarah   I think that between history and where we find ourselves in practice today is a very complex continuum of ideas. You can't have one without the other. You have what you're taught, your first introduction to history, and then you have the history you assemble yourself, as you go. As you become more autonomous in building your practice and identity, you also go back to or find different things. They can be active, present ideas. This may be especially important in a time when everything is so superficial, fast, flickering ... ahistorical.

Mark   That is exactly why we think history is more important and relevant than ever. Perhaps unlike historicism, where things are subsumed under a grand historical narrative structure, we see history as a horizon, open and accessible, with multiple entry and exit points. We also don't see history as being autonomous but rather as being actively engaged in current design practices, where the old and the new are in a cyclical relationship, or where the old becomes new when viewed through contemporary knowledge. For us, the model is close to the way Adolf Loos embraces progress—within a cultural and historical tradition.

Sarah   If you think about architecture criticism and journalism today, it's so much more about the image, as opposed to the ideas, context, and criticism of the projects. I think an exhibition is a way of bringing that dialogue back into architecture culture. When Joseph [Grima] and I were organizing the inaugural biennial, he quoted, I think it was James Stirling, saying that events are the new magazines. The conversations are being explored in a different format and happening in a different sphere, not in the remote circulation of ideas but rather within the actual space between you, the object, and the person next to you; the convening, therefore, is as important as the work.

Sharon   When we began thinking about this project, we considered how our program could move forward with the important conversations begun in the 2015 program. That inspired us to think not only about how we might engage the architectural legacy of the city of Chicago —as a crucial part of the history of modernism—but also how we might contribute to the future legacy of the city, both in terms of the intellectual discourse and the physical artifacts and interventions that would be created by the participants in the main hub of the exhibition, the Chicago Cultural Center [CCC], for continued use.

Mark   The aura of Chicago is exciting for us and many of the participants. I imagine it was essential that you were "from" Chicago to initiate the first biennial, together with Joseph, who was a bit more of an outsider. Our connection to the city has grown through our collaboration with the MCA [Museum of Contemporary Art] and with Theaster Gates and his Arts + Public Life program [at the University of Chicago]. We have come to understand a bit about how much Chicagoans value the architectural legacy of their city. It is always exciting to recognize how the old is always new when we see it through knowledge and fresh perspectives. We look forward to imagining how future curators who are less familiar with the city will take on this role and uncover different histories.

Sarah   Even I am a transplant. I only know the city to a certain extent.

Mark   When you invited Lacaton & Vassal to the biennial in 2015, they said, "Chicago is so important to us because we are modern." They hadn't even been to Chicago before, but Chicago is part of the canon. It doesn't matter where in the world you are, if you are studying or have studied architecture, you know the history of Chicago and its impact on modern architecture. Quite a number of architects that we invited will be coming to Chicago for the first time for this biennial.

Sharon   When Mayor Emanuel recently spoke about the biennial, he reminded us that Chicago is right in the middle of America, and there is a certain strength in that. Given our current political landscape, it seems very important to bring an open, international exchange to the center of the United States.

Sharon	Part of what excited us about this project, among all the projects we are engaged in, was how we can shape this year's biennial as a platform for exchange among architects and artists and eventually with the audiences who will experience the work. With so many long-established biennial programs around the world, we wanted to differentiate our project by bringing together architects to create environments for visitors to experience where the works build off one another and specifically engage the nuances of the Chicago Cultural Center. We strongly believe in supporting new voices and building opportunities as part of the exhibition program. Equally important to us is how we can bring new perspectives to historic material across a long and continuous historical arc.
Sarah	Often people talk about architecture exhibitions as if the thing is missing. That assumes that architecture is a building, not a set of ideas.
Mark	Yes, architecture is a building, it's a set of ideas, and it's a process. With this being our first curatorial endeavor at this scale, we also treat it as an architectural project, in the sense of the first biennial being part of the context we worked with. It's like a chess game. You and Joseph did something, and we did something to reinforce it. We hope that we have set up a precedent for the next artistic directors to build upon. We always envision that the Chicago Architecture Biennial is not just one biennial but rather four or five biennials that describe a decade, that come to describe an epoch. We're very excited to see how our move will trigger the next move, and then what happens in the coming years.
Sarah	Stanley Tigerman described it to me something like this: "I was in the Navy, and those aircraft carriers just catapult you out into the air. That's what the biennial should do." It really is like a two-way opportunity. It's bringing the best of the world to Chicago and the best of Chicago to the world, and they meet in the middle.
Mark	As architects, it is inevitable that we think of the exhibition design of the biennial as an architectural project. We see the exhibition design as a mediation between the long lifespan of the building and the much shorter lifespan of the exhibition. In a sense, the permanent and the ephemeral are treated as equals, they just have different modes of temporality. We have thus commissioned architects to design interventions into the Chicago Cultural Center, with the hope that some of these installations could stay after the biennial is over and affect the daily use of the center.
Sharon	This approach, which begins with the layout of the Chicago Cultural Center building, demands a design response, rather than

a purely curatorial, content-based response. We are architects, and we approach the making of the show from this perspective.

Perhaps here is a good place to talk about the in-between-ness of the experience; it's not simply works on the walls but also a collection of new environments in conversation with CCC, its users, and the multiple publics of the building.

Mark   Part of our approach to engaging with the specific context of the cultural center was to analyze the building in order to try to make the experience of moving through the exhibition clearer for visitors and perhaps draw out more specific kinds of projects from each participant. We envisioned a new taxonomy of spaces—a collection of rooms—that for us had inherent ideas about how work might be curated and displayed in each. The rooms included the archetypal spaces of the labyrinth—a collection of galleries on the first floor; the salons, which occupy a series of rooms on the second floor, including the Chicago Galleries; the arcades, which transform the north-south corridors on the west side of the building; the lounges, which will occupy not only the generous and readily accessible public spaces, like Randolph Square, but also some more unexpected pockets and landings through the building; and the collective projects, which will occupy the great halls.

Sharon   One of the first times we walked through the building, when we started talking about 2017, I was looking at Atelier Bow-Wow's play-ful insertion of ladders and ramps in the courtyard of the building, which remains on site today. I recall thinking, what do we do about that? With fragile tilting ladders, suspended bridges, and stairs to nowhere, the installation has such an intelligent and humorous way of engaging this courtyard, which was almost invisible as a space before this enigmatic piece was installed. It seemed like absolutely the right thing to do to have that project remain and invite somebody else to participate in that space and see it through a new lens. Obvi-ously, this approach of adding and transforming layers is embedded in the historical narratives of our theme. When we met with Mark Kelly and Michelle Boone, the current and previous cultural commis-sioners, we found that they were both open to how the building could evolve. Given the messy interweaving of exhibition and display spaces with functioning city offices, it's not a generic exhibition hall that's going to be filled up with stuff then be emptied out again in three months. It's a working building. Commissioner Kelly prompted us to think about other spaces, like the arcades, that could be more positive spatial environments for exhibitions and different city events that could remain after the run of the biennial. I think that deepens the mandate of the biennial and strengthens its connec-tions with the city. We feel there is a productive tension between the everydayness of the building and its life as a site for exhibition. It is a space for ideas and for experiences for multiple audiences.

Mark   It's kind of funny; when we asked participants to intervene with works that have remained since 2015, often they were initially deferential. Perhaps they were thinking, "Those are my friends; I don't want to step on their toes." In the case of Bow-Wow, Yoshiharu [Tsukamoto] and Momoyo [Kaijima] really loved the idea, but when Anne Holtrop first inherited their site, he was hiding in a corner a bit as he sorted out how to occupy the space with Bow-Wow.

Sarah   I think Commissioner Boone also understood the importance of rethinking the building. When we first started talking about the biennial, I recall there was carpet on almost every hard surface in the building. We embarked on a process of peeling back the layers that had accumulated in the name of function, like the covering of all the floors throughout. For example, whenever a trench was cut for plumbing, they hid it with carpet. The carpet has taken on a life of its own at this point. Commissioner Boone really encouraged us and gave us freedom. The rest of the staff at the cultural center, the custodians and stewards of the building, were really willing to move beyond the designated gallery spaces and take on the difficult circulation brought about by using a building for a purpose that it wasn't designed for.

Sharon   I was just going to say that this notion of in-between-ness in the cultural center and the utilization of these provisional, seemingly unglamorous spaces have prompted a lot of the stronger aspects of the different projects that have been developed for the site. Our task has been to take the participants' ideas and feed them through the particular programmatic challenges that the spaces pose.

Mark   You talked earlier about how reaching a larger public is important. The impression I got from the first biennial was that, even after the first two weeks of opening events, it was always filled with people, often the general public and school groups. I think there's something to say about that compared to other biennials where, after all the opening events, you go back and it's you, one other person, and a few cats.

Sharon   How do you reach out to a generally informed audience? This condition of accessibility is one of the things in the first biennial that we wanted to continue. There are many levels of entering the biennial. Those who are generally interested can grasp the architecture exhibition in a very straightforward way, based on an understanding about housing and houses from everyday life. Those who have deeper knowledge can get more. I think having this layered approach is our response to maintaining accessibility. It's not about oversimplifying, but rather having multiple layers to reach a broad audience. I think that's something that the Chicago biennial could continue to build upon.

Sarah   There's often an approach to architecture exhibitions that is an over simplifying or dumbing down of the ideas. It really misses the mark on understanding the public's relationship to architecture. It's not even a matter of the public necessarily being informed about architecture and design. It's just being in the world and experiencing the kinds of issues that emerge in the spaces that you live in, work in, and use in various other ways, and being able to read and understand the social and power dynamics at play in the designed environment.

Sharon   I think this is a very relevant point about cultural spaces today, in particular museums. We are working on several museum projects, including renovations to the MCA Chicago. So much of our conversation with the museum has been about breaking down the barriers between the institution and a public's experience with art and artists. I think what is powerful about the biennial taking place at the cultural center is that it is already a community building. Our emphasis on creating site-specific installations, like those in Randolph Square entry, is to let people slip into the exhibition, maybe without initially being aware they are within an installation, thereby eliminating the perception of boundaries between the gallery, the public life of the building, and the city. This challenge is something that a lot of cultural institutions are thinking about, through educational programs and different kinds of spaces that aren't galleries or auditoriums.

Mark   What you said about Stanley Tigerman is resonating with me. I'm thinking today that information is so much more accessible than it was in 1980. There are more biennials; there are more exhibitions. What would be an ideal role for the biennial to play today? When you talk about reaching multiple audiences, I feel it's so important to go beyond a certain architectural community, to avoid marginal- izing architecture as this insider, naval-gazing culture.

Sharon   The idea of fostering relationships for architects is really powerful. The first time that we participated in a collective project was probably in 2008, when Herzog & de Meuron and Ai Wei Wei bought together a group of international architects for the Ordos 100 housing project in China. For us, that experience sparked relationships and friendships that produced not only great adventures but also projects and collaborations. We are interested in the idea of exhibitions within the exhibition, for example our *Vertical City* project this year, where we asked 16 architects to revisit the Chicago Tribune Tower Competition brief. We were thinking about Paolo Portoghesi's Strada Novissima brief for the 1980 Venice Biennale (which was the first iteration of the Biennale to have a section dedicated to architecture), and how we might set each design team to work with a similar set of questions and reflect on one another's responses to the challenge. It creates another level of exchange around a shared and focused idea. At the same time, the works will be experienced as a powerful spatial encounter, and perhaps the public can begin to discern common questions and diverging interests based on the framework of the design problem.

When you think about it, architecture's own entry to the domain of the art biennials was really only 40 years ago. That inaugural exhibition, titled *The Presence of the Past*, was also about history in architecture! Even there you saw the expanding repertoire of theatrical devices and scenographic modes of display. The biennial format sits at the core of architecture's cultural project: a forum to reach and produce new audiences.

Mark   I'm very curious how you and Joseph began the process of inviting participants.

Sarah   I think it was reflective of the ways in which we both work, institutionally. We had the shared background of Storefront for Art and Architecture, which was, under both of our tenures there, really focused on single projects that together presented a diverse set of positions in the field. The Storefront is where I learned to embrace risk and the willingness to go there, to support what someone's trying to do. I came to see myself almost more as a producer. My approach to curation is not that I want to make a definitive statement and I'm going to select people who will demonstrate my opinion.

Sharon   That's a really important distinction. As I understand it, your primary goal is to bring projects to life and put them in dialogue within a show or amongst shows. There is a level of generosity and risk in this approach versus a more top-down narrative that a more traditional curatorial approach might assume.

Sarah   At the Graham Foundation, we have open submissions for the grants, but it's not about producing an ideological project. It's about producing or being willing to accept the diversity of work happening in the field that shapes the field, even if things are going in different directions or hitting each other head on. It's that willingness to invest in an idea and see what happens. We really tried to do that with the biennial. It produced consternation at times, but I'm totally fine with that.

Sharon   How do you approach these ideas over time, as a collection?

Sarah   The ideas we exhibit don't only exist in the moment they were created. Ideas have a life in the field that is very much present tense and waiting to be activated. We approached the Graham archive or network of ideas as a pool of potentiality, with ideas that could be activated at any moment. We tried to put them in dialogue with something new we might do today but that relates to a project that sat in a drawer unopened for 40 years. Now the idea finally may have its time in the light.

Mark   I really like how you described your curatorial approach. For us, it has a lot of parallels to the architectural process and the way in which we never have a purely deductive or inductive approach. As we began our selection process, we looked deeper and deeper at the field of our colleagues. We cut and edited, cut and edited, then the theme began to emerge. We also looked at the 2015 biennial and began to form groups or collections. For us, the title, *Make New History*, questions and solidifies a certain group of contemporary architects, but it also questions the demand of the project of the new.

Melancholia — Write New Theory
Philip Ursprung

I write of melancholy by being busy
to avoid melancholy.

— Robert Burton, *The Anatomy of
Melancholy* (1621)

For architectural history and theory, the biennial's
imperative "make new history" is a challenge. It
resonates with a growing interest by architects in
historical references of the nineteenth and twentieth centuries and earlier. This trend promises to
bring practice and theory closer again, and to be
an encouragement to write new theory. But how
can I embrace making new history without being
misunderstood as being nostalgic for a modernist
idolatry of progress or affirmative toward the planners and politicians who have confiscated the
notion of the new in our own time? At first sight, the
affinity toward history might imply that architectural
theory is recovering. However, I believe that we are
in an *a-theoretical* phase that goes hand in hand
with an increasing segregation and specialization
among the academic disciplines of architectural
design, architectural discourse, and architectural
history. The more specialized and self-absorbed
these disciplines become, the less their voices are
heard. If, from the late nineteenth century to the
1980s, architectural theory formed a horizon for the
entire field of architecture, a plethora of statements
by architects, the historicization of theories of the
past, and references to other disciplines such as
anthropology, sociology, and political philosophy
have since replaced it. Today, architecture theory
is evoked merely as a phantom that haunts us and
cannot find rest.

In the following pages, I will outline some
thoughts about a possible new theory. They emerge
from a seminar week that Alex Lehnerer and I
conducted in March 2017 with our students under
the title of Melancholia.[1] We traveled in a dark
grey double decker-bus from Zurich to Colmar,
Strasbourg, the Ardennes, Lille, Dunkirk, the Rhine
Delta, and Rotterdam. We wanted to find out if the
concept of *melancholia* could help us to address
the situation of the European Union, which, after
an optimistic phase of building up a peaceful aggregation of countries, is currently facing its possible
disintegration in the aftermath of Brexit. What
happens, we asked, when a political, economic,
and cultural project that has shaped the prospects
of hundreds of millions of people is on the verge of

1   The seminar Melancholia: Licht und Schattenbilder from Inner Europe
    took place March 20–24, 2017, with a group of 50 students and staff
    from the Department of Architecture of ETH Zurich, as well as some
    guests. I am grateful for Alex Lehnerer for our conversations over the
    past couple of semesters and to Tim Klauser, Sabine Sarwa, Berit
    Seidel, Emily Scott, Nina Zschocke, Li Tavor, and Samia Henni for
    their collaboration in conceiving and realizing the seminar.

dissolving? At the same time, we wanted to use the notion of melancholy to describe our attitude toward the architecture that was built in France, Belgium, and the Netherlands between the late 1980s and the early millennium. What happens when architecture that was synonymous with *contemporary*—Herzog & de Meuron, Zaha Hadid, Office of Metropolitan Architecture (OMA), MVRDV, and others—becomes the architecture of the recent past?

Melancholy is originally a medical term used in antiquity to describe one of the four temperaments. (The other three are sanguine, choleric, and phlegmatic.) Its broad spectrum of meaning includes the conditions of sadness, introversion, aimless passivity, and pause. Its lesser known attributes include the contrasting symptoms of passion, excitement, and humor. In fact, the polarity between extreme passivity and extreme activity is characteristic of melancholy, which is a condition that is never moderate but rather always beyond the norm—extraordinary. Since the Renaissance, melancholy has been considered a precondition for artistic creativity. As the art historians Rudolf and Margot Wittkower summarize in their classic book *Born under Saturn*, "Only the melancholic temperament was capable of…creative enthusiasm."[2] During the long hours on the bus, I explored the most comprehensive account of melancholy ever written: Robert Burton's *Anatomy of Melancholy*, first published in 1621. Burton offers an encyclopedic description of melancholy's innumerous definitions, causes, and symptoms, ranging from medicine to literature, history and the arts. Much more than a medical treaty, this book is a diagnosis of the human condition and a lens to better understand the author's own era. Although Burton rarely addresses the visual arts, he is known to art historians due to his inclusion of Albrecht Dürer's *Melancholia I* (1514). In the engraving, melancholy is depicted "like a sad woman leaning on her arm with fixed looks, neglected habit, &c., held therefore by some proud, soft, sottish, or half-mad…and yet of a deep reach, excellent apprehension, judicious, wise, and witty."[3] (fig. 1)

If it is accurate that the absent architectural theory is haunting us like a phantom, then the notion of melancholy adequately describes this status, not only because it implies silence and inertia, but also because, as Burton lets us know, the melancholic subject often feels haunted by ghosts. According to Burton, "These kinds of devils many times appear to men, and affright them out of their wits, sometimes walking at noonday,

sometimes at nights."[4] Can we consider figures such as Aldo Rossi, Rayner Banham, Manfredo Tafuri, and Adolf Loos as ghosts from a past where architecture theory appeared to form a solid ground? And can *melancholy* as a concept be made fruitful in writing new theory? Is it manifold enough to be more than a label and become a "miniature theory," in the sense of the Dutch art historian Mieke Bal, who, in her book *Travelling Concepts: A Rough Guide to the Humanities* writes:

Concepts are the tools of intersubjectivity: they facilitate discussion on the basis of a common language. Mostly, they are considered abstract representations of an object. But, like all representations, they are neither simple nor adequate in themselves. They distort, unfix, and inflect the object. To say something *is* an image, metaphor, story or what have you—that is, to use concepts to label something—is not a very useful act. Nor can the language of equation—"is"—hide the interpretive choices being made. In fact, concepts are, or rather do, much more. If well thought through, they offer miniature theories, and in that guise, help in the analysis of objects, situations, states and other theories.[5]

We made a stop at the European Parliament in Strasbourg, the very epicenter of political power in the European Union. I knew the cylinder-shaped building, with its shiny metal-skin and the rows of colorful flags in the foreground, as a backdrop of innumerable television interviews; I was somewhat surprised to see it in three-dimensional space. The Union Jack was flying merrily among the other flags, as if nothing had changed. The Japanese cherry trees were blooming. The state of alert was on "yellow" and the security guards were relaxed. A guide led our group to the Louise Weiss Building, designed by the Paris office Architecture-Studio and opened in 1999. Once inside the tower, the iconography of the building became evident. We were in a pastiche of the Coliseum—a paved oval courtyard surrounded by endless rows of office windows. (fig. 2) Inevitably, the vast space recalled the "lost center" that the late Diogo Seixas Lopes describes in his book *Melancholy and Architecture: On Aldo Rossi*.[6] The guide pointed to the open terraces that symbolize, as she put it, the "unfinished" state of the European Union and offer space for further nations to join (or for nations to leave, I thought). The guide reported that 26 languages were spoken in the Parliament and that the combination of languages translated into other languages was 650. I realized that the building not only

2   Rudolf and Margot Wittkower, *Born under Saturn: The Character and Conduct of Artists, a Documented History from Antiquity to the French Revolution* (New York: W. W. Norton, 1969), 103.
3   Democritus Junior (Robert Burton), *The Anatomy of Melancholy* (1621), Project Gutenberg, e-book no. 10800 (2004), 928.
4   Burton, 473.
5   See Mieke Bal, *Travelling Concepts in the Humanities: A Rough Guide* (Toronto: University of Toronto Press, 2002), 22.
6   Diogo Seixas Lopes, *Melancholy and Architecture: On Aldo Rossi* (Zurich: Park Books, 2015), 59–69.

resembled the coliseum, but also Pieter Bruegel the Elder's painting, *The Tower of Babel* (1563), which brings Burton to mind again: "The tower of Babel never yielded such confusion of tongues as the chaos of melancholy doth variety of symptoms."[7]

From the outside, the assembly hall takes the shape of a globe. I could not help associating it with Etienne-Louis Boullée's utopian project for a Cenotaph for Isaac Newton (1784), which foresaw a 150-meter-high globe, representing the universe. A handout featured the seating plan of the parliament. The new political faction of "Euro-skeptics" was placed on the far right and marked in brown, like a disease affecting the continent. We were led down endless corridors and up escalators to atriums, and meeting spaces. Plants hanging from the ceiling in an atrium were covered with dust. A toy airplane with the slogan "Fly with Europarl TV" stood in the hall. One of the students took a seat, but the screen that was supposed to show news of the parliament was dead. Besides some technicians repairing an elevator, the place was deserted. The guide explained that we were in a "mint green" week. According to the color code of the European parliament, that meant that the members of parliament are absent. The

7   Burton, 938.

European Union as an institution is frequently considered an apparatus of control, and the current trend of national isolation is seen as a symptom of the fact that many Europeans feel not represented but rather dominated by the EU. Yet its architectural spaces appeared fragile and vulnerable. A melancholic atmosphere prevailed, as if the building itself knew that it might someday be obsolete.

As we departed Strasburg, its disappearing silhouette reminded me how much the temporal horizon—both of the past and the future—had shrunk. The European Union was planned for decades before it was established in 1993. But its future is uncertain; it may last only a few more years. In Michael Hardt and Antonio Negri's book *Empire*, the authors theorize that the idea of progress has been absorbed into the realm of an ever-expanding present.

Empire's rule has no limits. First and foremost, then, the concept of Empire posits a regime that effectively encompasses the spatial totality, or really that rules over the entire "civilized" world. No territorial boundaries limit its reign. Second, the concept of Empire presents itself not as a historical regime originating in conquest, but rather as an order that effectively suspends history and thereby fixes the existing state of affairs for eternity. From the perspective of Empire, this is the way things will always

Fig. 1, Albrecht Dürer, *Melancholia I*, 1514

Fig. 2, European Parliament, Strasbourg, 1999

be and the way they were always meant to be. In other words, Empire presents its rule not as a transitory moment in the movement of history, but as a regime with no temporal boundaries and in this sense outside of history or at the end of history.[8]

The European Union was one of the primary engines driving the movement toward Empire; its demise could challenge the theory of the eternal present.

From the comfort of my reclining leather seat, I saw old factories filtered through the dusty windows of the bus. We were in Lorraine, once a hub of heavy industry in Europe. We had discussed the architectural quality of the parliament building and its eclectic use of historic references, which one of the students characterized as postmodern. The industrial ruins reminded us that the discourse of postmodernity was triggered by precisely the process of deindustrialization that took place in the second half of the twentieth century, particularly after the deregulation of the financial industry and the labor markets in the early 1970s, which accompanied the European unification process. The most influential interpretation of this shift argues that the ensuing recession, skyrocketing oil prices, decreasing salaries, and growing socioeconomic inequality constituted a "break" between the modern and the postmodern periods. Theoreticians such as David Harvey, Jean-François Lyotard, and Fredric Jameson depicted this shift as a crisis, yet they naturalized it as a *cultural* phenomenon. The dualistic model that they proposed—modernism versus postmodernism—fanned the flames of theoretical debate in the 1980s and 1990s. At the same time, it also narrowed the focus by turning historicity into the main criterion of the interpretation of architecture and art.

By using the term *postmodern*, we place ourselves *outside* the phenomena, as if, from the armchair of philosophy, we could overlook them unfolding in time from a distance. In reality, we are not detached; we are still located within the economic shift. We are subject to the ground moving under our feet. Melancholy is appropriate because it defines as situation *within* the phenomenon, as a situation that does not allow for distance. There is no outside in the space of melancholy, and the new theory should not be considered a realm outside reality. I found a fitting passage by Burton, who writes that melancholic states "keep the mind in a perpetual dungeon, and oppress it with continual fears, anxieties, sorrows."[9]

It was raining as we drove through the Ardennes, the heartland of Flanders. This extensive forest area, with rolling hills and meandering rivers, is a region—not a nation—that both divides and unites the French and the German parts of Western Europe with the Lowlands. The Swiss artists' collective U5, which was part of our group, had invited all of us to become part of a collective performance under the title *Europa—No Word Spoken from Now.* As part of the project, we were all obliged to remain silent for the day. Burton describes speechlessness as a key symptom of melancholy: "Melancholy is most part silent."[10] We passed the site where the last battle between the Germans and the Americans in the Second World War took place. Today, only the SMS on my phone announcing different roaming tariffs distinguished whether we were in France, Belgium, or the Netherlands.

Sitting silently in the bus, I had time to ruminate over the challenge of architectural theory. How can one juxtapose, on one level of representation, issues of economy, aesthetics, politics, history, and experience? How can we explain the renewed interest of architects in the historical dimension, in architecture from the nineteenth century, the Renaissance, and the Middle Ages? And how can we relate this interest in history to the current pressure exerted on the coherence of the European Union by growing nationalism and isolation, the move toward dictatorship in Turkey, and the hundreds of thousands of people fleeing the wars in Syria and Afghanistan and seeking asylum in the European Union? Does the architects' the interest in history represent an attempt escape from the challenges of the present? It is a reaction to the tendency toward an eternal present, in the sense of Hardt and Negri's *Empire*? Or is it a sign of increased awareness of historic dynamics? Our travel companion, the Belgian philosopher Lieven De Cauter—who was exempt from the silent performance—read from his essay "Small Anatomy of Political Melancholy," an homage to Burton: "Probably—that's our hypothesis—politics will become more bipolar by the day. The more extreme the situation gets, the more melancholy there will be: moments of hope and inconsolableness seem to succeed one another at an ever faster pace. And more and more they collide."[11]

In Lille, we visited Congrexpo, a huge convention center and exhibition hall for trade fairs and concerts, with restaurants and meeting facilities. Congrexpo opened in 1994 and marked the international breakthrough of architect Rem Koolhaas and his firm OMA. (fig. 3) Part of the ambitious urban redevelopment project EuraLille, Congrexpo exemplifies the enthusiasm of the early 1990s, when a provincial city like Lille could catapult itself to

8   Michael Hardt and Antonio Negri, *Empire* (Cambridge, MA: Harvard University Press, 2000), xiv–xv.
9   Burton, 994.
10   Burton, 345.
11   Lieven De Cauter, "Small Anatomy of Political Melancholy," *Crisis and Critique* 3, no. 2 (2016), 99–100.

prominence on the world map due to its position as a traffic hub between Paris and London. The skyline in the background, which features a row of five towers by Jean Nouvel and Christian de Portzemparc's Crédit Lyonnais Prism, reinforces the impact of the infrastructural sublime. This effect is typical for the early years of the European Union, with its massive investment in infrastructure projects, high-speed train networks, bridges, tunnels, highways, and higher education buildings that span the European continent. Congrexpo features prominently in *S, M, L, XL* (1995), the compendium of OMA's work. The book's description of Congrexpo amounts to an epic praise of infrastructure, and the notion of melancholy does not feature in the alphabetical dictionary that runs through the book. But a melancholic tone is woven into the quantitative description of Congrexpo, which shows that even the most cherished masterpieces of art history have become interchangeable commodities in a world that is ruled by money: "7 van Goghs, 18 de Koonings, or 6 Jackson Pollocks would buy Congrexpo. But for the price of its 1200 parking spaces in downtown Tokyo, 40 more Congrexpos could be built in Lille."[12]

On the building's façade, rustic cladding contrasts with an undulating plastic membrane and crystal-like glass. As in the European Parliament, the ground plan is oval, and the colossal order mimics antique grandeur. The difference is, of course, that Congrexpo's over-explicit rustic appearance is an ironic pastiche mimicking a Renaissance palace, while the Parliament building is un-ironic. Inside Congrexpo, I was nevertheless struck by the sublime atmosphere of the entrance hall, which recalls the prints of Piranesi and the spaces of Le Corbusier. The dimensions and organization of the pillars reminded one of walking through a forest of giant trees, and it was easy to imagine that the center was a hub, linking the metropolises of Paris and London. Our guide explained that the inside had undergone much change. The client, we were told, had been disappointed with the rawness of the concrete surface, which was unlike a convention center. Much cladding, color, and light had been added in view of generating "a higher revenue," as our guide explained. When we visited, one of the conference rooms had just been transformed and the original seating dismantled. The main hall was still unchanged, but one wonders for how long. The Netherlands Dance Theater in Den Haag (1987), the first building by OMA, was demolished in 2016, an event that went almost unacknowledged by the architecture community.

We reached the channel and visited Lacaton Vassal's FRAC Nord-Pas de Calais in Dunkirk (2015), a regional center for contemporary art located in the old industrial harbor. Instead of packing the dysfunctional wharf with exhibition spaces, the architects kept it as it was and added a second building with the same dimensions. The huge empty wharf, which echoes the Turbine Hall in Herzog & de Meuron's Tate Modern in London (2000), can be used for temporary exhibitions, large scale works of art, or performances, while the collection and the exhibitions occupy the newly constructed adjacent spaces. We were confronted with twin phantoms, so to speak—an echo of an echo. (fig. 4) As we started to walk along the beach, the sun was lighting the glass containers like two crystals that were simultaneously absent and present. It was a monument for the new theory, I thought, and also a monument for melancholy. After an hour, we came to some dilapidated bunkers. We recalled the history of violence that had informed this site, where hundreds of thousands of soldiers had been cornered by the Germans in World War II, then evacuated to the United Kingdom. During the war, both sides—the Allies and the Germans—referred to the notion of "Fortress Europe." Nobody seems to remember this, and the same term is being used today, in regard to the refugees seeking protection in Europe. Paul Virilio foresaw it in his book *Bunker Archeology*, in 1975: "The bunker has become a myth, present and absent at the same time: present as an object of disgust instead of a transparent and open civilian architecture, absent insofar as the essence of the new fortress is elsewhere, underfoot, invisible from here on in."[13]

After passing the Rhine delta and a large part of the country that lies below sea level, we met the artist Lara Almarcegui, in Rotterdam. Since the late 1990s, she has worked with the topics of wasteland, interstitial spaces, and *terrain vague*. Her installations shed light on the complexity of urban transformation and show how connections between economy, history, and biography are made manifest in the terrain. I found particularly striking her small booklets, *Guide to Al Khan*, *Guide to the Wastelands of the Lea Valley*, and *Guide to the Wastelands of the River Tevere*, which conduct readers through forgotten areas comparable to those I have encountered in Athens.[14] Unlike traditional travel guides, these works focus on the periphery, approaching sites

12   OMA, Rem Koolhaas, and Bruce Mau, *S, M, L, XL* (New York: Monacelli Press, 1995), 769.

13   Paul Virilio, *Bunker Archeology* (New York: Princeton Architectural Press, 1994), 46.
14   Lara Almarcegui, *Guide to Al Khan: An Empty Village in the City of Sharjah* (Sharjah Biennial 8: Still Life, Art, Ecology and the Politics of Change, 2007); Laura Almarcegui, *Guide to the Wastelands of the Lea Valley: 12 Empty Spaces Await the 2012 Olympics* (London, Barbican Art Gallery, 2009); Laura Almarcegui, *Guide to the Wastelands of the River Tevere: 12 Empty Spaces Await the 2020 Rome Olympics* (Rome, Fondazione Pastificio Cerere, 2011).

in transition that bear the traces of an industrial past and are subject to new uses in the future. For the Netherlands, she has published a small booklet documenting a collection of ruins and urging readers to see them before they are gone:

These ruins and abandoned buildings have no use, no function. This means that they are open to all kinds of possibilities. In a country like the Netherlands, in which every inch of land seems to be used with the utmost efficiency, the existence of these blank spaces is something to be grateful for. But it is important to remember that although some of these ruins will remain standing for some time, others will be renovated and many of them will be demolished before long. It is important to visit them as soon as possible.[15]

Almarcegui led us through her favorite terrain vague—a site near the river that was formerly used by factories and now awaits a developer to transform it. As we walked about on the grass, young men were walking their dogs, and someone was preparing to fish. Barges passed by, and on the horizon we saw the cranes of the Container Harbor. (fig. 5) A student inquired what Almarcegui would do if she was offered this site for free. The artist

15 Alma Almarcegui, "Ruins in the Netherlands," in Lara Almarcegui, *Ruins in the Netherlands, XIX–XXI* (Rotterdam: Episode Publishers, 2008), n.p.

responded that she would put it under protection and keep it as it is, without any intervention. She asked, in turn, what the students would do if they could use it for a design. "Build!" was their answer.

As we drove toward Schiphol airport and our seminar week approached the end, I reflected on the role of art for today's architecture. Many observers consider art and architecture to be overlapping disciplines. The discussion with Almarcegui had shown me that they are further apart than in earlier periods, such as the time of the avant-gardes in the early twentieth century and in the 1960s. They are institutionally separated and differ in matters of education, practice, wages, and the market. But what Almercegui's art works also make clear is that art has partially taken the role of architecture theory. It functions as a mirror of architectural practice, making visible its limitations and internal contradictions. Art can function as a medium of architectural critique, in other words, as a vantage point from which judgments are made, quality is evaluated, and historical relevance is discussed. The imperative to write new theory requires us to revise our understanding of the current relationship between art and architecture and envision a theory of integration that addresses visual art and architecture alike.

To paraphrase Mieke Bal, melancholy as a concept has traveled a long way from Robert Burton to

Fig. 3, OMA, Congrexpo, Lille, France, 1992

Fig. 4, Lacaton & Vassal, FRAC Nord-Pas de Calais, 2013

Sigmund Freud, Walter Benjamin, Susan Sontag, Alain Ehrenberg, and Lieven De Cauter. In view of the writing of new theory, melancholy must not be mistaken for despair, nostalgia, apathy, nihilism, or depression. Rather, as I see it, melancholy refers to the alternation of action and passivity, performance and stasis. It stands for a theory of the present, one that allows us to change an opinion and revise its judgements, to speculate, follow a path obsessively, and then change direction again. It is characterized by ambiguity and by internal contradictions. "Humorous they are beyond all measure, sometimes profusely laughing, extraordinarily merry, and then again weeping without a cause," Burton writes of melancholics.[16] And melancholy does not aspire to solve everything: "Melancholy advanceth men's conceits, more than any humour whatsoever, improves their meditations more than any strong drink or sack. They are of profound judgment in some things, although in others [they cannot judge adequately]."[17] It cannot be reduced to one meaning. It is about latency and therefore contains the potential of a new beginning.

16   Burton, 930.
17   Burton, 928.

Philip Ursprung is Professor of the History of Art and Architecture and designated Dean of the Department of Architecture at ETH Zurich.

Fig. 5, Lara Almarcegui with students from ETH Zurich, Rotterdam, March 2017

With our participation in *Make New History*, we want to highlight the idea of a dynamic practice that focuses on the production of space and on the organization of the necessary dialogues and processes supporting it. In our installation, symbolic objects that tell stories about two projects of very different scales are laid out in space and coupled with videos by contemporary artists intimately linked to these projects. With this particular setting we wish to reveal the pervasive interplay between history and stories and between forms and narratives of making, to expose the web of unseen interactions and conditions actively shaping the personal and collective experience of built space.

A dynamic interplay is shown in the installation and activated through encounters. We propose to set up our contribution as a platform to link people, to confront positions, and to produce new discourses and ideas—new personal histories.

This installation will thus become an open-ended, productive learning environment and a flexible setting for a collective reflection, allowing invited participants and visitors to generate new knowledge by going through an experience together.

As a whole, our contribution captures architecture as a transformation process that generates a productive friction—through design—in turn enabling new connections through dialogue. As such, it stands for every one of 51N4E's projects. It shows how a project in a changing society requires the creation of specific conditions to allow it to come to fruition, conditions which then outlive the project and become a new ground for further development. This approach draws freely from autonomous architecture as well as participatory design. It can be understood as an alternative and more ambiguous path: one that enables a multitude of alliances, encounters, and new histories to arise.

51N4E, First tests of the spring-fountains on Skanderbeg Square, Tirana, Albania. When the water starts flowing on the unpolished marble stones, it temporarily reveals the mosaic of colors making up the square.

Sorigué Foundation, Planta Project
Ábalos + Sentkiewicz and Armin Linke — Cambridge, USA/Madrid, Spain/Shanghai, China

The Planta Project, a 5000m^2 thermal machine, is located in the gravel pit of the Plana del Corb and was built with materials directly extracted from the quarry nearby, thus tying it back to the original topography. Organized according to Ábalos+ Sentkiewicz's concepts of form, matter, and flux, the building passively manages radiation, natural lighting, and ventilation with advanced thermodynamic concepts. The Planta serves as a museum space for the collection of contemporary art of the Sorigué Foundation, as well as an observatory of the entropic processes of time and human action. These twin functions tie the plastic experience with the productive-ecological one. This synthetic character of the building—uniting museum, observatory, and thermal machine—is performative and material, aiming to connect to the times and cultures of the site. It is built from the resources and iconography present in the local context that collect in the newly forged artifact whose new primitivism invites revision of the ways we value time (or of history, if it is preferred).

Armin Linke, *Planta*, Lleida, Spain, 2012

Ábalos + Sentkiewicz, Sorigué Foundation/Planta Project, 2016

Tropical Canonical: The Order of Ambiguity
AGENdA – agencia de arquitectura
— Medellín, Colombia

Colombia, as with many other tropical countries of the world, is trapped in a narrow definition of its architectural history and a very incomplete idea of its identity. This trap is mainly set between colonial (Iberic) architecture, informal vernacular architecture, modernist legacy, and less visible non-Pre-Columbian architecture heritage as in Mexico or Peru. This situation makes it difficult for a practitioner to engage in architectural history and derive a practice therein. There is space only for a present tense.

AGENdA suggests an alternative approach to history: not as a coherent narrative, but as a systematic adaptation of canons, process, or materials, so far away and distant from the original that, with time, it evolves creating an order of its own. This lineage is referential to the original in an imprecise architectonic way: distorting it so much either in form or by allowing language to be the only witness to the original—the engine of the foundational cause. For instance, the curtain wall—as stated and proved by architecture history and contemporary cities—is the epitome of modern architecture. From England to Germany and from Europe to the US and then to Latin America, its impact and influence still eagerly drive investors, citizens, and politicians by way of its global identity and power. The curtain wall—distorted, modified, and adapted into many other devices, types, or systems— suggests a beautiful contradiction lies in its inverted logic. Allow that transparency, rigidness, weather isolation, and precision are no longer driving the logic of the curtain wall. Let us imagine instead opaqueness, flexibility, porosity, and freedom as the structure's main characteristics once it is used in the tropics and modified due to the climate.

AGENdA Agencia de Arquitectura, *Canonical Tropics*, installation view, LIGA, Mexico City, 2017

In architecture, history is perceived from the present to the past.

Every memory, every influence, every reference reemerges from the work, in each project.

History has no time, no sequence, no place. It is an inexhaustible source of freedom: a field operable in all senses—which turns into our possibilities—expanding, verifying, and legitimizing our proposals.

Aires Mateus, House in Monsaraz, in situ, 2015

Aires Mateus, House in Monsaraz, 2015

Entrance Installation　Ania Jaworska — Chicago, USA

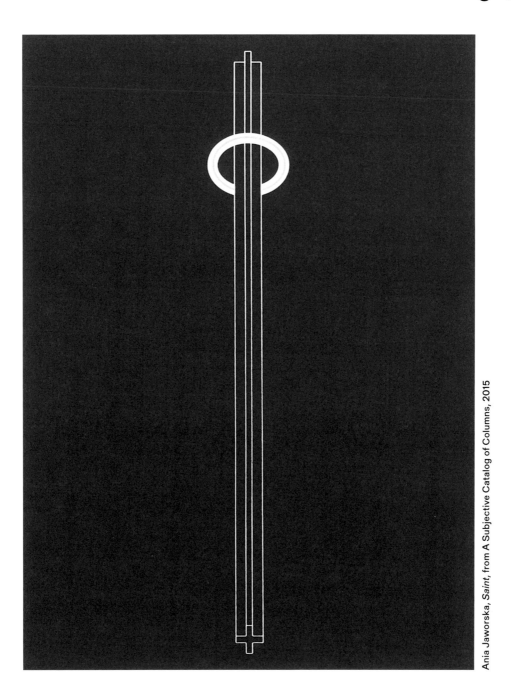

Ania Jaworska, *Saint*, from A Subjective Catalog of Columns, 2015

In her entrance to the Chicago Architecture Biennial, Jaworska uses two familiar iconic forms—the arch and column—to call on architectural history and establish meaning, while simultaneously undermining it. Because of their use, overuse, and reinvention throughout history, these two architectural elements function as both structure and symbol. She uses an arch to highlight and contradict the entrance; though it reads as an entry, it simultaneously creates a physical boundary. Similarly, her use of the column invokes an idea of stability and tradition, while the column itself requires support and provides no structure. Through a process of establishing and questioning architectural classification, Jaworska's installation entertains multiple and contradictory readings. In many ways, it is and is not furniture, a sculpture, or a pavilion. Its color, material, and form contrast its context, command attention, and divide the space. The installation literally contains a history inside, as it actually covers an existing Chicago Cultural Center information desk—hiding it, consuming it, overtaking it—while it remains, at the core, the genesis of the project.

Ania Jaworska, *Wooden Column on Fire (It Was Always Burning)*, from A Subjective Catalog of Columns, 2015

Aranda\Lasch and Terrol Dew Johnson
— New York and Tucson, USA

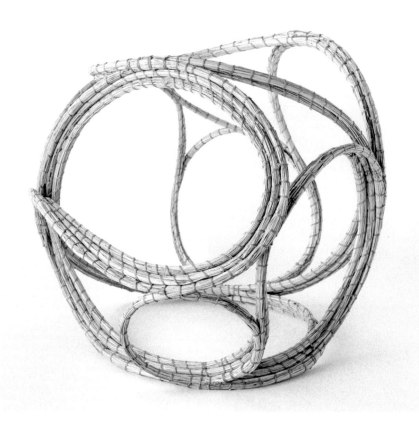

Aranda\Lasch continue a longstanding collaboration with Terrol Dew Johnson, a Native American basket weaver from the Tohono O'odham Nation in Sells, Arizona. Together, they produce work that blends their two practices and explores the role that ritual plays in both traditional Native craft and contemporary design. In traditional O'odham culture, the social, spiritual, and material become entwined through the ritualistic making of everyday objects. In this way, the collective knowledge of the society—its people and environment—is passed from generation to generation through creative experience. The foundational structures of the community are continually revitalized and embedded throughout O'odham material culture. Aranda\Lasch and Johnson seek to understand ritualistic making from a cross-cultural perspective and to illuminate ways in which similar processes are implicitly at work in contemporary design and architecture. At the heart of this project is the realization that, when architecture learns from indigenous craft, one comprehends that conventional divisions between craft and technology and between historical and contemporary technique are actually best understood as a continuum.

ArandaLasch and Terrol Dew Johnson, *Meeting the Clouds Halfway*, installation view, Museum of Contemporary Art, Tucson, Arizona, 2016

Robotic Craftsmanship: Making New History with Traditional Materials — Shanghai, China

Archi-Union Architects

Archi-Union Architects, Gallery of Chi She, Shanghai, China, 2016

From a genetic thread based in regional culture, new design research can continue local lineages of traditional materials while playing an important role in the global understanding of traditional cultures. In the digital age, design methods and robotic fabrication technology present new technical and expressive possibilities for traditional materials. This new path opens the possibility for extension and improvement upon traditional crafts, leading to design innovation, and an upgrade of what is familiar.

Technology, design, and culture form a three-way symbiotic relationship. As technology advances, new possibilities in design emerge and culture at large is influenced. Similarly, when the building blocks of culture shift, design swerves to meet current demands and new technology becomes available. In this way, the digital revolution that has matured over recent decades presents a new direction for critical thinking about traditional materials today. The mechanics of robotic real-time information sensing and feedback, combined with intelligent production methods, provide us with a wealth of new ways to approach future modes of construction using materials which are already at hand.

With a deep sense for the traditions of Chinese wood joinery, ceramics, and masonry, in addition to our long-term research in the field of robotic fabrication, we explore the possibilities for robotic fabrication to reshape how we use and experience traditional materials. Using digital tools to analyze traditional materials, we will wed our new understanding with innovative fabrication techniques to arrive at new design solutions. Used in this way, robotic fabrication not only demonstrates the potential for digital technology to construct new environments, but also assists in extending the historic narratives and craft based knowledge surrounding traditional materials.

Archi-Union Architects, In-Bamboo, Chengdu, China, 2017

Decor and Construction   architecten de vylder vinck taillieu — Ghent, Belgium

Jan De Vylder, photograph of Sol LeWitt at Gewad, 1992

architecten de vylder vinck taillieu continue to examine the relationship of décor and construction, the realms on either side of architecture that are seemingly opposite but always fundamental. The work hinges on two speculations: to propose the column as décor and the idea that one might reveal the nature of the column through a process of wall drawing. An earlier version of this project was first shown at ETH Zurich with the title *Carousel*

and later reproduced at Maniera in Brussels. *Carousel* took existing institutional columns that were sheathed in drywall to meet fire code, and marked on this surface abstract drawings that played perceptual games influenced by the wall drawings of Sol LeWitt. architecten de vylder vinck taillieu's drawings revealed an imagined geometry; looking beyond the surface of the drywall and constructing a view of the I-beam column beneath.

architecten de vylder vinck taillieu, *Ensemble* (detail), MANIERA 05, Brussels, Belgium, 2016

Building Portraits   Atelier Manferdini
— Los Angeles, USA

Building Portraits explores the potential of intricate scripted line work to depict building facades, taking as a point of departure nine iconic pictures of Mies van der Rohe buildings. The collection plays with the graphic potentials of woven colorful grids and scripted vector lines, while exploring the canonical relationships of shape versus form, ground versus figure, pattern versus coloration, and orientation versus posture. The title of the series *Building Portraits* alludes to two distinct disciplines: the field of architectural drawings of buildings and the one of fine art portraits. This body of work tries to claim a territory where these two attitudes find a common ground, where pixels and vectors get closer at the scale of perception. Mies's constructions are renowned examples of how the geometrical ordering system of the grid embodied a political meaning in our discipline. Mies's elevations, like many other modernist works, projected an egalitarian image of the built environment. At a time when the reading of a modern building was supposed to be a byproduct of its constructive technology, the modularity of its

assembly system was asked to reinforce the idea of technical efficiency and social democracy. Following this tradition, Mies's buildings assumed the generic attributes of production: the facade adopted readymade steel members as mullion systems, his elevations revealed the load-bearing structure, and its construction methodologies became their primary expression. On closer look, it is possible to discover that he often corrupted the functionality of his envelopes with ornamental fine grain mullions that had no use other than creating an interesting optical effect. This is the turning point where the *Building Portraits* suite of drawings began. The work is rooted in the belief that contemporary architecture has been able to produce new models of computational geometries: affect driven political forms that can no longer be structured on the traditional values of the grid. The work is not based on an historical interpretive methodology or logical argumentation, but wants to provide a working methodology towards a contemporary aesthetic of computational, directional, and dynamic grids.

Atelier Manferdini, *Portrait 12*, from Postures and Ground—III, 2015

Atelier Manferdini, *Portrait 04*, from Forms and Ground—I to III, 2015

58

Building Histories

Building histories take the as-found building as a locus of design and discursive activity; here the building is a palimpsest for its singular contextual history, as well as a typological artifact in the collective pool of existing realized and unrealized architectures. Projects engaged with this category examine the building in its signifying components, its material relation to time, and its potential for change and reinterpretation.

Reinvigorated interests in the building-as-edifice often appear alongside a return to formal languages of type within architectural classification. Typological problems are necessarily, like language, collectively derived, maintained, and extended. For example, the type of the tower is expanded by Christ & Gantenbein's project for *Vertical City* (p. 228) to include a found object: the Roosevelt Garagem Tower in São Paulo built in 1964 to deal with the increasing need for mass vehicle storage in the city. Designed for cars, the appropriation borrows measure and significance from the heightened rationality of structure and the attendant anonymity of expression as a result. In the same vein of typological inquiry, PRODUCTORA's tower, also in *Vertical City*, emerges out of what seems to be an exhaustive search for slab and profile-driven tower combinations in a series of drawings in everyday, blue office pens on grid paper (p. 240). In both cases, theories of type are built on a foundation of historical precedents in order to extend concepts of what might constitute the particular out of the generic.

To study building typology requires the understanding that forms cross and break historical periodization.[1] Several projects in the biennial reference the temporal categorization of architecture: from perpetual monuments to ancient forms, to ruins real and imagined. Aires Mateus interpret the strange stillness of the stalled building site as a ruin (p. 46). Their hazy filtered films call upon the productive redundancy born out of economic downturn, famously named by Robert Smithson as "ruins in reverse."[2] T + E + A + M similarly examine the ways that ruins—commonly aligned with nineteenth century romanticizing of authentic materiality—were always mediated through technologies of image production (p. 172). Their mise-en-scène model opens up and perpetuates the crisis of time embedded in ruins, and invites new image making from the visitor and their iPhone camera. The concept of the building and its image as an enduring monument is not new; indeed, there are few more persistent fascinations in architecture than those of the building as a marker of time, life, and change.

One of the unifying concepts shared between postwar art and architecture has been the site-specific

1   Colin Rowe's linkage of Palladio and Le Corbusier in "The Mathematics of the Ideal Villa" required the building matter of the drawings to literally disappear into the regulating lines on the page. Rowe's editorial move demonstrated the material facts of the building; their constitution and presence can be read as a marker and vessel of time, and their removal revealed deeper, unencumbered rules.
2   Robert Smithson, "Monuments of Passaic," *Artforum*, December 1967.

engagement of locations, contexts, and communities as it can be examined in a single building.[3] Adds and alts, once considered the sustenance of professional architecture, are being reinvigorated in the context of the exhibition. Close examination of the everyday locations of historical research, like permits, unravel layered narratives—often at scales beyond the building itself. In discussion of their columns for Chicago, Belgian firm architecten de vylder vinck taillieu refer to an office snapshot taken several years ago of a Sol LeWitt wall mural in a building entry in Gewad Gent (p. 54). The enjoyment in the photo is not only the expected appreciation of the LeWitt, but the interruption of the mural by electrical conduits and lighting infrastructure that creep down from the ceiling with utter indifference. Perhaps this move by the electrician destabilizes (like much of de vylder vinck taillieu's own work) the clear distinctions between what is deemed pragmatic and construction driven, and what is seen as the conceptual—and, thereby, rarified—site of autonomous design.

To appreciate these stories of building history is to appreciate the multi-agent layering of aspirations and intent, the planned and the improvised, and the things that occur over time through inhabitation that are embedded in the very materials of the building as site.

3   Sylvia Lavin has shown in her 2013 exhibition, *Everything Loose Will Land*, that many artists who engaged in site-specific work often required permits with drawn plans: an important intersection, she claims, in the procedures of art and architecture in the 1970s. The scale of some of these site-specific interventions was minor in material and rather major in effects. Then and now, this would be considered additions and alterations in architecture, a bureaucratic category that is distinguished by the fact that it occurs on an existing building.

Invisible Modern Architecture AWP office for territorial reconfiguration — Paris, France/London, UK

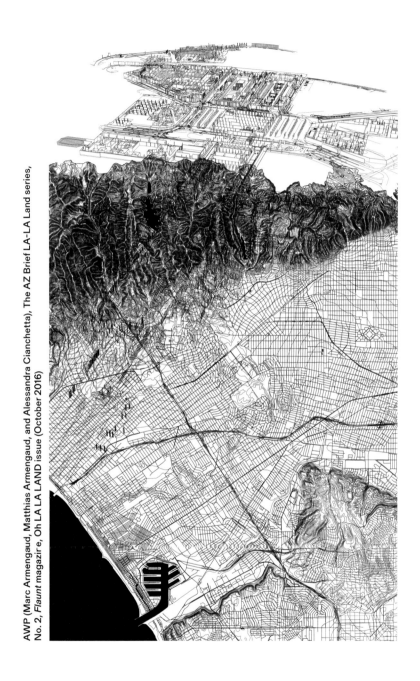

AWP (Marc Armengaud, Matthias Armengaud, and Alessandra Cianchetta), The AZ Brief LA-LA Land series, No. 2, *Flaunt magazine*, Oh LA LA LAND issue (October 2016)

Invisible Modern Architecture aims to examine the legacy and propose a forward-looking reuse of late modernist architecture, slab urbanism, underground infrastructures, and invisible structures. Part of a series, initially developed in collaboration with artist Ania Soliman, the project will continue exploration of post-digital architecture and post-digital institutions to open the field for a communal imaginary. *Invisible Modern Architecture*

takes on the contested topic of an urban thickness: slabs and deck typologies centralize criticism around the abandonment of natural reference in favor of abstract and artificial architecture. AWP confronts a strategic question concerning the underground, within the context of Paris' CBD La Défense: how to appropriate and reuse the thick, multi-layered, and highly infrastructural modern city towards contemporary discourse?

Desenhos de Trabalho (Working Drawings)
Bak Gordon Arquitectos — Lisbon, Portugal

In the realm of building practice, the work of the architect is more and more a collective activity. Given the extension of project teams, the number of external contributors, and the multidisciplinary nature of the process, it is easy to forget the component of intimacy in the daily work life. There is a more private and essential process of reflection and investigation—an intimate relationship—within the work of an architect. It is through sketching that Ricardo Bak Gordon finds this intimate space, which seems to be missing in the contemporary discipline. In sketching, he finds a fertile field for cultivation and for the clarification of the project that is sufficiently expressionist enough to create specific atmospheres. Ricardo Bak Gordon sketches are part of a process. They develop a possibility: always different from the previous designs, always looking for a new hypothesis. These drawings, as Ricardo Carvalho once wrote about them, feel the terrain—the surrounding buildings, the vegetation, the topography, the spaces of daily life, their materials, and colors. They infer any principles useful to the creative process. In each one of them, one can find a theme: an implantation scheme, a distribution plan, an exterior view, an interior perspective, or experimentation in constructive solutions and colors. They are done once and then redone, but never in the same way. They investigate both the encounter with the site and the program, and, later, are redesigned with the constraints of regulations and client desires. They correspond to temporal instances of a dynamic process belonging to many different projects of the studio. In them, one can trace superposition, annotations, and side notes as well as changes, indecisions, and desires. Autonomously exhibited, they live by themselves; they tell a story and they show another constructed world where one can wander around, imagining many possibilities.

Bak Gordon Arquitectos, Escola Secundária da Amora (Amora High School), Amora, Seixal, Portugal, 2009

Bak Gordon Arquitectos, Escritórios (Offices), Lisboa, Portugal, 2017

Housing History: Three Residential Towers
Barkow Leibinger — Berlin, Germany/New York, USA

Barkow Leibinger, *Timber Log Tower model*, 2017

Barkow Leibinger revisit three selected histories from the mid-twentieth century to inform three urgently needed affordable housing towers in Berlin. While the towers are similar in scope and programmatic content, they are differentiated by the selected historical models that inform contrasting outcomes and suggest alternative techniques for driving new architectural solutions. This is not a sentimental mining of history, rather a pragmatic and performative one.

Nancy Holt and Robert Smithson's seminal 1971 film *Thicket* follows Holt's walk through a swamp of tall grasses. The film depicts a labyrinth-like space delineated by a thatch of vertical lines of varying density. The goal became to translate this historical film into an architectural outtake, both physically and experientially, through strands of bundled steel wire that form dematerialized columns and walls supporting a series of stacked floor plates. Heinrich Tessenow's 1936 Festhalle is a timber pavilion resembling a constructed forest. This project is redeployed as an idea for stacked vertical housing defined by offset log columns using a repetitive copy-paste technique whereas each floor layout of column logs is independent of the other. Plattenbau construction of the 1950s to 1980s in Eastern Europe served as a method for affordable and redundant socialist housing. Today, using infra-light concrete, Barkow Leibinger propose sculpturally dynamic, precast forms to offer new ideas about wall making.

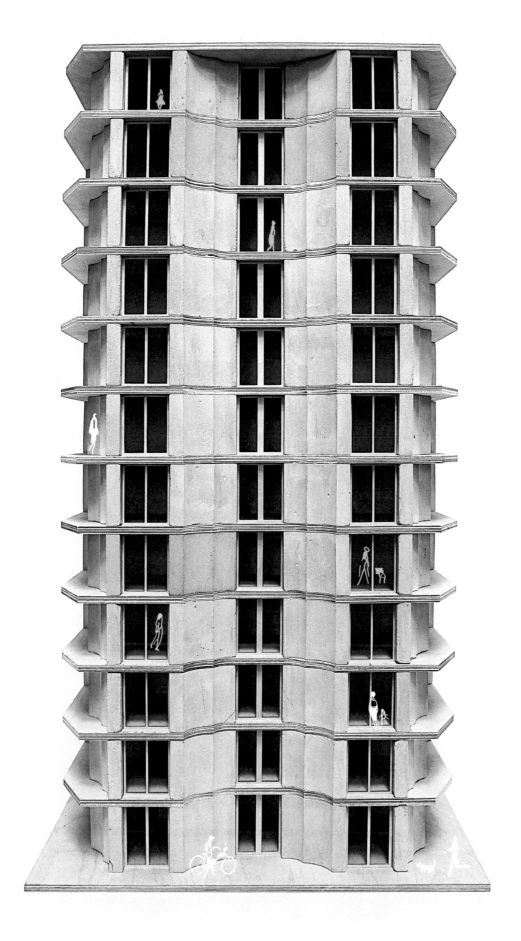

Barkow Leibinger, *Smart Material House* model, 2017

(Study for) Chapel for Scenes of Public Life — The Meeting of Enrico Mattei and the Queen of Sheba
baukuh and Stefano Graziani — Milan and Genoa, Italy

The Chapel for Scenes of Public Life imagines the production of spaces where gestures inside acquire public relevance. A project of public art, the chapel is designed to exhibit a cycle of photographs that describe the scenes (the places, the spaces, the volume occupied by human bodies) of an imaginary event that is explicitly staged in order to produce a spatial figure and, through this, becomes a collective project. This staged event is the imaginary (and impossible) meeting of Enrico Mattei and the Queen of Sheba. Enrico Mattei (1906–1962) was an Italian politician and entrepreneur who ran the state-owned oil company ENI. The Queen of Sheba is mentioned in the Bible (I Kings, 10:2 and II Chronicles, 9:1–9) in relation to her visit to King Solomon. Piero della Francesca painted the meeting of King Solomon and the Queen of Sheba in *The History of the True Cross* in the Basilica of San Francesco in Arezzo. There is a movie from 1959 by King Vidor titled *Solomon and Sheba*. It stars Yul Brynner as Solomon and Gina Lollobrigida as Sheba.

baukuh and Stefano Graziani, *Study for Chapel for Scenes of Public Life—The Meeting of Enrico Mattei and the Queen of Sheba*, 2017

BLESS N°60 Lobby Conquerors
BLESS in dialog with Artek furniture classics
— Berlin, Germany

BLESS create products and situations that connect people to surroundings and atmospheres that celebrate the *Jetztzeit* or the restless present. *Lobby Conquerors* are related to the *BLESS N°07 Livingroom Conquerors*, a series of options for dressing existing furniture for private use. In Chicago these ideas expand, not only providing furniture with garments but also fragmented architectural add-ons that allow them to transform from the classic Artek Kiki lounge chair into small interior/exterior "architurniture" units, or *Lobby Conquerors*.

These amended furnishings inhabit transitory spaces and invite interaction in two ways: some with the aim of connecting people and others, in contrast, are able to provide privacy and shelter. The aim is to make each element—the space, the furniture, and the visitors—of equal importance.

The Property Drama Brandlhuber+ and Christopher Roth — Berlin, Germany

Brandlhuber+ and Christopher Roth, film still from *The Property Drama*, 2017

It's time to ask who owns the ground!
In collaboration with Marc Angélil, Sandra Bartoli, Oana Bogdan, Peter Cabus, Sam Chermayeff, Adam Caruso, Tom Emerson, Isabella Fera, Yona Friedman, Renée Gailhoustet, Christian Kerez, Phyllis Lambert, Gaetano Licata, Juliette Martin, Luigi Snozzi, Jonas Staal, Milica Topalovic, Leo van Broeck, Jean-Philippe Vassal, Hans-Jochen Vogel, Anna Yeboah, Mirko Zardini, and many more.

Constructions and References
Caruso St John with Thomas Demand
and Hélène Binet — London, UK

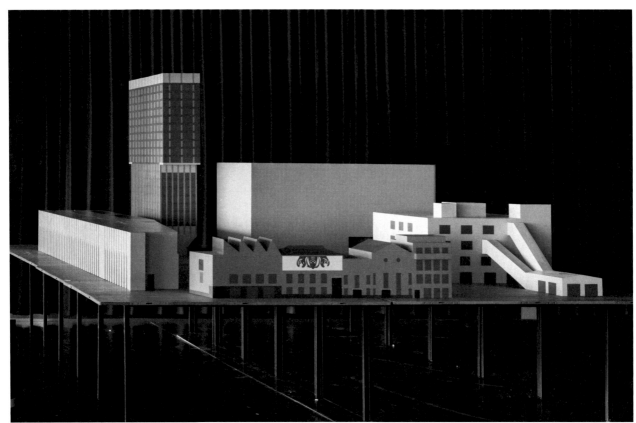

Caruso St John, Models, 2016

In the middle of the lofty interior of one of the Chicago rooms stands a constellation of figural volumes, a city-like tableau of five large models; a completed building, one whose design is currently being developed; and three competition designs. Stripped of their contexts, removed from place and politics, they are close to autonomous architectural thought. Their simple, almost monumental shapes of extrusions, distortions, and additions are neither obviously sculptural nor dispassionate representations, but somewhere between the two. This uncertain balance implies relationships to the endlessly fascinating world of real things. The space around the models, their stage, is dressed in a tall curtain: elegant and pleated in a classical manner. On second glance this backdrop turns out to be flat paper, wallpaper specially made by the artist

Thomas Demand, whose influence on us and on our working methods is evident in the exhibition. Demand's own work occupies the north wall of the room. A selection of reference images is mounted directly onto the wallpaper. These show places, art practices, and architectures from the wide history of Western culture. Details and forms from these references appear, sometimes with a shocking directness, in our completed buildings. Color prints of photographs by Hélène Binet are installed onto the remaining walls of the gallery. These show buildings that have recently been completed in London, Zurich, St. Gallen, Bremen, and Lille. These details of construction hold a microcosm of ideas about architecture, as well as ways of thinking that are informed by references and lie latent in the coarse forms of the big models.

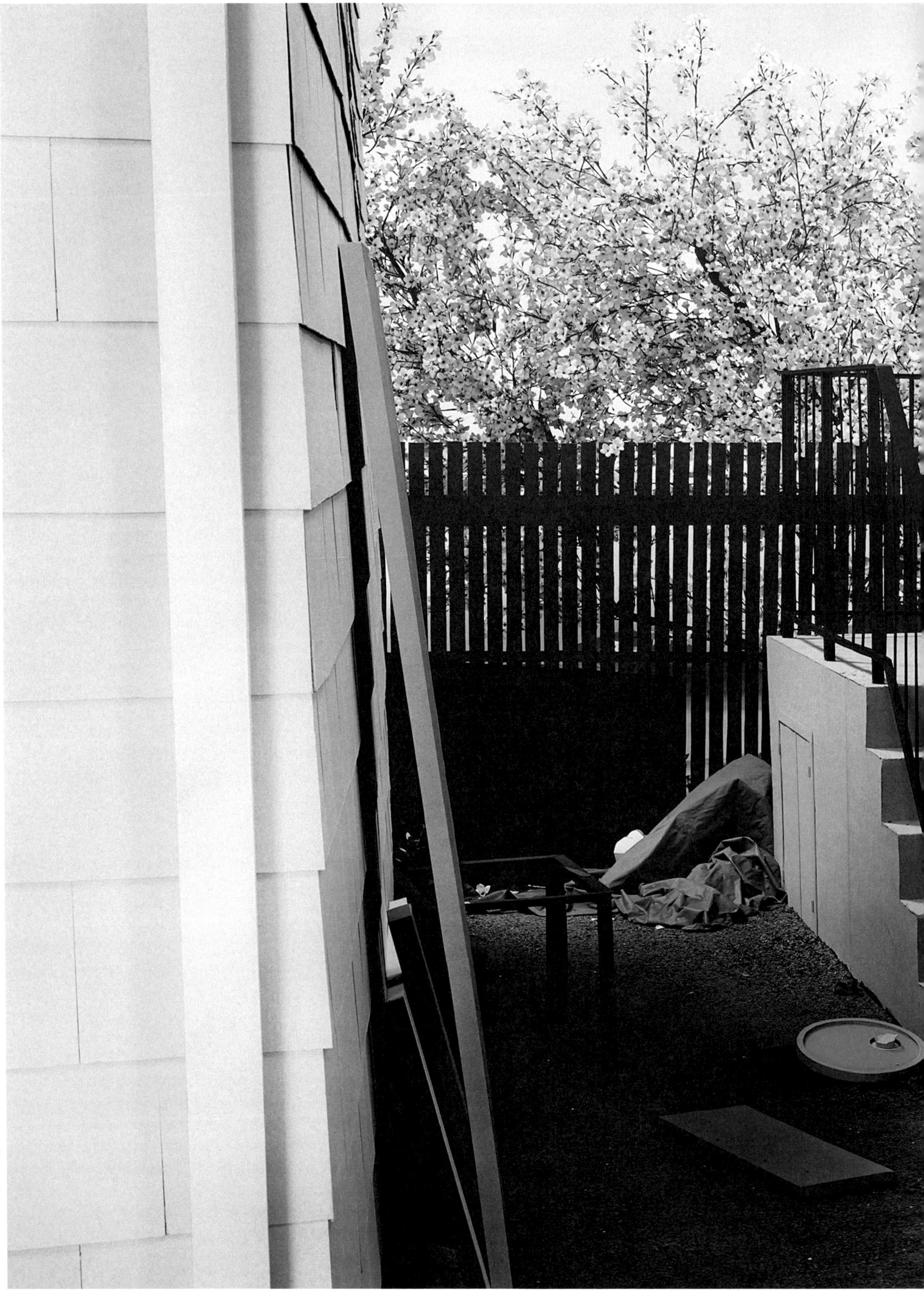

Thomas Demand, *Backyard*, 2014

Heliomorphic Chicago   Charles Waldheim with Office for Urbanization Harvard Graduate School of Design and Siena Scarff Design — Cambridge, USA

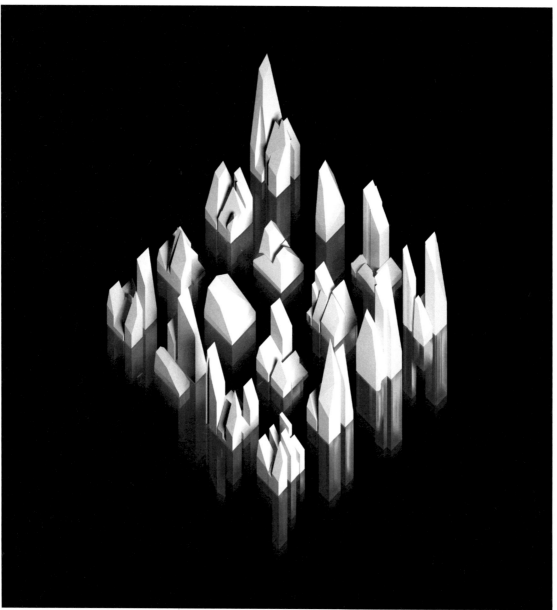

Charles Waldheim with Office for Urbanization Harvard Graduate School of Design and Siena Scarff Design, Study for Heliomorphic Chicago, 2017

Heliomorphic Chicago imagines the radical revision of Chicago's urban form through the optimization of solar performance. The project revisits the city's architectural history and proposes multiple potential futures for Chicago's architectural identity and collective urban form, each derived from the seemingly benign application of opposing relationships to solar energy.

The installation features two alternate versions of the Chicago Loop, modeled out of the optimization of solar performance criteria. These models are augmented with the projection of digital animations, drawings, and diagrams. The installation arrays a field of large format maquettes suspended from the ceiling. These maquettes describe alternative architectural identities and solar aspirations of many of the city's iconic tall buildings.

On the Definition of Structure in Architecture
Christian Kerez — Zurich, Switzerland

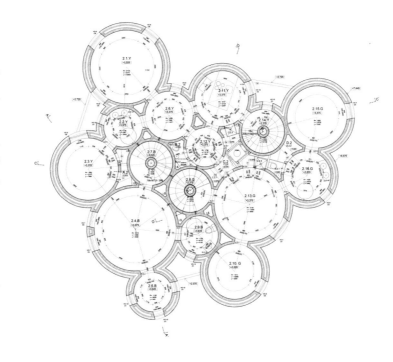

Christian Kerez, House Tomio Okamura, Prague, Czech Republic, 2013–15

Fundamentally, structure describes a system that is built on rules or experiential repetitions. Structure comprises an accumulation of equivalent or similar elements by which a building is put together. Structure defines these elements by describing how they relate to each other. Through this understanding of structure, a building has a loadbearing structure only when those elements stand in recognizable relation to one another and represent a comprehensible entity. Conceiving architecture as a structure that can be formed or defined by individual elements standing in a clear interconnection enables us to rethink architecture in an entirely open, unprejudiced way, eliminating both randomness and arbitrariness as well as formal rigor on the basis of simplification of content. This understanding of architectural structure enables us to address the basics of architecture without getting lost in gestures of archaic fundamentalism or minimalist rhetoric. But this definition of structure can only attain meaning when it becomes specific—when it is articulated.

If the structure of a building circumscribes it as an entity, this is naturally only achieved through the overlay of different kinds of structures—for example the loadbearing structure, the circulation structure, and the spatial structure. In a comprehensive practice of architecture, all these articulations are based on rules that relate to one another. They do not have to collide; they could also respond to each other in a complementary way.

A built structure has a definite extent, it has boundaries, it has an external volumetric appearance, and in addition to this limited extent, a building is always formed by exceptions. A stairway, for instance, is a fundamental break in a series of horizontal floor slabs, as is any elevator or service shaft. From the very outset, the tight spatial limitations and multitude of exceptions create the risk of a structure that is piecemeal and collaged. But these considerations aren't mere irksome obstacles in the way of creating a pure structure; instead they are the precondition for developing a multi-layered architecture out of a simple scheme, forming a complex entity from simple linear derivations. These breaks within an architectural system are imminently necessary; and it is only through these breaks that a complex system can be understood in its entirety.

This description of structure may seem cumbersome or abstract, but it can be a helpful tool to utilize when trying to understand and design a building that is a world unto its own, a coherent whole, which, while full of surprises and diversity, is derived from an overall architectonic entity rather than from arbitrary whims.

The Wallderful Dellekamp Arquitectos
— Mexico City, Mexico

Dellekamp Arquitectos, The Wallderful, 2017

Although they are doomed to crumble, humans have always built walls: along borders, across disputed lands, and around cities. Whether it was Hadrian, Qin Shi Huang, or Nikita Khrushchev, leaders often proclaimed the need to fortify their territories. And indeed they did, erecting formidable walls whose remains are largely relegated to the backgrounds of tourist selfies. In Chicago, Dellekamp Arquitectos hopes to reclaim the rhetoric of the wall in its ironic/iconic post-functional state. If anything, our morose political context serves as a point of departure to imagine a future where the border becomes a connection and the wall an invitation. The inhabited wall presents an inclusive threshold in its urban context, fulfilling a symbolic function while simultaneously creating public space for people to gather and build new memories.

Chicago Reframed Design With Company
— Chicago, USA

Design With Company, Study for Make New History, 2017

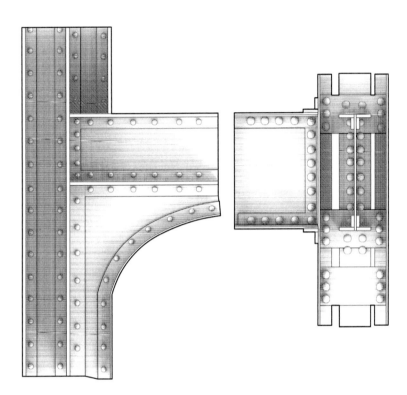

In this project, Design With Company uncovers the hidden biases of typical steel frame construction details, specifically those within Chicago School skyscrapers like the Home Insurance Building, Sullivan Center, Reliance Building, Rookery Building, etc. Too often these details— and the spatial matrix produced by their collection into a frame—are described as a neutral and infinitely flexible background for the life of business to unfold. Thinkers like Colin Rowe wrote about the "Chicago Frame" in these terms, further claiming that the American architects who proliferated its

development and construction only stumbled onto their architectural implications. They arrived at the modern technique of dislocating a building's structural elements (columns) from the elements which delineate space (walls) through necessity and economic pressures rather than ideological, disciplinary ambitions. In response to the repeated dismissal of the possibility of a frame having particular qualities and consequences, Design With Company is putting these hidden details on display and reconfiguring them to reveal their complexities, their differences, and their significance.

Rooms   Dogma — Brussels, Belgium

Dogma, Marcel Proust's Chamber, Living/Working, 2013–17

The room is perhaps the most obvious form of architecture. Both as dwellers and as architects, we have no choice but to live in and design rooms. If architecture means to make space, then the room is the most direct form that results from this claim. Etymologically, the words room and space are related, as the "room" refers to the capability of clearing space for oneself. In his text "The Room, the Street and Human Agreement," Louis Kahn identifies the room as the beginning of architecture.[1] But for Kahn the room is also a state of mind—the possibility to have one's own space of reflection. Kahn's description of the room comes close to Virginia Woolf's essay *A Room of One's Own* in which the writer links the room as individual space to the possibility for concentration and, more broadly, to the struggle of woman's emancipation from the patriarchal structure of domestic space.[2]

Woolf's reading questions the essence of domestic space as the place for reproductive labor where all the rooms are meant to support the management of the household, showing how the room is a historically produced space whose use and interpretation are determined by power relationships. The room is thus the best illustration of the twofold condition of architecture as both archetypical form and as the nexus of power relations through which society is organized. Dogma's contribution to the exhibition consists of a concise narrative about the history of the room as quintessential architectural space through relevant cases from antiquity to today.

1   Louis Kahn "The Room, The Street and Human Agreement," *a+u*, January (1973): 23–30.
2   Virginia Woolf, *Women & Fiction: The Manuscript Versions of A Room of One's Own* (Oxford: Blackwell, 1992).

Groundscapes — Paris, France

Dominique Perrault Architecture

Dominique Perrault Architecture, Empire State Building Fiction, 2016

In architecture, when we want to separate the outside from the inside we build walls and above them a roof. In this process we draw a line between two spaces: one remains open while the other is enclosed.

It is the same when we represent the independence of air and earth. By drawing this ground line that separates above from below, we inadvertently use a model for representing reality, which, in fine print, expresses the only thing that does not exist.

And yet, this model is efficient as it corresponds to the limits of our vision; thus, we perceive the landscape as a surface even though it hides a volume.

However, below this simple ground line hides a universe of possibilities, of unexplored places —existing or awaiting creation. As the surface of the planet has been entirely brought to our knowledge, what we are dealing with here is the very last frontier yet to conquer for our cities, be they historic or metropolitan.

The perception of the underground of cities may well raise concerns at first, as we imagine it dark, damp, and uncomfortable. But if we go beyond this fantastical prejudice, we will find another image of the underground: one that is more physical and sensitive. We have called this territory the groundscape as a foil to the landscape of the grounds. *Groundscapes* offers a potent catalyst for urban networks: a naturally ideal thermal inertia, an unrivaled respect for the landscape, an elegant enhancement of our architectural heritage, and a unique palette of lights.

Front Door Fiona Connor and Erin Besler
— Los Angeles, USA

First opened in 1897, the Chicago Cultural Center occupies an entire city block with main entrances at both Randolph and Washington streets. It connects public transport, workplaces, and hotels. The section of pedestrian walkway below the building opened in 1989 as part of an existing, but noncontinuous, network of subterranean commuter corridors that encompass forty blocks of Chicago's downtown. Known colloquially as the Pedway, this underground network is clad in a varied material palette: tile, brick, terrazzo, and glass. The transitions in the finishes and fittings point to the continuously phased construction of the underground system and delineate the boundaries of properties and buildings above. Below ground, fluorescent lighting provides constant illumination throughout, but a closer reading reveals inconsistencies between fixtures. Connor and Besler survey the environmental elements from the Chicago Pedway system and the Chicago Cultural Center and situate them anew in order to heighten attention beyond that of utilitarian purpose. What is taken for granted is seen afresh.

The CTA tunnel connecting the Washington/Randolph mezzanines of the State and Dearborn subways.

The Daley Center Concourse - CTA subway is to the left, City Hall to the right, and the Brunswick Building straight ahead.

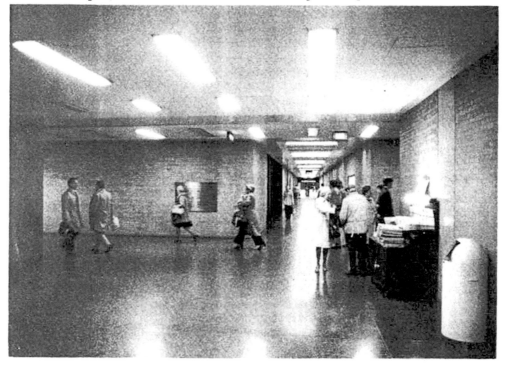

J'ai Pris Amour (I took love)
Fosbury Architecture — Milan, Italy

Today the boundaries between public and private are vanishing. The home is becoming more and more a place for work and an instrument of subsistence. Domesticity invades every field of human activity: with shops that are camouflaged as lounges, offices as game rooms, and restaurants as kitchens. The traditional "work/consume/death" human agenda is shifting towards an endless and sneaky productive leisure. Social media has put *otium* to work twenty-four seven. The sharing economy has, on the one hand, completely distorted the housing market and, on the other, converted intimacy into an economic asset. The Internet has produced an unprecedented physical space: a comfortable, comprehensible, homogeneous, and generic geography that allows us to travel from New York to Bali, with stops in London and Singapore—frictionless.

In this contemporary panorama of co-working —with its coffee shops, IKEA furniture, vintage leather sofa, craft beer, avocado sandwiches, and free Wi-Fi—the last authentic private spaces are environments of resistance for social individuals (private in the sense of deprivation of public presence) designed through exceptional pieces of furniture with the sole purpose of accommodating the idiosyncrasies of their occupants.

This scenario is investigated through an update of the *Studiolo di Federico da Montefeltro* in Urbino. Dedicated to *otium* and *studia humanitatis*, the room is completely lined with wood inlays depicting everyday objects, idols, fetishes, allegorical scenes, and external views aimed to celebrate the union of *arma et litterae* in Federico's dukedom. Just like in the *Studiolo*, the installation reassembles an up-to-date set of both mundane and allegorical oddities, giving us the opportunity to reconsider the relationship between immaterial needs, ambitions, and desires within the current models of living.

Air Houses: Design for a New Climate
Francois Perrin — Los Angeles, USA

Throughout most of human history, architecture has developed in response to nature. From the writings of Vitruvius in ancient Rome to the indigenous design practices documented in Bernard Rudofsky's 1964 book and exhibition *Architecture Without Architects*, civilizations have traditionally built sustainably: utilizing local materials and engineering techniques that work with—not against—landscape and climate.

The birth of modernism changed all this. Even if the early ideas of the movement were concerned with air quality and light, the concept of an international style—and the advent of air conditioning—turned architecture away from the environment and climate in the twentieth century. The postwar avant-garde proposed alternatives, such as Yves Klein's *Air Architecture*—which imagined traditional building materials replaced with air, water, and fire—and the techno-utopianism of Buckminster Fuller, which explored new forms and construction techniques and their connection to the environment. Yet, a culture of mass consumerism continued to produce buildings disengaged with their context, at ever greater environmental cost.

Now, in this era of climate change, energy crisis, population growth, and political uncertainty, it is necessary to re-examine age-old traditions of climate-responsive construction—such as the Korowai tree houses of Papua New Guinea—in order to create new architecture and design that engages with economic and environmental realities of the present. The Palm House at the Garfield Park Conservatory—and its microclimate—provide the setting for an experiment that proposes a new direction for building in harmony with nature.

Air Houses: Design for a New Climate looks back to look forward, referencing vernacular traditions and radical twentieth century thinkers while prototyping a new direction for the design and fabrication of buildings. Suspended in the canopy, the Air Houses demonstrate a lighter, more flexible approach to building structures that not only provide shelter but also interact with climate conditions: accepting, rejecting, or repurposing sun, wind, and rain to optimize comfort and make the most of natural resources. They also provide a framework for plants to grow and become part of the architecture, reactivating the symbiosis between nature and structure.

Figuring Modern Urbanism: Chicago's Near South Side — Sarah Whiting

Platted in 1830, Chicago's urbanism was firmly grounded in the gridiron tradition systematized by Thomas Jefferson's 1787 Northwest Ordinance, which subdivided the Western Territories into townships of 36 square miles. This gridded system divided the landscape into commodifiable parcels, thereby facilitating rapid and rampant land speculation. Published in 1933, Homer Hoyt's *One Hundred Years of Land Values*—a surprisingly fascinating read that resulted from his University of Chicago dissertation in economics, which surveyed the hundred-year history of Chicago—meticulously documents the many ways blocks were divided. Hoyt's detailed study offers few surprises: absent are the urban innovations that one would expect of a modern city.

Despite the implied rigor of the grid's mathematical substrate, Chicago's blocks are not entirely homogeneous today. In *Manual of Surveying Instructions*, written over a century later, the Bureau of Land Management described Chicago's grid with the oft-repeated phrase "usually," suggesting regularity but admitting aberration. If New York's unyielding grid "force[d] Manhattan's builders to develop a new system of formal values, to invent strategies for the distinction of one block from

another,"[1] Chicago's was essentially the opposite: the grid itself was manipulated in order to distinguish one project from another. Because Chicago's grid resulted from a territorial organization that expands outward—unlike Manhattan's, which is directed inward from its island configuration—the city's urban logic is one of multiplication rather than division.

It was architecture that awakened Chicago's latent modern urbanism: Mies van der Rohe's campus plan for the Illinois Institute of Technology (IIT, 1939–58) changed the course of Chicago's urban history. The campus is sited in Chicago's Near South Side, just south of the Loop. Even fans of the campus read the project as an autonomous island, a tabula rasa that utterly disregards its physical and social contexts. This interpretation is reinforced by Mies's presentation collage, which ruthlessly eliminated one hundred acres of the city's dense urban fabric, clearing the way for his expansive, low-density campus. (fig. 1) Each campus building in this collage announces its own isolation in turn: each is indifferent to the blank, white ground upon which it sits or hovers; indifferent to its neighboring pavilions; indifferent to the streets; and indifferent to the blocks of the city beyond.

1   Rem Koolhaas, *Delirious New York* (1978) (New York: Monacelli Press, 1984), 20–21.

When read within the context of Chicago's Near South Side of the 1940s, however, another understanding of IIT emerges: rather than an autonomous singularity, this campus exhibits an integrated form of urbanism that is architectural in its logic and modern in its effect. Mies's plan for IIT exploited Chicago's flat immediacy to offer an urban model that was at once autonomous and situated, figure and ground, figural and abstract. A simple way to characterize what results from the combination of these several pairings is that it forms an urban-scaled bas-relief, deliberately inflecting the flatness of Chicago's incessantly horizontal ground plane. Extending this model, the Near South Side of Chicago developed over about a twenty-year period into one of the first modern urban plans to be built in the United States.

Understanding IIT and the Near South Side of Chicago as a horizontal bas-relief of interconnecting and overlapping superblocks foregrounds Mies's urban project for the campus, which has been overshadowed both by the initial process of land clearance that made the project possible and by the architecture eventually installed there. At this historical moment, immediately following World War II, this part of Chicago was reconfigured as a collection of large entities—superblocks or campuses—but the particular way that these superblocks came to be simultaneously meant that they were interdependent, not autonomous entities. It is a figural landscape, but not a figurative one: while the figures that it forms are not recognizable as typical urban forms, they are nevertheless differentiated, unlike the homogenous uniformity of a typical gridded city. In his essay, "The Superblock," first published in 1971, architectural historian Alan Colquhoun attributes the rise of the superblock as an urban form to the growing concentration of capital and to the increasing scale of urban investors: corporations, developers, and speculators. He argues that the superblock necessarily harms the public realm through this large-scale privatization of the city into discrete units; the Near South Side of Chicago, however, offers a productive counter example whereby the plan's superblocks were, at their origins, not autonomous in their form, their financing, and their management.[2]

Although the trope of the bas-relief is most striking as a formal analogy, it additionally operates as an urban manifestation of political overlaps and economic contingencies. From the late 1930s through the early 1950s, this part of the city was

2   Alan Colquhoun, "The Superblock," *Essays in Architectural Criticism* (Cambridge, MA: MIT Press 1981), 83, first written in 1971 and first published in Alan Colquhoun, *Arquitectura moderna y cambio historio: Ensayos 1962–76* (Barcelona: Gustavo Gili, 1978).

Fig. 1, Mies van der Rohe office, IIT campus: photomontage aerial view showing model within Near South Side (detail), 1947

developed into a collection of institutions. The fact that these institutions had frequently coincident corporate boards suggests that what might look to be separate superblocks in the urban fabric were in fact quite interconnected. (fig. 2) Beginning with IIT, and later including Michael Reese Hospital, Mercy Hospital, Chicago Housing Authority public housing projects, and several private-housing developments, a group of institutions collaborated to plan and execute one of the first large-scale modern urban plans in the United States. This seven-mile-square plan paved the way for federal slum clearance, redevelopment, and urban renewal legislation, including the Housing Acts of 1949 and 1954. In addition to Mies and Ludwig Hilberseimer from IIT, key figures involved in the conception, development, and promotion of the Near South Side Plan included Chairman of the Harvard Department of Architecture Walter Gropius, planners Reginald Isaacs and Walter Blucher, real-estate developer Ferd Kramer, IIT President Henry Heald, and University of Chicago sociologist Louis Wirth, among others. The strategic alliances of the Near South Side Plan projected a protean synthesis of otherwise autonomous social, political, and aesthetic tableaus. This synthesis forged a postwar corporate-municipal-state cooperation that extended to the federal realm.

Flatland: The Impenetrable Density of Chicago's Near South Side

The gridded urban fabric of Chicago's Near South Side, untouched by the Great Fire of 1871, had constituted Chicago's original "Gold Coast," but by 1947 restrictive covenants that limited locations where African Americans moving up from the South could live had turned it into the city's "Black Belt." Large homes that had previously been mansions were divided into small, overcrowded apartments. Recognizing that the city's urban ills offered a way to tap into Roosevelt's federal work-relief program, the Chicago Plan Commission (CPC), a private organization comprised primarily of the city's most prominent businessmen, initiated a land-use survey in 1938.[3] Already within this survey one can find the seeds of the powerful, albeit often unbalanced, Keynesian triumvirate of federal policy and monies, private monies and interests, and social interests and ends that would define most American urban planning—particularly large-scale municipal improvements—at least until the economic recession of the 1970s. Business was neither willing nor

3   The editors of *Pencil Points* in collaboration with the Chicago Plan Commission, "Chicago Plans Today for Tomorrow," *The New Pencil Points* (March 1943), 35.

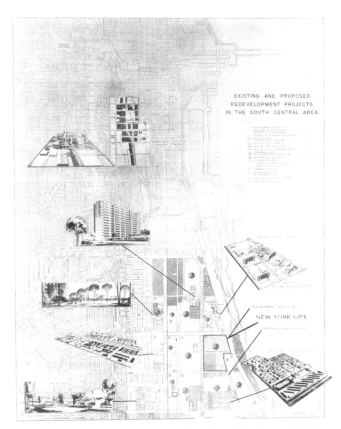

Fig. 2, SSPB Redevelopment Plan for the Near South Side. In John McKinlay, *Redevelopment Project No.1: A Second Report,* *The New York Life Insurance Company Redevelopment Plan*, 1950

able to spend its own money on such research; the federal, state, and even municipal governments, meanwhile, lacked the resources and the special interest to undertake it. By using federal money, the CPC could afford to assess the city's properties, which was in its own private interests.

The conclusion of this statistical analysis, which used the urban sociology methods of University of Chicago professors Robert Park and Louis Wirth, confirmed that the Near South Side was the largest area of blight in Chicago, and perhaps in the whole of North America. This conclusion led to the CPC's comprehensive slum clearance and redevelopment policy of 1941 and the Illinois State Legislature's Neighborhood Redevelopment Corporation Law, passed at the same time, which "enable[d] private enterprise to do much of the job of rebuilding Chicago's older neighborhoods" and broadened measures introduced by New Deal legislation, such as the 1937 Housing Act, which had initiated federal assistance to cities for slum clearance.[4] Although its constitutionality was eventually challenged on the grounds that it promulgated racial segregation,[5] the Illinois Neighborhood Redevelopment Corporation Law would eventually pave the way for additional state and, more significantly, federally mandated, privately assisted slum-clearance legislation, including the Federal Housing Act of 1949.

Manifest Destiny: IIT and the Urban Frontier

As early as 1933, the Armour Institute of Technology (AIT, which became IIT when it merged with the Lewis Institute of Technology in 1940) had hoped to move away from the area because the neighborhood's decline was affecting faculty and student recruitment. But by 1937, the Institute had concluded that it couldn't afford to move because its land was worth so little. Their strategy shifted to expansion and neighborhood rehabilitation.

They instigated a quiet land grab, using foreclosure suits and sheriff's sales to bid on properties that were abandoned and tax delinquent. In order to keep prices from rising, they purchased through third parties, including members of the institute's board of trustees.[6]

The development committee used two initial campus schemes designed by AIT faculty members to raise funds for land purchasing. The first, dating from 1937, was by Holabird and Root; the second, of 1940, was by Alschuler and Friedman. While both of these schemes are sited in the gridded field of Chicago's Near South Side, they both favor formal courtyards, strong axes, and clear hierarchies. The awkwardness of inserting this Beaux-Arts vision into the city's grid reveals the campus's design challenge: how to give IIT an identity while fitting it within Chicago's urban logic.

Mies's IIT: Bas-Relief Campus

When Mies was hired to design the campus, he did not start by designing the plan. Instead, he began by studying the program, which was just being developed and would continue to evolve over the twenty years that he directed the project. After considering and testing various alternatives, Mies determined that a 24-by-24-foot square module could be used to accommodate the full spectrum of the campus's varied requirements. He then moved wooden blocks around a large piece of gridded paper that represented the site.[7] (fig. 3) Although Mies once claimed that site was not "that important,"[8] the combination of the gridded background and the gridded blocks gives an impression that the figures of the buildings were emerging from the ground plane.

Shared programs—the library and student union—define the edges, not the center, of the campus's courtyard. Mies's perspectival views of the campus similarly emphasized edges rather than centers, with multiple side axes promising endless possibilities lying just around any given corner. Mies's perspectives are mostly two-point constructions that lead the eye off the page, away from any central focus. Even when a building's entrance is centered on its façade, the drawing's vanishing point does not lie in the center of the image, and

4   *Annual Report of the Chicago Plan Commission, 1941*, Chicago, IL, 15. The 1937 act provided federal assistance to states for low-income housing.
5   As early as 1935, federal housing policies, introduced under Roosevelt's New Deal legislation, maintained that it was important to respect existing racial and ethnic neighborhood definitions: "Called the Neighborhood Composition Rule, it was formulated by Secretary of the Interior Harold Ickes, and provided that a housing project would not be permitted to alter the racial character of its neighborhood." Devereux Bowly Jr, *The Poorhouse: Subsidized Housing in Chicago, 1895–1976* (Carbondale: Southern Illinois University Press, 1978), 27. See also Martin Meyerson and Edward C. Banfield, *Politics, Planning, and the Public Interest: The Case of Public Housing in Chicago* (New York: Free Press, 1955), esp. 20–21. For the most compelling and thorough analysis of the racial repercussions of urban policy, see Arnold R. Hirsch, *Making the Second Ghetto: Race and Housing in Chicago 1940–1960* (Chicago: University of Chicago Press, 1983). For a specific case study, focused on the Mecca building (site of the current Crown Hall on the IIT campus), see Daniel Bluestone, "Chicago's Mecca Flat Blues," *Journal of the Society of Architectural Historians* 57, no. 4 (December 1998), 282–403.

6   Board of Trustees Executive Meeting Minutes, May 7, 1937, addendum 2, 7. See also Bluestone, "Chicago's Mecca Flat Blues," 394.
7   "We ... made wood blocks of the volume of the building, and on a plot of the whole site I drew up, he would work those out in some arrangement within the spaces of the buildings, having had that plot from— what was it?—31st Street down to 35th, State Street over to the tracks to the west, drawn up in a modular system that he had found workable for the contents of the program." George Danforth in conversation with Kevin Harrington, CCA Oral History Project.
8   Mies van der Rohe, interview with Katherine Kuh, in Kuh, *The Open Eye: In Pursuit of Art* (New York: Harper and Rowe, 1971), 35.

framing elements are always uneven: a cut-off building to one side or an asymmetrically composed array of figures whose opacity competes with the spectral, lightly penciled buildings behind them. When perspectives do focus upon a building's entry, the material of the ground plane slips through the door into the lobby, suggesting a continuum rather than a boundary. In the earliest schemes, many of the buildings were lifted on pilotis, or piers; the campus's entire ground plane would then be a single surface, interrupted only by the glass walls of the lobby spaces and stairs. Each building would then have a transitional space between the exterior, public world and the interior, private or academic world. Once the decision was made to eliminate the piers, Mies put the buildings directly onto the ground, aligning the ground floor slab with the ground itself. Even the detailing of the doors does not interrupt the flow of space between outdoors and indoors, as with the centered, pivot-hinge doors to Lewis (now Perlstein) Hall: the door handles are kept vertical and in alignment with the doorframe, avoiding any interruption of the view. Only a slight change in surface texture marks the transition from outside to inside. The asymmetrical campus plan, as conveyed through Mies's drawings and detailing, constructs a new urban type where pedestrian movement across campuses, into and

through buildings, is fluid and where every building oscillates between being foreground and background and between figure and ground. (fig. 4) This urban bas-relief became the blueprint for the entire Near South Side.

Contours of Proliferation: Chicago's Near South Side

Chaired by IIT's president, Henry Heald, and initiated jointly by IIT and Michael Reese Hospital, the South Side Planning Board (SSPB) was formed on "June 11, 1946 as an inter-racial community planning organization which was incorporated as a not-for-profit agency with the objective of inaugurating and guiding an orderly redevelopment program for the Central South Side community as a better place to live and work and do business."[9] As an organization of interested private individuals, the SSPB put itself forth as a mediator between the public (municipal and legislative realms) and private (institutional and corporate, as well as individual)

9 SSPB News Release draft, 1, Heald papers, Box 62, SSPB folder, IIT Archives, Paul V. Galvin Library. Although it was titled the South Side Planning Board, the group initially focused on the Near South Side area. In the 1950s, they turned their attention further south to redevelopment in the Hyde Park neighborhood.

Fig. 3, Mies van der Rohe and Ludwig Hilberseimer with a preliminary model for the IIT campus, 1945

Fig. 4, IIT campus: aerial view looking north, 1986

realms. Hardly masking her astonishment, architecture critic Ada Louise Huxtable described the board as being composed of "Catholic, Protestant, Jewish, Negro, Labor, Railroad, Industrial-Commercial, Real Estate, and Public Housing" interests, all focused on the re-planning of the seven-square-mile area of Chicago that surrounded IIT.[10] Beginning in 1947, the board began holding public meetings and also issuing booklets, leaflets, and pamphlets; these materials presented easy-to-grasp graphic analyses and boldly rendered planning proposals, including mile-square super-blocks, mixed-rise blocks composed of row houses and skip-stop slabs (housing blocks that had floor-through duplexes that were made possible by having elevators skip every other floor), and an extensive array of community facilities, including parks, beaches, and museums. (fig. 5) Although blamed for pushing African Americans out of the South Side, the SSPB openly aspired to racial integration, all the while representing the institutions, businesses, and community organizations that had motives of self-interest for remaining in

this area just south of the Loop.[11] The board included Chicago Housing Authority Executive Director Elizabeth Wood, who was not shy about her integrationist platform for public housing in Chicago. And the board's vice chairman was the black columnist Willard Townsend from the progressive black newspaper the *Chicago Defender*, who supported the SSPB in his columns on race and redevelopment.[12] The SSPB had no official municipal status; it was merely a civic association, an example of what Alexis de Tocqueville had admired a hundred years prior as being the backbone of local American politics.[13]

Looking at the board memberships of these various organizations reveals otherwise hidden alliances. Henry Heald, for example, was vice-chairman of the Chicago Land Clearance Commission. And in addition to the heads of both

10   Ada Louise Huxtable, *Two Cities: Planning in North and South America* (New York: MoMA, 1947): 13.

11   See, for example, the far more homogenous membership of the Metropolitan Housing and Planning Council, which was another civic-oriented organization of Chicago business leaders consisting primarily of the heads of commercial and corporate interests in the Loop. For an excellent discussion of the MHPC, see Hirsch, *Making the Second Ghetto.*
12   For Willard Townsend's defense of the SSPB on the issue of race and the SSPB's goals, see Townsend, "Southside Planning Board Gets Airing," parts 1 and 2, Chicago Defender (November 29 and December 4, 1948).
13   Alexis de Tocqueville, *Democracy in America* (1835), trans. Gerald Bevan (New York: Penguin Classics, 2003).

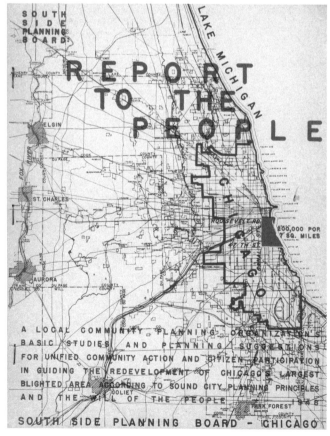

Fig. 5, SSPB: Report to the People, 1949

the Chicago Housing Authority (CHA) and Michael Reese Hospital being members of the SSPB, a complex liaison was forged between these two organizations that enabled the hospital to acquire land for its expansion. After procuring some adjacent properties through public auction, it became clear that the hospital would have trouble obtaining the land that it needed to fulfill its vision of an expansive campus complex. Under the provisions of an amendment to the Illinois Cities and Villages Act of 1945, the CHA could condemn slum land for redevelopment purposes that did not necessarily have to include public housing. Finding a way to profit from this amendment, the hospital agreed to pay the full cost of land assembly, relocation, and overhead for a four-block area adjacent to their property.[14] The deal looked as good to the CHA as it did to Michael Reese Hospital: slums would be cleared and housing provided that, even if it was private (for hospital employees) rather than public

housing, nevertheless promised to improve the general quality of the neighborhood.[15]

In addition to IIT and the mixed-rise campus (combining buildings of different heights) of Michael Reese Hospital, which was designed with assistance from consultants Walter Gropius and Walter Blucher, the Near South Side Plan included Lake Meadows, a mixed-rise, private housing development designed by Skidmore, Owings, and Merrill between 1950 and 1960 (fig. 6) and built on the first land parcel to be appropriated by the Chicago Land Clearance Commission[16]; the mid-rise towers of the CHA project, Dearborn Homes, designed by Loebl, Schlossmann, and Bennett and completed in 1950; the combined-height buildings (elevator buildings, two-story buildings, and row houses) of Prairie Courts, another CHA project, designed by Keck and Keck in the early 1950s; and the five private-housing slabs of Prairie Shores, also designed by Loebl, Schlossman, and Bennett, in the later 1950s.[17] The South Side Planning Board also envisioned the development of a light industrial

14   Reginald Isaacs, "Progress Report," *Michael Reese Hospital Planning Board* (August 1945–December 1946), 12. In "A Hospital Plans," Isaacs takes note of the CHA's power of eminent domain: "The [Chicago Housing] Authority has the necessary power, through eminent domain if necessary, to assemble property, tear down slum structures detrimental to the welfare, health and morals of the public, and dispose of the property by sale or lease to public or private redevelopers who submit plans in conformance with proper land use and community requirements" (338).

15   Bowly Jr., *The Poorhouse*, 59.
16   For more about Lake Meadows, see Sarah M. Whiting, "Invisible Superblock," *SOM Journal* 4: 168–78.
17   According to Ferd Kramer, whose firm Draper and Kramer developed Lake Meadows, Gropius was a much more influential figure in the South Side Planning Board meetings than either Mies or Hilberseimer. Kramer in conversation with the author, November 20, 1998.

Fig. 6, SOM, Scheme 1 of Lake Medow Housing Development, Chicago, 1950

park that would be located at the northern end of the Near South Side, between the Loop and the proposed housing projects, aimed at stabilizing the area economically.

An extensive green carpet provides a common denominator to the entire plan—the field for the area's bas-relief. Landscaping was a quick and effective way to demonstrate progress in what was otherwise a very slow process. The Near South Side Plan's seemingly infinite park was proffered as public space, accessible to all: not one of the plan's campuses was fenced off; nothing but the public streets and the footprints of the buildings interrupted the carpet's verdant horizontal plane: the urbanized horizon of a redirected manifest destiny. (fig. 7) Michael Reese Hospital's campus even set up a transition between the "man-made landscape" of Chicago's grid and the "natural land-scape" of the lakeshore: the alignment of the hospi-tal's buildings shift from one to the other as one moves eastward across the site.

The land acquisition methods of each of these campus developments in the Near South Side plan added to an evolving strategy of what could be called "inner-city landfill." Until the passage of the Illinois State Blighted Areas Redevelopment Act in 1947, large-scale land-acquisition strategies for private institutions were limited to IIT's

underhanded method of third-party buying and Michael Reese's loophole partnership with the CHA. The cost of acquiring land otherwise was out of the reach of these institutions. Attesting that "neither the demolition nor repair of an occa-sional building changes the character of a blighted neighborhood," the act made the acquisition of large parcels of land available through purchase, the powers of eminent domain, and "the use of public funds to squeeze the water out of the inflated values of land and structures."[18] This legis-lation thoroughly transformed the dynamics of urban development in Chicago, and furthermore served as a model for subsequent federal legisla-tion that would enable large-scale urban-renewal projects throughout the country during the 1950s.[19]

18   John McKinlay, Chairman, Chicago Land Clearance Commission, *Redevelopment Project Number 1: A Report to the Mayor and the City Council of the City of Chicago and to the Illinois State Housing Board* (March 1949), 5–6.
19   A diagram of dynamic arrows depicts the process underwritten by the act: based on information gathered via surveys and studies, the Chica-go Land Clearance Commission (CLCC) determined what properties should be condemned and how they should be redeveloped, subject to the approval of the City Council and the State Housing Board. The CLCC's powers of land acquisition, tenant relocation, demolition, construction, and sale were funded by city bond issues and money al-located from the state; federal support was included after the Federal Housing Act was passed in 1949.

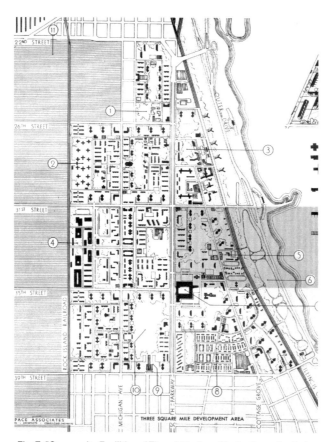

Fig. 7, "Community Facilities of Three Mile Area." In *An Opportunity for Private and Public Investement in Rebuilding Chicago*, 1947

Much American postwar urban renewal has been rightfully vilified for replacing without improving. Chicago is host to a number of such examples, mostly of public housing projects, such as the Robert Taylor homes, which opened in 1962. Its 4,500 apartments were spread across 28 sixteen-story high rises in a two-mile-by-two-block corridor just south of IIT's campus. (fig. 8) The earliest design for this project closely resembles the projects from the Near South Side Plan: "eight-story high-rises and two-story apartment buildings...[with acreage set aside] for public spaces such as park areas and playgrounds, waterways and ponds, and winding pathways that moved through the natural landscapes."[20] Cost cutting eliminated all of these amenities, resulting in the complex being un-programmed and lifeless at the street level. Those factors, combined with famously negligent maintenance and the drug wars of the 1970s, led the project to become one of the more notorious in the city and, in so doing, rendered modern public housing towers synonymous with crime in the public imagination.

The projects that constituted the Near South Side Plan remind us, however, that we should not abandon re-envisioning the city at a large scale. The diversified, mixed-rise urbanism idealized in the Near South Side Plan and exemplified in some of its projects offered up an entirely new way of living in the city. Unlike the Chicago Plan Commission, the SSPB was not trying to suburbanize the city. In a 1941 proposal for the very same area, the CPC created curvilinear subdivisions, in a vain attempt to jump onto the suburban American Dream bandwagon that was sapping cities during those years.[21] The SSPB not only saw such neighborhood planning as impractical and nostalgic, they also believed that this idyllic vision was often used to mask and manipulate urban racial demographics. In 1948, board member Reginald Isaacs, who was also the planning director of Michael Reese Hospital, argued that defining neighborhoods along racial or

20 Sudhir Venkatesh, *American Project: The Rise and Fall of a Modern Ghetto* (Cambridge, MA: Harvard University Press, 2000), 17–18.

21 For an analysis of the CPC's proposals, particularly in terms of its "neighborhood definition," see Bruce Biossat's *Remaking Chicago*, a reprinted series of articles published in the *Chicago Daily News*, February 13–March 6, 1945, especially page 15, which provides a "before and after" analysis of a southwestern Chicago neighborhood, depicted in grid form in the "before" image and in curving streetscapes in the "after" image. See also a similar evaluation in *The Chicago Sun*: "The Sun Looks Ahead to Postwar Chicago," by Milburn Ackers: "In those unoccupied subdivisions ... the commission projects a type of development that would give the city many neighborhoods similar in design to the best found in the suburbs. It suggests the amendment of the city's building code in a manner permitting the substitution of the curvilinear for the rectilinear or gridiron development." *Chicago Sun* reprint, September–October 1943, 6.

Fig. 8, Exterior of Robert Taylor Homes public housing, Chicago, July 1, 1964

religious lines—a common proposal among adherents to the subdivision model of planning—was no different than prescribing ghettos and preventing the social mobility of minority groups. "The notion that man is happier if he shares the same values as his next door neighbor is peculiar—John Doe living in suburb 'A' shares the same keep-up-with-the-Jones ideal as neighbor John Smith in their Veblenian state of 'conspicuous leisure,' vying with each other in 'conspicuous consumption'—and in constant anxiety."[22] Rather than forsaking modernism, Isaacs and the rest of the SSPB embraced it, envisioning a concomitant lifestyle.

Fragile Future

The Near South Side Plan is an urban story without a fairy tale ending. The seven-square mile area was never a resounding success and its history was overshadowed by that of the CHA high-rise projects built subsequently around it. But it's a story that embodies the complexities of urban renewal, canonical modernism, postwar economics, and the

22 Reginald Isaacs, "Are Urban Neighborhoods Possible?" *NAHO (National Association of Housing Officials) Journal of Housing* (July–August 1948), 178.

particular circumstances of Chicago—the grid, the lakefront, the politics, and its changing racial makeup. Storytelling has a tendency to simplify, and when this tale gets told, it is cast merely as a barren *tabula rasa*. The complexities underlying the planning of the entire area, however, reveal that blame for failure or credit for success can hardly lay with a single figure, a single institution, a single scheme, or a single legislative act.

Between 1939 and 1958 (when Mies retired from IIT, by which time Henry Heald had left IIT for New York University, Reginald Isaacs had left Michael Reese for Harvard, and Elizabeth Wood had been fired from the Chicago Housing Authority), the Near South Side's urban bas-relief wove together the different institutions sited there, differentiating the seemingly neutral and totalizing traits normally ascribed to the Chicago grid and to canonical modernism. The topography that the early plan threw into relief included the multiple layers of networked relationships among the institutions, the architects, the planners, and the agencies involved, as well as the formal terms of the space itself.

If the bas-relief of the Near South Side failed in certain respects, that does not warrant totally abandoning its prescient if perhaps naively optimistic urban strategy. Its prescience lies in its

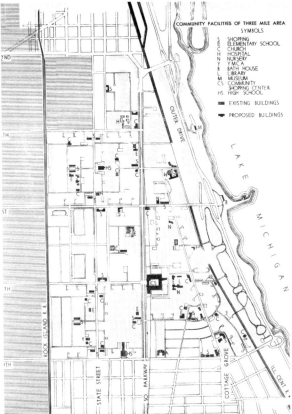

Fig. 9, "Three-Square Mile Development Area." *In An Opportunity for Private and Public Investment in Rebuilding Chicago*, 1947

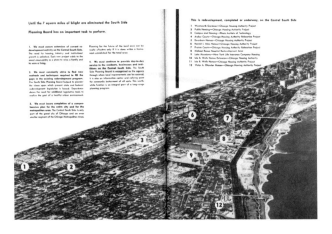

Fig. 10, "Central South Side Redevelopment Projecs." In *A Redevelopment Proposal adjacent to Michael Rees Hospital*, 1952

susceptibility to the complexities of urban space and its complicity in the different networks that it spun within that space: its effort to engage the collective and the individual simultaneously, to link institutions with institutions, local politics to federal politics, and private economies to public ones. The figured fields of the campus superblocks provided a means of balancing the individualism of the real-estate parcel with the collectivity of the shared public realm. Beginning with IIT, the Near South Side Plan pulled the lakeshore's green belt inland, creating a nexus of semi-public open spaces funded by a Keynesian combination of municipal, state, and federal politics with private, local institutions. The topography of this ground plan—the seemingly inert park of the tower becomes instead a charged, infrastructural carpet, reflecting the complex relations underlying the entire area.

But this modulated topography constituted a fragile ground. Although the story cannot be attributed to a single person or moment, it depended on individuals, as evidenced by the roles of Mies, Heald, Isaacs, and Wood. The delicate nature of the personal relations that underpinned the institutional ones is particularly visible in the example of Wood at the Chicago Housing Authority. Upon her dismissal, the precariously balanced terms of urbanism in the Near South Side were stretched to the point of snapping. The CHA projects of the 1960s and later, which consisted of undifferentiated high-rise towers combined with no other programs, returned the bas-relief to a field condition: the figures of these towers sit directly on top of an unactivated tabula rasa. One would be hard pressed to find ground-level perspectives of these latter projects because there is no ambiguity, no differentiation in the experience of their spaces and therefore no need to place the individual within their sites. For a short while, when the South Side Planning Board was most intact, Mies's model turned the tabula rasa into a bas-relief of susceptible but provocative semi-figures, thereby transforming modernism's homogeneous field into an articulated, proactive network. The success of this bas-relief comes from its variegated scales, which included high density but always in partnership with low-rise housing and amenities, including commercial and recreational amenities and landscapes. (fig. 9–10)

Today, what little that remains of the Near South Side Plan is being demolished: IIT is mostly intact, but Michael Reese has closed and is being razed, Prairie Courts came down years ago, suburban-scaled townhomes are being added the campus of Lake Meadows, and Georgian trim has been added to Dearborn Homes to hide its modernism. Seventy-five years after the South Side Planning Board was just beginning to come into existence, how can we find a way to return to its optimism, to its comprehensive mix of constituents that managed nonetheless to produce uncompromised futures, to large visions for the city, and to modern visions for the metropolis?

Sarah Whiting is the Dean and William Ward Watkin Professor at the Rice University School of Architecture.

Randolph Square   Frida Escobedo
— Mexico City, Mexico

Frida Escobedo, Study for Randolph Square, 2017

This intervention departs from a question—what happens when different systems of demarcation intersect? What does it mean to inhabit such a space of convergence? Frida Escobedo began by interrogating the grid, which is the most recognizable agent of an absolute and Cartesian notion of space: modern urban planning, private property, and other such territorial organizations. As Rosalind Krauss wrote, "...the grid does not map the space of a room or a landscape or a group of figures onto the surface of a painting. Indeed, if it maps anything, it maps the surface of the painting itself. It is a transfer in which nothing changes place."[1] It is, perhaps, exactly this remove from the real conditions of a site that so ideally suit the grid to reveal the contradictions inherent in rational public space.

By inscribing the grid onto a plane which cuts through Cartesian space, Escobedo draws from this intersection a more complex, embedded terrain. The result echoes what Sarah Whiting called "Chicago's elastic grid," a heterogenous fabric wrested from Jeffersonian uniformity.[2] The intervention is therefore not intended as a purely abstract expression of Cartesian logic, nor as a mere functional object designed to fulfill a prescribed program. Rather, it is an ambiguous ground—a landscape intended to encourage improvisation and play and to respond over time to the various ways, predictable and otherwise, in which it will be occupied.

1   Rosalind Krauss, "Grids." *October*, vol. 9 (1979): 50–64.
2   Sarah Whiting, "Chicago – Superblockism: Chicago's Elastic Grid," in *Histories of Cities: Design and Context*, ed. R. El-Khoury and E. Robbins (London: Routledge, 2004), 57–76.

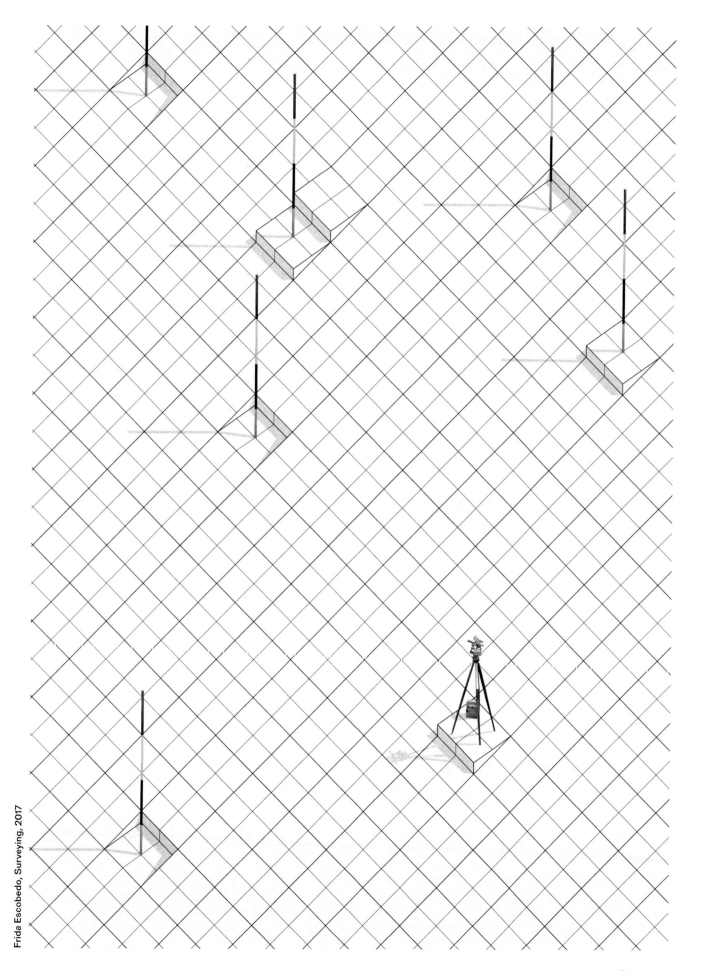

Modern Living   Gerard & Kelly — Los Angeles, USA

Gerard & Kelly, *Modern Living*, 2016. Performance view, The Glass House, New Canaan

Manifesting as site-specific events, videos filmed on location, and drawings of performance scores, *Modern Living* explores intimacy and domestic space within legacies of modernist architecture. Structured in chapters, each situated in a modernist home, the project is driven by the question, "What would a home have to look and feel like, today, to protect and produce intimacies and relations that don't fit within dominant narratives of family, marriage, or domesticity?"

The first two chapters of the project unfolded at the Schindler House in West Hollywood, California, and The Glass House in New Canaan, Connecticut, in 2016. Both homes sheltered relationships that were as radical and experimental as their designs. The Schindler House was built in 1921 by Rudolph M. Schindler to house two families who shared a kitchen, garden, and other common spaces—an early example of communal living. The Glass House protected its architect Philip Johnson and his partner, David Whitney, in a relationship that preceded the Stonewall rebellion and endured for more than forty years.

At each site, Gerard & Kelly work with a variable numbers of dancers to create a choreographic score spread throughout the interior and exterior spaces of the house. Falling in and out of sync, the dancers use the choreography of a "clock"— a series of twelve movements customized for each individual dancer and corresponding to the face of a clock—to generate rhythms, spoken memories, and temporary constellations of duos, trios, and quartets. Future chapters of *Modern Living* are planned for the Watzek House in Portland (designed by architect John Yeon) and villa e.1027, Eileen Gray's home in the South of France.

Gerard & Kelly, *Score for the Glass House*, 2016

Parking & More   HHF Architects — Basel, Switzerland

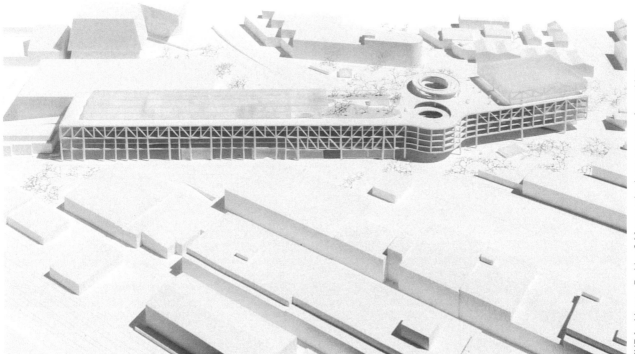

HHF Architects, *Parking & More*, a mixed-use structure for parking and a variety of public and private programs, 2014

In 1964, Bernard Rudofsky criticized the narrow focus of architectural history, which suppresses the non-representative—or, in Rudofsky's words, "non-pedigreed architecture."[1] That is, it suppresses what is erected by non-Western cultures as well as the buildings of pre-antiquity, and, even more, all the architecture that is not linked to the names of architects or master builders, whether rural buildings or anonymous dwellings. Today, the spectrum of typologies analyzed by Rudofsky requires extension to include suburban single-family houses, artistically inconsequential commercial properties, and banal factory architecture. These are buildings that surround us every day and which rarely attract our attention. They develop out of economic logic; they serve their purpose, but usually achieve no more than that.

One of these is Dreispitz, an extensive logistics and warehousing area in the south of Basel that covers fifty hectares and extends into the neighboring community of Münchenstein. Established as a public materials storage yard in 1901, the site has been subject to years of structural transformation due to changes in the logistics business and later its conversion into a cultural depot. Increased visitor traffic on the Dreispitz site, triggered by the above transformation processes, necessitates the construction of a new parking garage over the site of the existing Ruchfeld one. *Parking & More* provides an open structure for an open future. It incorporates the anonymous historical infrastructure of the surroundings, but rather than remediate and hold in an ideal state, the site is transformative: allowing future processes that are not entirely foreseeable today.

1   Bernard Rudolfsky, *Architecture Without Architects: A Short Introduction to Non-Pedigreed Architecture* (Garden City, New York: Doubleplay & Company, Inc., 1964).

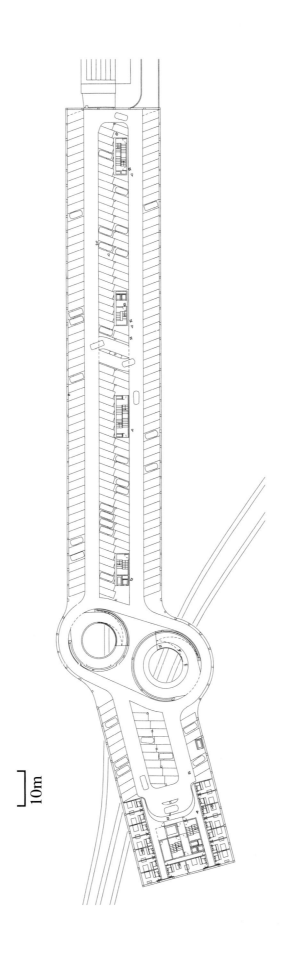

HHF architects, *Parking & More*, Upper floor plan with parking structure and built-in hotel, 2014

10m

Beehives with Asteroid, 2013–17
Iñigo Manglano-Ovalle — Chicago, USA

Iñigo Manglano-Ovalle, *Beehives with Asteroid, 2013–17*

The modern day Langstroth beehive was an invention of Rev. Lorenzo Lorraine Langstroth, an apiarist, clergyman, and teacher, considered the father of American beekeeping. His patent of the modular and movable comb hive in the late nineteenth century revolutionized beekeeping and fostered the growth of commercial honey production on a large scale in both Europe and the US. Like other commercial/industrial innovations of the time this simple beehive aligned itself with the modernist industrial movement as an unwitting adherent to form follows function.

Beehives with Asteroid, is a functioning set of structures, an installation which may or may not be put to use. It can stand within architecture or find itself outside of it. It is a readymade, repurposed, waiting to be put to purpose.

Manglano-Ovalle's minimalist white hives are set in a LeWittian grid and refer to Sol LeWitt's frequent use of open, modular structures originating from his study of the cube. The grid promotes a sense of intersecting complexity, historically contextualizing and pragmatically theorizing on instances of mapping, accounting, screening, and other standardized modes of containment. The phenomena of the grid explores sensoria that are constantly ordered and liberated by structures. Navigating it creates an interactive understanding of the relation between the ordering of physical space and the intangible network of self-sustaining beliefs and assumptions that underpin our everyday perceptions and practices.

Cosmic Latte J. MAYER H. und Partner, Architekten and Philip Ursprung — Berlin, Germany/ Zurich, Switzerland

Colour Coordinates for Cosmic Latte, the Colour of the Universe CMYK (0, 2.7, 9.6, 0), 2002

After the modernist paradigm of white architecture, the built environment today is characterized by the off-white of beige architecture. Beige is not radical and purist like white; it is moderating and popular. Beige allows formal nuances, the play with materials, subtle response to the spatial, and historical context. But while beige acts as emblem of harmony and the removal of conflict in architecture, it is omnipresent in the media as the color of violence—in the form of war images from the desert regions and the destroyed monuments from the time of the origin of our civilization.

Where does beige come from? According to the *Oxford Dictionary*, it is rooted in French and is "of unknown ultimate origin." And yet it is a universal color. Astronomers Karl Glazebrook and Ivan Baldry, in 2002, referred to the color of the universe as a "pale turquoise," then because of an error in the white balance as "light beige."[1] After a survey for name suggestions, they agreed on "Cosmic Latte." The universe is beige.

Our manifesto goes back to a design studio with Marc Kushner at Columbia University and is produced together with the artists Wermke/ Leinkauf, tho photographer Tobias Wootton, and students from ETH Zurich. It wants to expand the horizon of the architectural discussion and visualize the inner contradictions inscribed into the seemingly smooth façades of our buildings, from experimental architecture to developer architecture. It does not join in the lament of the homogenization of architecture, but quite optimistically outlines its potential. It wants to locate a new architectural paradigm and show the big in the small and the small in the big. It is a cosmology of the architecture of our time.

1   Ivan K. Baldry et al., "The 2dF Galaxy Redshift Survey: Constraints on Cosmic Star Formation History from the Cosmic Spectrum," *The Astrophysical Journal*, 569 (April 2002): 582–94.

The Ethics of Dust — New York, USA   Jorge Otero-Pailos

My work is guided by the insights of psychoanalysis, specifically, how we transition as people from one phase in life to another. Transitions are often difficult, maybe even scary.

I focus on the objects we take along with us while we are in transition. Think of how a child's teddybear helps them transition from being awake to sleeping, how refugees carry family jewels into their new lives, or how religious buildings help us cope with death. These are very special objects because they help us make sense of transitions, and when they are particularly hard, or even traumatic, they help us make them bearable.

I am more concerned with larger social groups: with what we call culture, rather than individuals. I gravitate towards monuments, the objects that entire cultures latch onto in order to transition into new phases, to remember, to celebrate, to come together, to imagine a new future.

The Ethics of Dust is a series of casts resulting from the cleaning of pollution from monuments around the world. Each cast is a piece of the polluted atmosphere deposited on a particular monument over time. Taken together, the series of casts show us the atmosphere as a cultural and architectural material creating its own new history: that of pollution's past and future effect on the environment. The lesson of the anthropocene is that pollution is our longest lasting civilizational product, more enduring than our buildings. *The Ethics of Dust* invites us to consider atmospheric pollution as an object accompanying our civilization's transition into the future, and to imagine ways we might change its course.

The Chapel junya ishigami+associates
— Tokyo, Japan

junya ishigami+associates, Study for *The Chapel*, 2017

The Chapel is a study in the way that the valley form envelopes a space: capturing its interior through different forms resulting in a variety of spaces. We designed a chapel that sits at the base of a very small valley in the Shandong province of China. From the beginning, we wished to create a new environment as if expanding the valley's terrain. We wanted to emphasize the tranquility of the existing environment, by designing a space with mysterious light that leads to the valley floor. The grandeur of this space exceeds the scale of the existing valley and also the human scale that was not previously present at the site. Both scales can now coexist in the chapel. Two closely curving concrete walls run alongside each other to form a narrow entrance at a height of 45 meters.

We designed the structure with walls gradually moving further apart from one another, then merging to enclose the altar space. This becomes a new valley between thick concrete walls as a continuation of the existing valley. The entrance and the ceiling remain open to the elements, and the chapel's form interacts with the light, wind, and rain in the production of various atmospheric and climatic moods; from spaces of darkness to gentle hazy light.

Just as the existing valley lies between two mountains, the chapel seen from afar appears as a new slender mountain.

A Purloined Argument — New York, USA   Keith Krumwiede

Keith Krumwiede, Don Barthelmismo Meets with Workers at the Palace, Freedomland, after Capital and Labour, by Henry Stacy Marks (1874), 2016

We come now to speak … of imitation, [of] borrowing a particular thought, action, attitude, or figure, and translating it into your own work. …It is generally allowed, that no [architect] need be ashamed of copying … works [that] are considered … common property [and] open to the public.[1]

[An architect] who borrows an idea … and so accommodates it to [their] own work that it makes a part of it, with no seam or joining appearing, can hardly be charged with plagiarism; poets practice this kind of borrowing, without reserve. But an [architect] should not be contented with this only; [they] should enter into a competition with [the] original, and endeavor to improve what [they are] appropriating to [their] own work. Such imitation is … a perpetual exercise of the mind, a continual invention.[2]

To find excellencies, however dispersed, to discover beauties, however concealed by the multitude of deficits with which they are surrounded, can be the work only of [one] who … has extended [their] view, … select[ing] both from what is great, and what is little, … making the universe tributary towards furnishing [their] mind and enriching [their] works with originality, and [a] variety of inventions.[3]

It is indisputably evident that a great part of every [architect's] life must be employed in collecting materials for the exercise of genius. Invention, strictly speaking, is little more than a new combination of those images that have been previously gathered and deposited in the memory. Nothing can come of nothing; [an architect] who has laid up no materials can produce no combinations.[4]

1   Joshua Reynolds, "A Discourse, Delivered … December 10, 1774," in Seven Discourses Delivered to the Royal Academy by the President, (London: T. Cadell, 1778), 234–235.
2   Ibid., 234–36.
3   Ibid., 243–44.
4   Ibid., 36.

Keith Krumweide, Plan showing a typical three-mile-square town in Freedomland, 2016

0   ½   1   1 ½ mi.

113

Paris Haussmann LAN with Franck Boutté Consultants and produced by Pavillon de l'Arsenal Paris — Paris, France

LAN with Franck Boutté Consultants, *Paris Haussman*, Pavillon de l'Arsenal, Paris, 2017

Produced by the Pavillon de l'Arsenal, the exhibition Paris Haussmann explores the Haussmann urban system at all levels through the lens of the current social and environmental challenges that our cities face in the present day. The architects Umberto Napolitano, Benoit Jallon (LAN), and the engineer-architect Franck Boutté conducted an analysis through drawings and development, which they paired with technology and calculations. Their study counts more than it recounts and yields a new definition of the Haussmann model. They looked at Paris from the large scale to its smallest dimension using contemporary criteria of connectivity, accessibility, consumption, practices, and uses. The analysis compares the Paris model's capacities to other cities across the world and other contemporary urban forms, providing a novel portrayal of a landscape that they use and admire, but do not fully know. The data confirms some hypotheses, disputes other assumptions, and invokes the criteria of contemporary urban design and architecture. Paris Haussmann thus offers renewed responses to the challenges faced by tomorrow's cities today.

N

0   50 M

PARIS 18

RUE EUGÈNE SUE ET RUE SIMART

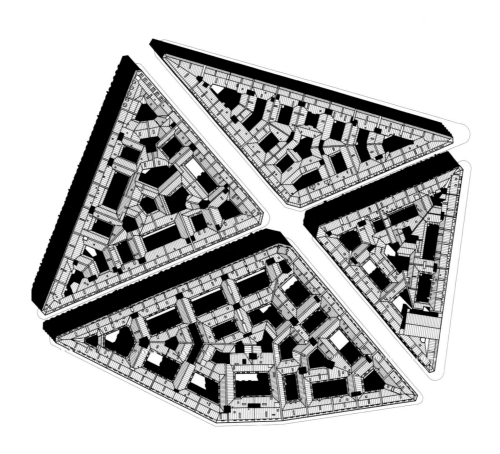

Machine Project — Los Angeles, USA

Machine Project collaborates with artists to do fun experiments, together with the public, in ways that influence culture. Founded in 2003 by artist Mark Allen, Machine Project began with the desire to create an informal community space where the public could participate in the creative process, generate ideas, and connect with contemporary art and culture in all its varied forms. Over the last 14 years, it has evolved into an informal collective of artists working together at locations ranging from beaches, to museums, to parking lots. Machine has produced shows with the Los Angeles County Museum of Art, the Hammer Museum, the Museum of Contemporary Art in Denver, the Walker Museum in Minneapolis, and the Tang Teaching Museum in Saratoga Springs, New York, as well as over 1,000 events in Los Angeles at the Machine Project storefront space.

During the 2017 Chicago Architectural Biennial, Machine is creating a series of events and actions, in and around the projects and site of the biennial, which will interpret, reimagine, or discuss the themes and pavilions. These events may or may not include indoor self-sailing blimps, an opera singer on a raft, and a cinematic psychic reading of the Chicago Cultural Center building.

Machine Project, The spiral staircase that connects Machine Project's storefront to the Mystery Theater below, 2017

Made in — Geneva and Zurich, Switzerland

Made in, *Airfield, Vaux Le Vicomte (1661)*, 2011

This project is a byproduct of the pervasive theatricality of the metropole in its relentless need for the new.

By indulging in an often-irrelevant alterity, metropolitan actors seem to have made any meaningful formal difference hardly legible; however legitimate discordances may be, they are nonetheless bound to the prerequisite of repetition as the dominant marker of singularities.

Derived from the late latin *repertorium*, meaning storehouse, a repertory is the entire assortment of things available in a field or of a kind. Inasmuch as the manifold identities of a repertoire account

for its protean expertise—its range so to speak—its most essential attribute lies in its availability: a repertory has the potential to be constantly reactivated.

In its search for a dynamic consideration of time, withstanding the contemplative view of the collective memory and its sententious unfolding of events, manner advocates for a deflective handling of history—of its canons as much as of its failures—and generates anexact figures, or "inexact by essence and not by accident."[1] History is a beat.

1   Gilles Deleuze and Félix Guattari, *Mille Plateaux* (Paris: Les Éditions de Minuit, 1980).

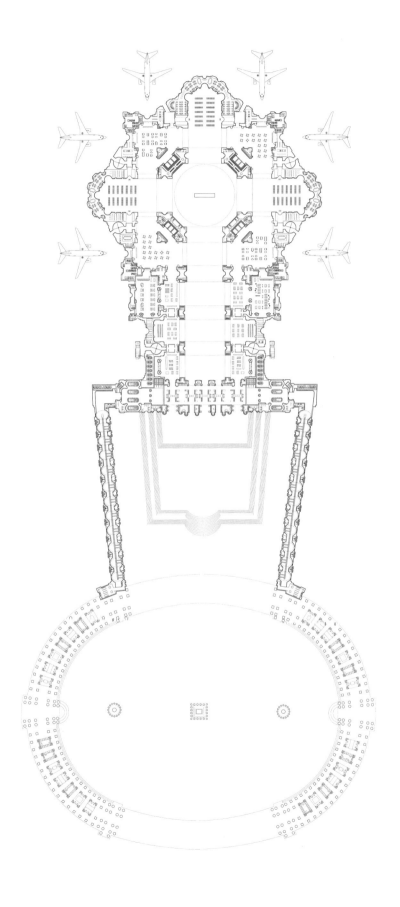

Made in, *Of Other Spaces: St Peter's Basilica (1626)*, 2011

The Architecture of Creative Miscegenation
Marshall Brown — Chicago, USA

Marshall Brown, *December 26, 2014*, from the Chimera series, 2014

Every instance of architecture is infected with references from history. Today's crisis of copyright has made the notion of origins both highly unstable and indeterminate, as originality is increasingly difficult to claim and influences are far easier to trace. Marshall Brown's collages foretell architecture that, in the words of writer Jonathan Lethem, embraces "filiations, communities, and discourses."[1] The works are grounded in what Brown calls a theorem of creative miscegenation. Miscegenation is, of course, an archaic term typically associated with racist laws that forbade racially mixed marriages and interbreeding. In this context, it serves as an adequately subversive name for Brown's sublime world of architectural half-breeds. The theorem's first assertion is that a work of architecture cannot be understood outside of the larger field of which it is part. The theorem's second assertion is that a work is not limited by its references, but it does create a new set of relations between them and itself.

Though these images begin with cutting, tearing, and dissection, they result in constructive acts of world-making. One hundred years ago, Dadaist and constructivist artists used collage to create shocking juxtapositions that represented the disruptive forces of modernization. Postmodernist architects used collage toward the end of the twentieth century to create parodies of history. Brown's architecture has a different agenda. Even if the samples are sometimes identifiable, all parts are synthesized within new wholes. Creative miscegenation is architectonic—an art of joining. This approach expands the role of history in design by positioning architecture as the formation of new alignments and new legibilities.

1   Jonathan Lethem, "The Ecstasy of Influence, A Plagiarism," *Harpers* (February 2007): 59–71. Lethem argues that creative works exist within a gift economy that establishes a bond between two people, which does not necessarily occur in a market economy, for example.

Material Histories

Once considered either the resources of a site, the means of construction, or the finishes and fabrics of the interior, understanding material in architecture today requires a larger field of reference.
A contemporary viewpoint incorporates the trend of repurposing, the subsequent practice of conflating making and curating, as well as new sensibilities and sourcing methods. For *Make New History*, participants emphasize considerations of the lifecycle of materials, their organization, and the way concepts of natural materiality are reproduced through a present-day architectural lens.

Select projects in the biennial examine the material life of architecture: sourcing, distribution, and assembly. For example, the heroicized histories of Chicago's famed timber and steel frame construction is a point of departure for Stan Allen and Design With Company. While Allen's timber stud frame model (p. 164) of aggregated rooms takes the notion of standardized timber framing through its iterative paces, Design With Company (p. 79) see design expression in the specific details of the universal steel joint. Besler & Sons LLC shift the material conversation to the participatory end, as seen in their examination of the DIY building industry of big box building supplies, as well as the amateur community built up around instructional videos on

YouTube (p. 289). Underneath this commercial argument for participation lies a challenge and expansion to the traditional notions of architectural knowledge and expertise.

If modernist ordering systems like the grid favor universalizing abstraction, the contemporary ordering systems follow a more idiosyncratic and qualitative model of association. It has been suggested that contemporary material orders are akin to the flea market: with new and often surprising associations between material forms and organization.[1] BLESS' *Lounge Conquerors No. 60* (p. 70) takes commercially available furniture to dress and compose in strange postures that disrupt conventional readings of leisure, rest, and comfort while also indicating at the frivolity of the new-and-next. This type of sampling is written into modern architecture's very logic through design tools including catalogs, interior mood boards, and specifications that have allowed for the quick selection and consumption of a plethora of finishes and material treatments. Greek office Point Supreme (p. 139) carefully compose selected vernacular materials, textures, and fixtures; their ad hoc totems operate as ex post facto material boards merging with the contemporary appeal of curation and display. These acts of recycling also shift the way we think about the life of buildings. Building parts, in their individuality as well as in

1   Nicolas Bourriaud, *Postproduction* (New York: Lukas & Sternberg, 2002).

recombination, may be read as carriers of very literal historical information in the marks of their former ownership and location: what Walter Benjamin called the magic encyclopedia of its provenance.[2]

Ábalos + Sentkiewicz exemplify the projects that consider the environmental scale of architecture. Their *Planta Project* (p. 40) continues the office's interest in thermodynamic models by recirculating the stone from the quarry site to the building—specifically, a museum—effectively gesturing towards the material distribution of the contemporary museum's redevelopment of postindustrial sites. The consideration of large-scale influence of industrial development on the landscape indicated in the project above is perhaps the impetus of architectural projects that appeal to fabrications of naturalism. Several projects in the biennial share a formal appeal to the geological, prehistoric, and primitive forms, such that they might have splintered off into another category of natural histories. Formlessfinder consider a type of naturalism in the possibilities of matter: often utilizing sand or gravel as something that has facts and properties, like entropic forces (p. 276). Since these elements do not behave according to constructive traditions of architecture, they indicate a desire to destabilize the tendency toward formal ordering that comes alongside questions of material.

2   Walter Benjamin, "Unpacking My Library," in *Illuminations*, ed. Hannah Arendt (New York: Schocken Books, 1969), 59.

Rooms for Books   MG&Co. — Houston, USA

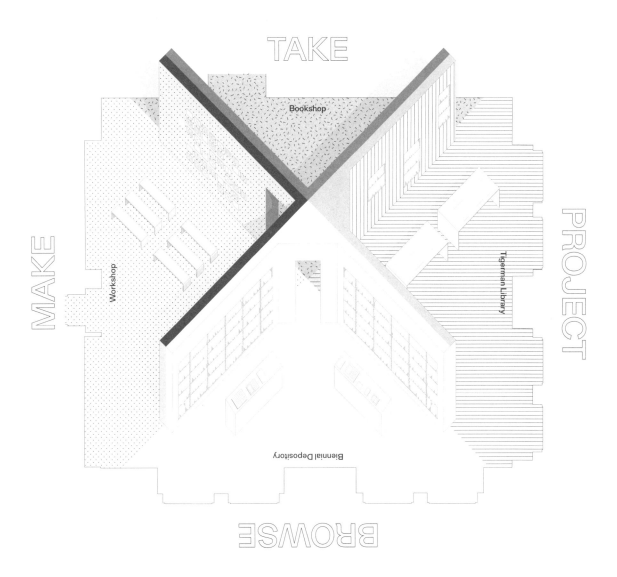

MG&Co., *Rooms for Books*, 2017

Books and architecture are intricately intertwined. Despite prophetic claims that printed matter would disappear in the age of electronic media, the book—in its material presence, durability, and its spatial and temporal qualities—persists. It remains an ideal medium for architects to use as they discuss, reflect, clarify, organize, and broadcast their ideas. The book can equally be a vehicle to advance architectural discourse and to critically address larger audiences, both within and outside of the discipline. *Rooms for Books* transforms the traditional bookshop into a platform for reflection and for the presentation, documentation, production, and dissemination of the architecture book. It is made up of four separate spaces: a repository that houses resources on the participants of the show; a room

dedicated to the analysis and display of Stanley and Margaret Tigerman's library; a room to advance the creation of new content, including talks, roundtable discussions, and interviews, and its translation into printed matter; and a bookstore offering a selection of titles for sale. The installation, divided into this series of discrete but closely connected rooms, stages the book as a decisive medium in the negotiation between practice and theory, between the discipline and its history, and between architecture and precedent. Each of the four spaces, every one in itself a room for books, is meant to produce a different context from within which to consider the architecture book as such and its relationship to the past, the present, and the future.

Make No Little Plans Monadnock — Rotterdam, Netherlands

This is not a proposal for a building, nor it is referring to the reality of the building industry. This object is to be understood as the carrier of allusions, architectural gestures, and narratives: alluding to an elaboration of stacked chapters, fragments, or architectural orders: deliberately seeking for the distortion of scales, in order to provoke reflections on the possibilities and functionalities of architecture. The result is an object that is both symbolic and decorative; it refers to a possible structure of a building.

The theme of signage plays a specific role as it has the ability to change the architecture of a building. The silhouette is complemented with a counter-form of contrasting character and appearance; sometimes refined, most of the time this will be an undesired temporary passenger with great impact. The signage refers to a famous quote by Daniel H. Burnham, one of the architects of the Monadnock building and director of the World's Columbian Exposition in Chicago of 1893. The full quote by Daniel Burnham reads,

"Make no little plans. They have no magic to stir men's blood and probably themselves will not be realized. Make big plans; aim high in hope and work, remembering that a noble, logical diagram once recorded will never die, but long after we are gone will be a living thing, asserting itself with ever-growing insistency. Remember that our sons and grandsons are going to do things that would stagger us. Let your watchword be order and your beacon beauty. Think big."[1]

1   Charles Moore, *Daniel H. Burnham Architect Planner of Cities*, vol. 2 (Boston and New York: Houghton Mifflin Company, 1921).

Monadnock, Model for *Make No Little Plans*, 2017

Building (Hi)story: Before and After Architecture
Nuno Brandão Costa with André Cepeda
— Porto, Portugal

The protagonist of history is time. Architecture adds a fourth dimension to its essence in its process and construction. Timelessness is a value whose identification in architecture is the validation of its quality. In order to make architecture, we must deal with the architecture that has already been made beyond the superficiality of the fleeting, epidermal images that we are confronted with on a daily basis.

The new project always looks at the old or the recent, finding its bearings, criticizing, or appropriating history.

This act of looking corresponds to the process of construction of the project, a cultural act involving memory as a prime vehicle of conception. The architect is almost always a collector of memories and he builds the work like an oarsman; he rows forward, looking backwards.

Nuno Brandão Costa and André Cepeda propose to present a selection of constructed works with different briefs, scales, and times from two fundamental elements: the concept drawing (done by hand) and the current photographic record documented by Cepeda. The drawings and the photographic record exist as two temporally opposed moments: the embryonic moment of the construction of an idea and the work constructed and in use. The drawing is a synthesis of the idea, and essentially adds the references of the project and the work constructed, finished, already used, or still under construction.

Nuno Brandão Costa, Sketch for House in Sobrado, 2006

Nuno Brandão Costa, Sketch for House in Melgaço, 2010

Unconnoted Happiness
Pascal Flammer — Zurich, Switzerland

The main goal of the office is to produce form based on our understanding of life and our wishes for it. The representation of these goals is what we call a proposal. It contains either a physical or a mental manipulation of the world. The design process is focused on three parts:

A. Analysis
The first part is purely analytical and self-reflective without the consideration of form yet. We try to define what we fundamentally care for and to understand, rationalize, and verbalize our preoccupations and fascinations. This method is a psychological analysis of mind and behavior. The psychology unfolds the personal relevance and is a tool for description of universal relevance. The more explicit and inclusive the distilled analysis, the more powerful it is to serve as a guideline to the second part of the design—the manifestation of the form.

B. Manifestation of the Form
The abstract and formless analysis is transformed into a mental and physical manifestation—in the most holistic and feasible form possible. Site, space, function, and construction are developed according to the guidelines of the analysis with the goal to maximize its intensity by virtuosity and elegance of the architect's craft. The full gamut of architectural tools shall be considered; the most powerful method and style shall be used.

C. Representation
The transformation from analysis to form exists only in the author's mind and remains undefined in many aspects. In the process of representation, the creator sifts through the mental form to clarify and communicate his thoughts to others. With the means of language, the process finds its final form: that which we call proposal.

These three parts are described as a seemingly consecutive method. More often they are not; they are non-linear, largely interpretive, and incomplete.

Pascal Flammer, *The owls are not what they see*, BALTS projects, Zurich, Switzerland, 2014

METROPOLITANA
Piovene Fabi with Giovanna Silva — Milan, Italy

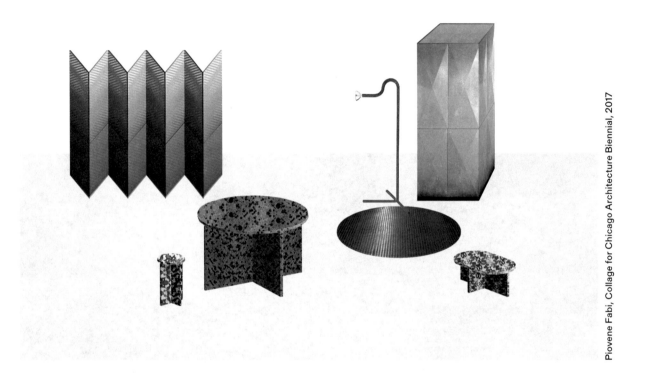

Piovene Fabi, Collage for Chicago Architecture Biennial, 2017

There was a time in Italy—during the booming 1950s and 1960s—where everything was possible. Emerging architects, artists, writers, and graphic designers, the cultural avant-garde of the time, were invited by companies and institutions to define a new manifesto of modernity. A modernity with no compromises, far from the difficult years of the war. Production was customized, precise, and ready-made. The future was there.

The first subway line in Italy, the M1 (or Red Line), was opened in Milan on November 1, 1964.—the M1 (or red line). At that time, the new infrastructure injected the idea of an Italian metropolis in a country that previously had little to do with it.

The project of the subway stations was assigned to the architects Franco Albini and Franca Helg and to the graphic designer Bob Noorda. Aiming to give an outstanding identity to the new Milanese transport vector, their intervention was a light but resistant superstructure which dressed an already built infrastructural void. The subway finishes were "designed searching for the standardization of materials, to achieve a certain repeatability."[1]

Production companies were proud to be part of such a challenge: new materials were tested for the occasion, such as the Silipol—a colorful stained concrete—or the Pirelli black rubber floor—which later became a mainstream flooring choice.

Within the different reality of today—just fifty years later—such a productive effort appears as pure archeology.

METROPOLITANA is a series of furniture pieces, which reinterprets the project for the Milanese Subway lines 1 and 2. As an act of appropriation, every single component of the Albini-Noorda project is removed from its context and transformed into a mono-material object standing on its own. The metropolitan project is therefore dismantled and recomposed in parts, performing as a series of individual pieces in a new domestic landscape.

1   Franco Albini as quoted in, "Gallery," Metro Milano, accessed May 15, 2017, http://www.metromilano50.com/scopri-la-rossa/architettura/.

Franco Albini, Loreto Metro Station, Milan, 1969

Five Rooms   Paul Andersen and Paul Preissner — Chicago, USA

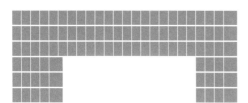

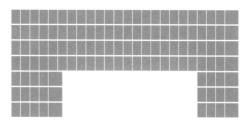

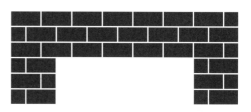

The Landmark Gallery in the Chicago Cultural Center suffers from an ambiguous identity as both a gallery and a corridor. It is too wide to be a hallway and too narrow to comfortably view exhibitions. Paul and Paul's project creates an enfilade of small galleries, which are conducive to viewing small or detailed works that might be overwhelmed by the Cultural Center's main galleries. The new rooms are defined by five pairs of heavy walls with curious forms—wiggly, stacked, thick, corduroy, and bent— and roughly equal openings that nearly line up along the length of the space. The walls are visually suspended in the existing gallery, so that each of the five rooms is defined by a pair of walls and the art works exhibited in between. All of the walls are made of structural glazed tile—a material commonly used in train stations, public schools, recreation centers, and other municipal buildings—in two colors per gallery, with the seam between the two sets consistently at eye level. The unconventional use of tile and the enfilade layout, which has been a defining form of museums and urban thoroughfares for centuries, sharpens the gallery's unique convergence of fine arts and public works.

Paul Andersen and Paul Preissner, *Five Rooms*, 2017

Finite Format 04 Pezo von Ellrichshausen Arquitectos — Concepción, Chile

We have never used precedents, concepts, or metaphors to produce our work. We have simply preferred to assume every case as a discrete one: as a self-referential system within our own shared, and certainly naïve, domain of intuitions and inventions. Since then, and with a rather short and impulsive memory, we have chosen to refer to the things we do by means of the things we have done. Thus, we look back to the thousands of pages of our early sketchbooks to try to understand our own motivations, our architectonic fictions, daydreams, and denials. "The fate of all paper, from the moment it leaves the factory, is to begin to grow old," as written in José Saramago's 2001 novel *All the Names*.[1] Ideas start as curiosities, then become fascinations (sooner or later obsessions), to only later erode and become obsolete. Why? We do not know. As far as we can recall, we only portrayed this inverted T-shaped tower after inhabiting it. Its silhouette is a double format: a figure that is no more than the outline for a field of action, the room contained within a laconic building, with a latent human scale given by its openings. Its identity is both singular and familiar. Each figure of the painted series is internally the same as the others yet with a highly specific and unique formal character. Since every object is successively transformed according to three pervasive sizes (small, medium, and large), the most basic three-dimensional figure (i.e. a cube) becomes twenty-seven variations of volume and direction. As the figure becomes more complex, the resulting series of transformation increases proportionally. Hereafter, a figure defined by four factors produces eighty-one variations. A figure with five factors, two hundred and forty-three. The one presented here, with an outline described by six factors, results in 729 variations. In order to highlight the individuality of each building, a seemingly random combination of 81 different colors separate its continuous surface into planes. If the figure would be a sign, it would be pointing towards itself—tower and plinth, and everything else in between.

1   José Saramago and Margaret Costa, *All the Names* (New York: Mariner Books, 2001).

Thermodynamic Tectonic
Philippe Rahm architectes — Paris, France

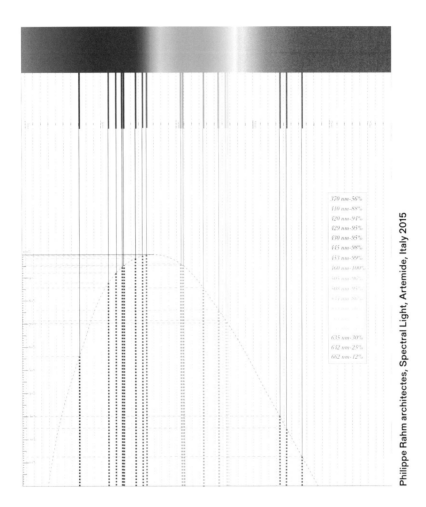

370 nm-56%
410 nm-88%
420 nm-94%
429 nm-95%
430 nm-95%
445 nm-98%
453 nm-99%
460 nm-100%
505 nm-96%
508 nm-95%
555 nm-96%

635 nm-30%
642 nm-25%
662 nm-12%

Philippe Rahm architectes, Spectral Light, Artemide, Italy 2015

A large part of the history of architecture is about the aesthetic history of the solid.

Our purpose today is to take up this history in the face of the new energy and climate issues that are changing our era, and forcing us to establish a new phase in the history of the architectural building solid. This new phase commenced when architects were forced to thermally insulate their buildings from the outside.

Thermodynamic tectonic is an introduction in this renewed field of the materiality of the solid used in building, conditioned by the climatic and energy stakes of today. What we want to bring into the definition of the solid—and the physical expressivity of a building—are thermal and climatic values, such as those of reflectance, emissivity, or effusivity, in addition to conductivity to join the established definition of exterior insulation. The aim is to facilitate the human climate production inside the building, to reduce the energy consumption, and to improve the outdoor comfort in front of the facades of buildings.

Thermodynamic tectonic is a manifesto. We propose not to choose materials according to analogue or memorial criteria, but according to energy and climatic criteria. For instance, the gradient effusivity carpet proposes a highly perceptible gradation of four materials according to their intrinsic property of effusivity, from the coldest to the warmest, between a white woolen floor, a light gray wooden floor, a dark gray stone floor, and a black steel floor. Each material will qualify slightly the space around it by modifying the climate and the tactile experience of the inhabitants.

Totems   Point Supreme — Athens, Greece

Point Supreme, *Totems*, 2016

Totems consists of three vertical lists of things: all material samples that were used in the recently built Petralona House. Most of the elements were self-made: collected in markets or islands, donated, or sponsored by shops and companies. This method provided the architecture with an alternative modus operandi that overcame the limitations of building during the financial crisis and informed the design. The samples range from artificial and market-produced to natural and handmade; they are new or reclaimed, original or copies, Greek or imported, traditional or provocative, valuable or insignificant, designed or accidental, whole or modular, and are processed in ways both traditional and experimental. They make formally defined figures, treated as equal whether they are decorative or structural, interior or exterior, and regardless of their scale or value; a marble statue is sitting across from a plastic pot, together with a hose, a stone, poured concrete, antique tiles, a plug, a piece of graffiti, a bronze handrail. Each of these abstracted objects corresponds to precise pieces of the world. The relationships between the elements and the design of the house are dense and systematic, uncanny but familiar. The three totems vaguely correspond to three areas: exterior, ground, top. They form an alternative representation of the house that reveals how it is made by incorporating different histories and traditions into one and the same project.

Reuse of the Dom Revolucije — Ljubljana, Slovenia   SADAR+VUGA

On the 30th anniversary of the liberation of Nikšić, the Municipal Assembly voted to build a memorial to the fallen fighters for freedom and the socialist revolution. The works on the Home of Revolution commenced in 1978, following the ambitious design of Slovenian architect Marko Mušič (1941–). The center was planned to contain various social functions and cultural venues, catering to the needs of the growing industrial Montenegrin town.

After 11 years, the construction works were suspended and the memorial was left unfinished. The current state of the structure, even when decaying, is a magnificent reminder of the technical capabilities of the twentieth century, which effortlessly transformed the voluptuous drawings by Mušič into fascinating ambiances. The structure, now embellished with shattered blue glass, moss carpets, and colorful graffiti, offers a sensory experience similar to a cathedral.

The winning competition design for the structure's reconstruction by SADAR+VUGA and HHF Architects in 2016 proposes a gradual adaptation strategy. This approach of adaptive reuse has many focuses: firstly, it respects the original idea of the author and is reluctant to appropriate his work. Secondly, it is in awe with the current state of openness that makes the building appear as it was a covered public space. Thirdly, it takes into account the current size of Nikšić and its needs; it refuses to program the whole structure, but rather allows organic occupation according to future needs. Thus, this strategy is pragmatic towards its past, takes its inspiration from the present, and is excited about the open-ended future.

Marko Mušič, Concept design for Dom Revolucije, 1979

A obrazovni centar
B velika dvorana i
  svečani prostori
C klub mladih

SADAR+VUGA, HHF Architects, and Dijana Vučinić, Adaptation and reconstruction
of Dom Revolucije, Nikšic, Montenegro, 2016

143

Casa Âncora   SAMI-Arquitectos with Paulo Catrica — Setubal, Portugal

For many decades, Casa Âncora was the only place where the people of São Roque do Pico met, playing an important role in the society of this isolated small village. Following the client's brief for a new building, we proposed to maintain the social and urban importance of the historical building, giving back to the village a relevant place of its history: the café where they all felt at home. Our design reimagines what it is to produce a timeless architecture that is deeply specific to the local notion of everyday life, yet follows the tradition of the European Grands Cafés of the nineteenth century. For the past few years, Pico Island has been in the process of growing tourism. As the only contemporary building in the village, this structure is now conceived as a meeting place for locals and tourists, again.

Working for more than 15 years on this black-rock island in the middle of the Atlantic Ocean has shaped our way of thinking about architecture. In the presence of such a strong natural and rural context we seek to be adequate, insisting on design so that it disappears. In a land where everything has a purpose or function and basalt rock defines both the landscape features and the archaic built forms— in the words of Portuguese architect Eduardo Souto de Moura, "the Island functions as a machine" —the process of understanding this context, its topography, its volcanic roots, its rural society, its weather, its ambitions, seemed the only way possible to make architecture.

Paulo Catrica, Casa Âncora, São Roque do Pico, Azores, 2016

South Park: Proleptic Notes on the Barack Obama Presidential Center — Edward Eigen

The report might also have stated, with perfect truth, that men had been hired by the Government and paid out of the public Treasury, *to pick up the falling leaves...*

— Speech of Mr. Ogle, of Pennsylvania, on the Regal Splendor of the President's Palace: Delivered in the House of Representative, April 14, 1840

Let us begin at Hyde Park. Not the imperfectly neighborly home of the University of Chicago, the one that "owes name and existence" to the lawyer, real estate promoter, and "father" of the South Park system, Paul Cornell.[1] Whatever share he had in its origination, Cornell was outvoted by his fellow commissioners when they elected to redesignate South Park's lake-facing lower division, then still "mainly an uncultivated country," in honor of "Old Hickory," General Jackson. A more protracted process led to the recent announcement of Jackson Park as the future home of the Barack Obama Presidential Center.

In its natural state, wrote South Park designers Frederick Law Olmsted and Calvert Vaux, the site contained many trees of "considerable size." But not one of them was of a "character which would be high value in a park," and most of them were "struggling for mere existence,"[2] beset by "unfortunate influences" acting on their foliage and roots. What belongs in a park once it is subjected to cultivation and patronage, when the trees "at present on the ground" are not fit to remain? What belongs in the presidential library? When it comes to claims of heritage and, relatedly, with the propriety of place names, matters tend to become unsettled. And which Hyde Park? We refer, for the moment, to that "little village on the Hudson River," the site of the Franklin D. Roosevelt Presidential Library and Museum. By one account, published in conjunction with the Chicago International Exposition of 1933, this prototypical spot of the American picturesque, then "much in the public eye" as the home of newly elected president,[3] was Cornell's inspiration for his leafy commuter suburb of Chicago, rather than the "aristocratic London district, as is commonly supposed."[4]

The "Century of Progress," the 1933 Chicago World's Fair exposition, unapologetically

1   "How Chicago's Suburbs Were Planted and Named," *Chicago Daily Tribune*, March 4, 1900, 37.
2   Olmsted, Vaux, & Co., "Report Accompanying Plan for Laying Out the South Park," 1871, 10.
3   John Ashenhurst and Ruth L. Ashenhurst, *All About Chicago* (New York: Houghton Mifflin, 1933), 165.
4   Ibid.

celebrated the Treaty of Chicago of 1833, by which, according to the provisions of the Removal Act, signed by President Andrew Jackson, the Potawatomi, Chippewa (Ojibwa), and Ottawa (Odawa) peoples gave up title to their land and commenced their fatal emigration beyond the Mississippi River, the so-called Father of Waters (by mistaken reference to an Algonquin word).[5] George B. Porter, Governor of the Territory of Michigan, solicitously advised the assembled chiefs, "Your Great Father, the President of the United States, has a perfect knowledge of the condition and interests of his red children." Thus, he wanted to see them "made happy and removed far beyond the evils which now surround them."[6] There they could enjoy freedom from fear, provoked by the Great Father himself.

As for how Chicago's Hyde Park came into itself, a series in the *Chicago Daily Tribune*, titled "How Chicago's Suburbs Were Planted and Named," allowed that Cornell himself hardly recalled "whether the American or the English town most influenced him."[7] But one thing was certain: Cornell had "christened the seemingly hopeless region of sand and swamps where he meant to build a suburb, in June 1855."[8] In proper recognition of this redemptive act, "no one has ever successfully disputed" Cornell's "familiar title of the 'father of the south parks.'"[9] This once hopeless region will soon be the institutional home to the visionary who had the audacity to "reclaim the American dream." In announcing the choice of the South Side for his library, the president reflected, "All the strands of my life came together and I really became a man when I moved to Chicago."[10] Some rather more frayed strands of American history connect Obama to Jackson Park, named for the master of the Hermitage. While the word traditionally refers to a hermit's retreat, a place of spiritual or philosophical retirement, "Hermitage" was briefly adopted by Thomas Jefferson to adorn his Palladian plantation outside Charlottesville, Virginia. The name first appears in his garden books, in a memorandum on inoculating cherry buds into "stocks of large kind."[11] Jackson's Hermitage was originally a modest

plantation, purchased in 1804, chosen "for its perfect accord with his feelings; for he had then actually withdrawn from the stage of public life."[12] He was for a time in the wilderness. A graceful estate, but no state of grace, the Hermitage developed into a thriving theater of rural industry. Like Monticello, it was also a theater of cruelty sustained by slave labor.

Where does Obama's own legacy to history belong? Unlike Augie March, that somber city's most famous literary son, Obama cannot muscularly assert, "I am an American, Chicago born." A native of Hawai'i, his self-told story of race and inheritance is altogether more Ismaelitish. In Obama's own words, he is the "son of a black man from Kenya and a white woman from Kansas," and married to a "black American who carries within her blood the blood of slaves and slave-owners."[13] He made his name as a community organizer, working in the physically degraded and dispiriting Altgeld Gardens Homes, a public housing project at Chicago's southernmost edge. A corner of South Park, once the site of a temporary and illusory White City, is now set aside for the stewards of Obama's legacy to tend. To properly situate this development, we begin, as earlier mentioned, in Hyde Park, or rather Krum Elbow, as Franklin Delano Roosevelt wished the place to be known, where the idea of domesticating the messy paperwork of presidential history had a fitful home birth.

Krum Elbow

On December 10, 1938, during a special press conference held in his oval study on the second floor of the White House, President Roosevelt announced his intention to present his papers to the Federal Government and donate land for a library to house them.[14] Roosevelt realized that the Library of Congress, The National Archives, and the New York State Historical Society would probably be glad to have the collection. Depending on how they are read, the principles of archival provenance more or less dictated to which of these repositories belonged the papers produced during his time in office as Assistant Secretary of the Navy, governor of the state of New York, and finally as president. Yet the Harvard historian Samuel Eliot Morison made the compelling argument for keeping together, or "intact," all of Roosevelt's papers and other historical material (including books, works of art, ship models, plats, maps and other similar material)

5   Muriel H. Wright, "The Naming of the Mississippi," *Chronicles of Oklahoma* 6, no. 4 (1928), 529–53.
6   "Journal of the Proceedings of a Treaty between the United States and the United Tribes of the Pottawottamies, Chippeways, and Ottowas, Chicago, Cook City, Illinois, September 13, 1833," in James Ryan Haydon, *Chicago's True Founder: Thomas J. V. Owen* (Lombard, IL: Owen Memorial Fund, 1934), 242–43.
7   "How Chicago's Suburbs Were Planted and Named," 37.
8   Ibid.
9   Ibid.
10   "Obama Foundation Announces South Side as Home for Library." https://www.youtube.com/watch?v=d2Q3xFpf-KE&feature=youtu. be (Accessed May 1, 20017).
11   Edwin M. Betts, ed., *Thomas Jefferson's Garden Book, 1766–1824: With Relevant Extracts from His Other Writings* (Philadelphia: American Philosophical Society, 1944), 6.

12   Thomas Benton, *Thirty Years' View; Or, A History of the Working of the American Government for Thirty Years, from 1820 to 1850*, vol. 1 (New York: D. Appleton, 1886), 736.
13   "Barack Obama's Speech on Race" (transcript), *New York Times*, March 18, 2008.
14   "Roosevelt Estate to House Archives, Go to Public Later," *New York Times*, December 11, 1938.

as the cohesive product and portrait of a remarkable and singular life of public service and leadership. At the news conference, Roosevelt called on Morison to address a more general and dire problem, the "losses that had occurred in the past and the mutilation that presidential papers and records had suffered."[15] In his published remarks endorsing the library project, Morison draws on the famous autumnal simile from John Milton's *Paradise Lost* to address the urgent need to keep things in order, safe from the scattering effects of time and mischance. "Once thick as autumn leaves at Vallombrosa," he writes, "the papers of the presidents have for the most part gone with the winds of housecleaning and neglect. Some have been the victims of fire; only those of recent times have been preserved in anything approaching their one-time completeness in the White House."[16]

In making arrangements for the perpetual housekeeping of a presidential legacy, the planners of Roosevelt's library looked forward to a future if not also a final state of completeness, the institutional identity of which would ultimately transcend Roosevelt's own life in and beyond office, and indeed his own person. Thus House Joint Resolution 268 (April 19, 1939) provided for the establishment and maintenance of the Franklin D. Roosevelt Library "and other purposes," defined Roosevelt as the "donor" of certain "historical material," and authorized archivist of the United States, "for and in the name of the United States," to accept title to a tract of land located on the New York-Albany Post Road, in the town of Hyde Park, Dutchess County, State of New York.[17] The Franklin D. Roosevelt Library, Incorporated, organized for that purpose, was correspondingly authorized to construct a building, or buildings, to be designated as the Franklin D. Roosevelt Library, and to landscape the grounds.

Granted a corporate birth certificate, an operating agency was put in place to carefully tend to the housing and holding of the donor's effects.[18] A non-profit membership corporation, a sort of legal fiction, is not as morally and physically intimate as the "joint stock company of two," which was how Herman Melville described the tense "monkey rope" that binds together the oddly mated crewmen Ishmael and Queequeg.[19] But what it accomplished in this instance was to gather together the separate and perishable historical sources of personhood and the distinct personages of the president, real and symbolic, living and dead. "Roosevelt Estate to House Archives, Go to Public Later," ran the headline of the *New York Times* article covering the White House announcement. As the President explained, "that part of my family's country place at Hyde Park on which we live will, without doubt, eventually go the Federal Government to be maintained for the benefit of the public by the Federal Government."[20] The only inevitability of history is the eventuality of its own revision.

The choice of Hyde Park was at once patently obvious and beset by second thoughts. If traveling to this rewardingly remote spot, about four and a half miles north of Poughkeepsie, the Queen City of the Hudson, presented some inconvenience to history students who wished to consult its unique collections, Morison observed, then it needed to be weighed against the "sentimental value" of having the library at Roosevelt's home, at Krum Elbow.[21] The force of sentiment is more typically overcome by the imperious dictates of practical necessity, even as expressed or understood by hidebound historians. But as the future Pulitzer prize-winning newspaper correspondent Anne O'Hare McCormick noted, "Roosevelt...rooted in land settled for generations, living all his life in the house his grandfather had lived in, looked out from Krum Elbow on such a prospect, scenic, social, and spiritual, as Washington might have seen from the pillared porch of Mount Vernon. He grew out of this setting, was perfectly at home in the world; his fluent charm is the fruit of assurance and savoir-faire."[22] Let us keep in mind the Lukan pericope, "For every tree is known by his own fruit" (Luke 6:44 KJV), which Andrew Jackson remarked was a "favourite adage with me."[23] That this ancestral setting, which Roosevelt grew out of but never outgrew, was a source of self-possession is best revealed by his pre-occupation with changing its name. Where was this Krum Elbow, after all?

15   *Hearings before the Committee on the Library, House of Representatives. Seventy-Sixth Congress, First Session on H. J. Res. 268 A Joint Resolution to Provide for the Establishment and Maintenance of the Franklin D. Roosevelt Library, and for Other Purposes* (Washington, D.C.: Government Printing Office, 1939), 14.
16   Samuel Eliot Morison, "The Very Essence of History," *New York Times Magazine* (March 19, 1939), 4.
17   *Hearings before the Committee on the Library*, 1.
18   Waldo Gifford Leland, "The Creation of the Franklin D. Roosevelt Library: A Personal Narrative," *The American Archivist* 18, no. 1 (1955), 17.
19   A lover of the sea, Roosevelt considered whaling ships an "American epic symbol." See Franklin Delano Roosevelt, Introduction to Clifford W. Ashley, *Whaleships of New Bedford* (Boston: Houghton Mifflin, 1929), vi.
20   "Roosevelt Estate to House Archives, Go to Public Later," *New York Times*, December 11, 1938.
21   Samuel Eliot Morison, "Memorandum on the Proposed Franklin D. Roosevelt Library at Hyde Park, New York," in *Hearings before the Committee on the Library*, 24.
22   Anne O'Hare McCormick, "Two Men at the Big Moment," *New York Times Magazine* (November 6, 1932), 1.
23   Andrew Jackson to James Monroe (Nashville, January 16, 1817), in Harold D. Moser, David R. Hoth, and George H. Hoemann, eds., *Papers of Andrew Jackson, Volume IV, 1816–1820* (Knoxville, TN: University of Tennessee Press, 1994), 81.

In a letter published in the *New York Times* (January 12, 1933), in response to a competing claim to the name Krum Elbow made by Howland Spencer, who was Roosevelt's neighbor, boyhood friend, and distant relative by marriage, Mrs. Walter Graeme Eliot (Maud Stoutenburgh) vigorously suggested that the "contention that Krum Elbow is or ever was on the west bank of the Hudson River is erroneous."[24] Spencer was dismayed by the President-elect's attempt to assume the name Spencer himself had long used for his estate directly across river. Krum Elbow Creek winds in and out at Hyde Park, Mrs. Eliot explained, and was identified by early Dutch settlers as *Kromme Elboge*, meaning Crooked Elbow.[25] The name properly belonged to the place, as if by natural right. But Mrs. Eliot's real concern seems to have been to establish the presence of her Stoutenburgh ancestors, one of the Great Nine Partners who received the patent for what became Hyde Park, in papers that had "been in her family since 1697."[26] As for the President-elect, who was invariably said to be of old Dutch Stock, Mrs. Eliot was confident that Roosevelt was certain of his historic knowledge of Dutchess County. This fact was demonstrated later that year, when Roosevelt delivered an "extemporaneous speech" at the Hyde Park Methodist Episcopal Church, in which he detailed his efforts as the town's Official Historian. Working with the pastor, he had compiled records of the Methodist Episcopal and other churches in the township, for the reason that in the "old days," when Hyde Park was still known as Krum Elbow, the only "statistics relating the births and marriages and deaths were to be found" in the churches' registers.[27] Access to the records was his un-self-conscious historical birthright.

In response to Mrs. Eliot's letter, Spencer wrote to the *New York Times* to point out that the first maps printed by the United States government clearly show the location of Krum Elbow Point on the west side of the Hudson, and that her own discovery that British war maps labeled the east side as Stoutenburgh was a compelling "reason why that name might be taken instead of appropriating an estate name already established and

cherished by a neighbor."[28] Evidently sensing that historical documents might prove unpersuasive, as is often the case, Spencer appealed to the rule of law. In yet another letter, he asserted: "This property I inherited and make my home. Pursuant to Chapter 145, Laws of 1912, concerning names of real property, the name Krum Elbow mentioned as a definite boundary in the original patent of 1678 is registered legally as belonging to me."[29] But Spencer was finally willing to make a concession. "As an inaugural present and a token of neighborly good will, I wish the President-elect to share this name if he chooses, provided, of course, the dignified and gracious lady, Mrs. James Roosevelt, who owns the property, concurs."[30] As it happens, Sara Delano Roosevelt (Mrs. James Roosevelt) overruled her son the President, insisting that the correct and proper name for their family home was Hyde Park.[31]

As president, however, Roosevelt enjoyed a special prerogative, exercised within indistinctly prescribed administrative limits, to redesignate the inherited and/or inherent order of things. He put the matter of Krum Elbow before the Board of Geographical Names, a division of the United States Department of the Interior. After some deliberation, the fairness and transparency of which was speculated on in the press, the board issued a decision: "Crum Elbow Point: a point on the east bank of the Hudson River about four and a half miles above Poughkeepsie, Dutchess County, N.Y."[32] When his neighborly if not also Solomonic offer of name-sharing was rebuffed by Roosevelt, whose New Deal for America he detested, Spencer shifted the terms of the dispute. Out of both principle and prejudice, on July 29, 1938, he sold Krum Elbow to Reverend Major Jealous Father Divine, the charismatic and entrepreneurial leader of the Harlem-based Peace Mission Movement. The movement's newspaper, the *Spoken Word*, frequently attacked the Roosevelt administration and its social welfare programs, which it saw as depriving honest but needy downtrodden people of the work ethic conducive to self-respect. The purchase of Krum Elbow, to serve as a rural "Heaven" where members of his flock, or "Angels," could enjoy and cultivate the land, realized Father Divine's long battle against residential segregation.[33] Yet, despite his avowed support of Father Divine's (highly profitable)

24 Mrs. Walter Graeme Eliot, "Krum Elbow Creek," *New York Times*, January 12, 1933, 16. According to Mrs. Eliot, Hyde Park was originally known as Clinton, and this name was changed to Stoutenburgh, which can be seen on "ancient maps and on the British war maps." The place derived its present name from the country seat now belonging to Frederick Vanderbilt, which was named Hyde Park by its then owner Peter Fauconnier, secretary to Edward Hyde, Viscount Cornbury (1661–1723), the royal governor of colonial New York and New Jersey

25 Ibid.

26 Ibid.

27 Franklin Delano Roosevelt, "Extemporaneous Speech at the Hyde Park Methodist Church. Cooperation from the Churches. September 29, 1933," *The Public Papers and Addresses of Franklin D. Roosevelt*, vol. 2 (New York: Random House, 1938), 366.

28 Howland Spencer, "The Krum Elbow Controversy," *New York Times*, January 16, 1933, 14.

29 "Closing the Controversy," *New York Times*, March 1, 1933, 35.

30 Ibid.

31 "President Overruled by Mother on Krum Elbow," *New York Times*, August 3, 1933, 1.

32 *Decisions of the United States Board on Geographical Names. Decisions Rendered Between July 1, 1936 and June 30, 1937* (Washington, DC: Government Printing Office, 1937), 10.

33 Jill Watts, *God, Harlem U.S.A.: The Father Divine Story* (Berkeley: University of California Press, 1995), 158.

utopian vision, Spencer's racially tinged motive was readily apparent.[34] As the *New York Times* plainly stated it: "Negro Test Urged of New Deal Ideas."[35]

Life magazine reported, "Squire Spencer swore it was not malice" that led him to sell his estate to the prominent black religious leader. Instead, his stated purpose was "to test the theories of Franklin Roosevelt against those of Father Divine.'"[36] If Spencer sought to disturb the First Family by his "deal," the article continued, then he received small satisfaction. Eleanor Roosevelt offered, "It must be pleasant to feel that in the future this place will be 'heaven' to some people, even if it cannot be to its former owner.'" As for Father Divine, he beamed: "I couldn't have a finer neighbor, could I?"[37] In terms that Newburgh on the Hudson resident Andrew Jackson Downing would have understood, Father Divine had a direct and pleasing view across the majestic river to the Summer White House. And as was Spencer's intention, Roosevelt had a corresponding and un-self-flattering view to Father Divine's pleasance. A more dispiriting and perhaps more honest perspective on the situation was offered in a *Time* magazine item titled "Black Elbow," which reproduced a cartoon from the *Chicago Daily News* showing a pickaninny-type child on Roosevelt's front porch, a plaque reading "Crum Elbow" above the doorbell, with a word bubble reading, "Fatha Divine wants t' know kin he borry yo' lawnmo.'" The caption: "Don't forget your good neighbor policy, Franklin."[38]

Jackson Park

In an article titled "There Goes the Neighborhood," the historian of modern conservatism Rick Perlstein provides a *The Wire*-like account of site selection for the Barack Obama Presidential Center. The grimly hopeful campaign on behalf of the South Side of Chicago pit constituency against constituency, self-determined communities against entrenched interests, with Obama's own former chief of staff, Mayor Rahm Emanuel, keeping score.[39] Arguably, the battle was won or lost long ago.

It would have been easy to overlook mention of the routine vote by which Jackson Park, the site ultimately chosen for the next presidential library,

came by its name. "Bowen A Thief," ran the bold headline in the February 10, 1881, edition of *The Chicago Times*; it was followed by several column inches laying out the financial irregularities committed by Chauncey T. Bowen, a founding member of the South Park Commission. In 1869, Bowen and Paul Cornell went to the state legislature in Springfield to lobby for the passage of an Act to Provide for the Location and Maintenance of a Park for the Towns of South Chicago, Hyde Park and Lake.[40] The improprieties in question arose from the administration of a bond issue devoted to acquiring parcels for the 1,000-acre plan envisioned by Olmsted and Vaux. Bowen promised that if "time and opportunity were given him," he could "produce the evidence from the banks with which these transactions were made." Yet this evidence not having been produced, the article noted, the specially appointed investigatory committee was "obliged to regard it as the defalcation of Mr. Bowen."[41] His failure to produce exculpatory documents was as damaging to Bowen's reputation as were the bank records adduced by the investigators. Following the lengthy elaboration of Bowen's misdeeds, in which Cornell was also implicated, there followed a single line in the article indicating that at its regular February 9 meeting, the South Park Commission voted to affirm John B. Sherman's motion, by which "the east of the South parks was named Jackson, and the west, Washington."[42]

To judge from the South Park Commission's own internal expense reports, the setting for its meetings, in office space at no. 94–96 Fifth Avenue, where rent was paid to Wilbur F. Storey, proprietor of the *Chicago Times*, all but foretold this outcome.[43] From the moment it opened in 1873, as part of the vast rebuilding campaign after the Great Fire, The Chicago Times Building, the work of architect by James R. Willett, was the subject of speculation. The *Chicago Tribune* ran a series of articles examining the above-market rates Storey received for rooms in the building leased to the Cook Country Recorder of Deeds.[44] The very space that housed the bureaucratic apparatus of civic order—responsible for maintaining land records, preserving chain of title, and protecting property rights—was itself a clearinghouse of political influence; the *Times*'s printing presses occupied the basement. As the leading Republican paper in

34 See Thomas W. Casey, "F.D.R., Father Divine and the 'Krum Elbow Flurry," *The Hudson Regional Review* 8, no. 1 (1991), 45–56.
35 "Negro Test Urged of New Deal Ideas," *New York Times*, July 30, 1938, 15.
36 "President Roosevelt Gets New Neighbors Across the Hudson," *Life* (August 22, 1938), 17.
37 Ibid.
38 "National Affairs: Black Elbow," *Time* 32, no. 6 (August 8, 1938).
39 Rick Perlstein, "There Goes the Neighborhood: The Obama Library Lands on Chicago," *The Baffler* 28 (July 2015), 100–12.
40 *Charters, Ordinances, and Resolutions of the South Park Commissioners* (Boston: South Park Commissioners, 1887), 3.
41 "Report of the Special Commission Appointed to Investigate Complaints Against the Commissioners of Parks, Thursday, May 15, 1877," *Journal of the Senate of the Thirtieth General Assembly of the State of Illinois, January 3, 1877* (Springfield, IL: D. W. Lusk, 1877), 916.
42 "Bowen A Thief," *The Chicago Times*, February 10, 1881, 8.
43 *Report of the South Park Commissioners to the Board of County Commissioners of Cook County from December 1st, 1882 to December 1st, 1883* (Chicago: Rand, McNally, 1883), 36.
44 "The New Records Office," *The Chicago Tribune*, October 9, 1873, 3.

Chicago, Joseph Medill's *Tribune* was keen to expose Storey's manipulations. The antagonism was born of Storey's violent Copperhead opposition to the Civil War and Abraham Lincoln, who was legendarily said to have visited the *Tribune*'s own modest offices and complimented Medill for abandoning the newspaper's former Know-Nothing slant.[45] The *Times* for its part responded to Secretary of War Edwin Stanton's September 18, 1862 order for escaped slaves ("contrabands") and freed slaves to enter Illinois by warning his readers that they "must set their faces against immigration if they would preserve the state to the uses of their children and from the blight and mildew of Africanization."[46]

With the exception of Cornell, the South Park commissioners who voted on renaming South Park were prominent members of Chicago's Democratic establishment.[47] Martin J. Russell was an active member of the Iroquois Club, founded in 1881. The Iroquois name was a winking reference to the competing Democratic interests of the Tammany Society of New York, with its political boss known as the Grand Sachem.[48] Tammany was derived from Tamanend, Sachem of the Turtle Clan, which stood at the head of the Lenni-Lenape nation. Among the club's early efforts was a successful campaign to secure Chicago as the site of the 1884 National Democratic Convention, at which Grover Cleveland was eventually nominated. After all, the choice of Chicago as the host of the 1860 Democratic National Convention, held in a purpose-built wooden-frame "Wigwam," proved decisive in Lincoln's nomination. But the Iroquois club's initial symbolic and consolidating act was to host a banquet at the Palmer House in honor of Andrew Jackson's birthday, on March 15, 1882.[49] In a letter read at the banquet Samuel J. Tilden, the Democratic candidate in the disputed election of 1876, extoled the "beneficent Jeffersonian philosophy which prefers that nothing shall be done by the General Government which the local authorities are competent to do."[50] The sectional passions that defined the Reconstruction era were subsumed into the Compromise of 1877—brokered in secret at the eponymous Washington, DC, hotel run by the free-born black entrepreneur James Wormley—which granted Rutherford B. Hayes and the Republicans the presidency at the inestimable expense of restoration of "home rule" to former Confederate

states.[51] But the local authorities evoked by Tilden evidently did not include the native peoples of Chicago—the name of which comes from the Ojibwe word "Shikako," or "skunk place"—to whose removal Jackson had given sanction.[52]

Word of the South Park Commission's vote to honor Jackson might have taken longer to become widely known had not the *Tribune* made its own proposal to change the name of South Park to Garfield Park, days after the assassination of the newly elected Republican president, James A. Garfield, on September 19, 1881.[53] A compromise candidate, Garfield won the nomination at the 1880 Republican National Convention—held in Chicago's Interstate Industrial Exposition Building, the so-called Glass Palace—on the thirty-sixth ballot. The editors of the *Tribune* had assumed that the divisions of South Park were simply known as east and west because it had been "impossible to settle upon a name of a person that would be proper under the circumstances."[54] At one time, General Grant's name had been suggested, but as the former president was still living, in this instance considered a liability, the proposal was abandoned. The untimely death of President Garfield thus made it "eminently proper that his name should be given to the South Park at least, and if it be considered proper the East Park could be reserved to take Gen. Grant's name when he passes away."[55] But the *Tribune*'s proposal prompted the recognition that South Park had already been renamed Jackson Park and Washington Park. A follow-up article observed that in any case the Democratic commissioners would have been reluctant to commemorate Garfield. As an alternative, the editors suggested the West Park System, designed by William LeBaron Jenney, as the only pleasure-ground in the city that still lacked any "authorized name"; what was then popularly known as Central Park was "officially anonymous." On October 3, 1881, the commissioners of West Park voted to rename it Garfield Park.[56]

But the editors of the *Tribune* were not done with the vexing matter. They dispatched a reporter to determine why the South Park Commissioners had "in their wisdom fixed on the name of Jackson Park" and which Jackson in particular was meant. Speaking on the condition of anonymity, one of the commissioners allowed that "the names were given without much thought, and I never supposed that

45 Newton MacMillan, "Recollections of Lincoln as Furnished by Joseph Medill," *The Chicago Tribune*, April 14, 1895, 43.
46 "Shall Illinois Be Africanized," *The Chicago Times*, October 14, 1862.
47 "South Park Board," *The Daily Inter Ocean*, February 10, 1881, 7.
48 "Tilden and the Iroquois," *New York Times*, June 27, 1883, 4.
49 Alfred Theodore Andreas, *History of Chicago: From the Earliest Period to the Present*, vol. 3 (Chicago: A. T. Andreas, 1886), 402.
50 John Bigelow, ed., *The Writings and Speeches of Samuel J. Tilden*, vol. 2 (New York: Harper and Brothers, 1885), 514.

51 C. Vann Woodward, "Yes, There Was a Compromise of 1877," *The Journal of American History* 60, no. 1 (1973), 218.
52 H. A. Allard, "Chicago, A Name of Indian Origin, and the Native Wild Onion to Which the Indians May Have Had Reference as the 'Skunk Place,'" *Castanea* 20, no. 1 (1955), 28–31.
53 *Chicago Tribune*, September 25, 1881, 4.
54 Ibid.
55 Ibid.
56 "Garfield Park," *Chicago Tribune*, October 2, 1881, 19.

they were intended as formal names."[57] Pressing on the state-sovereignty Democrats' sympathies with the plight of the Confederacy, the reporter asked if it were not Old Hickory but rather Stonewall Jackson whom they meant to honor.[58] While giving voice to the "universal protest" against the "offensive partisan name," the editors finally proposed to honor a seemingly neutral but eminently worthy American hero: Benjamin Franklin.[59]

The same idea occurred to the Board of Commissioners of the Department of Parks for the City of Boston, for what were more transparently transactional than partisan reasons. The scheme was to draw on the so-called Franklin Fund, a bequest to the "inhabitants of the Town of Boston" made by Benjamin Franklin in a codicil to his will dated June 23, 1789. It stipulated that in a century's time an accumulated sum of 100,000 pounds would be available to expend on "public works which may be judged of most general utility to the Inhabitants."[60] In 1885, the board resolved in "the manner of naming the so-called West Roxbury Park, which title has been considered only a temporary one, suggested by the location of the lands," that it should be designated Franklin Park, "in perpetual recognition of the generosity of the great Bostonian to his native city."[61]

Native son or not, Franklin's legacy was not an unambiguous one. As historian David Waldstreicher has shown, Franklin's carefully crafted public persona was profoundly shaped by the cruelty of his apprenticeship to his brother, a Boston printer. In his *Autobiography*, Franklin portrays himself, after having slipped the bonds of his indenture, a "runaway servant," constantly under suspicion.[62] But as the publisher of the *Pennsylvania Gazette*, he profited handsomely from advertisements placed by owners to recover escaped slaves. As Waldstreicher writes, "The advertisements often catalog the known aliases of runaways with a sense of inquiry and outrage. Masters wished to reserve the privilege of naming property: 'He always changes his name, and denies his master.'"[63] Olmsted, the architect of what was to become Franklin Park, described this same practice in his *The Cotton Kingdom: A Traveler's Observations on Cotton and Slavery in the American Slave States*.

"When the hunters take a negro who has not a pass, or 'free papers,' and they don't know whose slave he is, they confine him in jail, and advertise him."[64] The right kind of papers will set one free, if not entirely free one from suspicion. They allow one to pass, assume a name, acquire a position, overcome the past, level the field.[65]

In what the *Tribune* editors seemingly regarded as their most compelling argument, they objected to the pairing of the names Washington and Jackson. "American history does not place Gen. Jackson upon the same plane with Washington, 'the Father of his Country.'"[66] This evaluation is not as self-evident as it may at first appear. In Philip Hone's remarks on Jackson's tumultuous visit to New York City in the summer of 1833, the diarist and one-term Whig mayor of New York City took keen note of the mobile force of popular sentiment. "Talk of him as the second Washington! It won't do now. Washington was only the first Jackson."[67] The very laws of succession, from the "Father of his Country," who was "superior to the homage of the populace" (Washington), to the fatherless people's president, who was a *"gourmand of adulation"* (Jackson) were fit to become reversed.[68] The nativist Hone feared the still more shocking reversals that could ensue from the influx of "unpatriotic" immigrant populations, "low Irishmen" in particular. Already they had interfered with the efforts of the Native American Democratic Association, formed in New York in 1835, to promote a distinct American-born ticket.[69] "The same brogue which they have instructed to shout 'Hurrah for Jackson!'" Hone predicted, "shall be used to impart additional horror to the cry of 'Down with the natives!'"[70]

One person who would not allow himself to become a second General Jackson was Andrew Jackson Downing, Olmsted and Vaux's mentor, landscape gardener, editor, and inspiration for their "peoples' [sic] park."[71] "What most branded Downing as an American-born author," writes his intellectual biographer Judith K. Major, "was hidden from the reading public, for he signed his correspondence and published works simply

57 "Jackson Park," *Chicago Tribune*, October 6, 1881, 8.
58 "The Names of the South Parks," *Chicago Tribune*, October 23, 1881, 4.
59 Ibid.
60 William Temple Franklin, *Memoirs of the Life and Writings of Benjamin Franklin*, vol. 1 (London: Henry Colburn, 1818), 421.
61 "Eleventh Annual Report of the Board of Commissioners of the Department of Parks for the City of Boston for the Year 1885," *Documents of the City of Boston, for the Year 1886*, vol. 1 (Boston: Rockwell and Churchill, 1887), 17. The available funds amounted to $350,000.
62 Leonard W. Labaree, ed., *The Autobiography of Benjamin Franklin* (New Haven, CT: Yale University Press, 2003), 73.
63 David Waldstreicher, *Runaway America: Benjamin Franklin, Slavery, and the American Revolution* (New York: Hill and Wang, 2005), 11.
64 Frederick Law Olmsted, *The Cotton Kingdom: A Traveller's Observations on Cotton and Slavery in the American Slave States*, vol. 1 (New York: Mason Brother, 1861), 157.
65 Ibid.
66 "The Names of the South Parks," 4.
67 Bayard Tuckerman, *The Diary of Philip Hone 1828–1851*, vol. 1 (New York: Dodd, Mead, 1889), 76.
68 Ibid.
69 Thomas Richard Whitney, *A Defense of the American Policy as Opposed to the Encroachments of Foreign Influence, and Especially to the Interference of the Papacy in the Political Interests and Affairs of the United States* (New York: De Witt & Davenport, 1856), 241.
70 Tuckerman, *The Diary of Philip Hone*, 184.
71 On the "peoples' park" see Edward Eigen, "Claiming Landscape as Architecture," *Studies in the History of Gardens & Design Landscapes* 34, no. 3 (2014): 226–47.

'A. J. Downing.'"[72] Born October 31, 1815, ten months after his namesake's great and glorious victory at the Battle of New Orleans, Downing came to resist any association with General Jackson. His wife Caroline was the grandniece of John Quincy Adams, whom Jackson defeated in the remarkably ugly election of 1828. As a sign of his preferred lineage, Downing dedicated his masterwork, *A Treatise on the Theory and Practice of Landscape Gardening, Adapted to North America* (1841) to the ex-president, a "Lover of Rural Pursuits."[73] But how was gardening, or parks for the people for that matter, to be adapted to the very exceptional conditions of North America?

While Downing wrote with great sensitivity on the respective virtues and proper placement of native and exotic plants, his principle concern seems to have been with the national original of the newly founded nation's gardeners.[74] In an article in *The Horticulturist*, titled "American Versus British Horticulture," Downing observed that "when a man goes into a country without understanding its language—merely as a traveler—he is likely to comprehend little of the real character of that country."[75] It is no slight to Downing to suggest that John Quincy Adams possessed a somewhat more nuanced notion of what is true of the traveler's perceptions, as opposed to the truth of the conclusions drawn by the traveler. Adams's conclusion was that the American character would be greatly improved once "wealth comes to be more generally *inherited* than *acquired*," that is to say, when Americans become less self-made.[76] Downing stuck to documented facts, when and if they were to become available. "The statistics of the gardening class, if carefully collected, would, we imagine, show that not three percent of all working gardeners in the United States, are either native or naturalized citizens." Having himself engaged in the nursery trade for nearly two decades, Downing concludes that he could not remember an instance of an "American offering himself as a professional gardener."[77] For the most part, they were the very "natives of Ireland," whom Hone despised, and a "few Scotchman, and a still smaller proportion of English and Germans."[78] A scattering of peoples, a democratic diaspora.

Vallombrosa

Jackson's presidency came to an end on March 4, 1837, with the inauguration of his former vice president, Martin Van Buren. History might ultimately judge Van Buren's greatest accomplishment in office to have been the inspiration for Pennsylvania Whig Representative Charles Ogle's uproarious speech to the House on "The Regal Splendor of the President's Palace." The executive mansion's ornamental garden did not escape Ogle's withering attention, with its very expensive and "choice collection of both native and exotics, many of the latter having been gathered from almost every clime."[79]

Two weeks later, on March 19, 1837, William Wordsworth set out on a tour of Italy. In late May, he arrived at the famous Vallombrosa Abbey, in Italy, where the monks recalled "with pride" Milton's sojourn there in 1638 or 1639. (Milton's stay remains unconfirmed by historical documents.) Wordsworth's versified reminiscence of his own visit is headed by the same lines from *Paradise Lost* alluded to by Morison as an argument for keeping "intact" the papers intended for Roosevelt's library:

> Thick as Autumnal leaves that strow the Brooks
> In *Vallombrosa*, where th' *Etrurian* shades
> High overarch't imbowr[80]

It is not a question of poetic persuasion that finally concerns us here. Rather, there is a lesson to be drawn from Wordsworth's careful examination of the place, of what is and what seems, as read in the texture of the Etrurian shades and the Tuscan foliage. For Milton, *shades* inevitably summoned the presence of spirits, though perhaps of a different sort than "spooks," the innocent evocation of which condemns Coleman Silk, the protagonist of Philip Roth's *The Human Stain* (2000). Silk, a light-skinned black man passing for white, is a classics professor at the fictional Athena college. The groves of academe prove an imperfectly sheltering but ultimately shadowy bower. For Wordsworth, the monastic fastness had to be visited and seen to be properly known. The very name Vallombrosa ("shady valley") distilled its evocative essence, but only careful attention to the trees "at present on the ground," to use Olmsted and Vaux's words, but also those they replaced, betrayed its cultivated nature.

Let us return to the topic with which we began, Hyde Park. The article "How Chicago's Suburbs

72 Judith K. Major, *To Live in the New World: A.J. Downing and American Landscape Gardening* (Cambridge, MA: MIT Press, 1997), 2.
73 Andrew Jackson Downing, *A Treatise on the Theory and Practice of Landscape Gardening, Adapted to North American with a View to the Improvement of Country Residences* (New York: Wiley and Putnam, 1841).
74 Major, *To Live in the New World*, 1.
75 Andrew Jackson Downing, "American versus British Horticulture," *The Horticulturist* 7, no. 6 (June 1, 1852): 249.
76 John Quincy Adams to Alexander Hill Everett (St. Petersburg, April 10, 1812), in Worthington Chauncey Ford, ed., *Writings of John Quincy Adams*, vol. 4 (New York: Macmillan, 1914), 310.
77 Downing, "American versus British Horticulture," 251.
78 Ibid.

79 Charles Ogle, "Speech of Mr. Ogle, of Pennsylvania, on the Regal Splendor of the President's Palace: Delivered in the House of Representative, April 14, 1840" (n.p., n.d.), 3.
80 John Milton, *Paradise Lost: A Poem, in Twelve Books* (London: S. Simmons, 1674), 11.

Were Planted and Named" suggests that its name was inspired by both by Hyde Park, New York, and Hyde Park, London. "The former Mr. Cornell had seen, the latter he had reach much about."[81] What we read, especially what appears in the papers, can only be verified after the fact by consulting the sorts of documents collected in libraries. The most damaging sorts of stories often have to do not with misleading accounts but rather with mislaid documents, the erasures of history that provide infinite room for suspicion. Like the traveler who forms passing impressions of a foreign nation's alien customs, the reader is easily and often willingly misled by what appears in print. Thus, Wordsworth was attentive to the "charge which has been brought against [Milton]," with respect to the famous lines: "Thick as autumnal leaves that strew the brooks." According to his critics and denigrators, Milton had "erred" in speaking of the trees there being deciduous, whereas they are, in fact, evergreen pines. Inspecting Vallombrosa, the alleged scene of Milton's unhappy error, his empiricist's fall from grace, Wordsworth is especially attentive to what is indigenous and what introduced—what is native and what it cultivated—though these distinctions are as unstable as they are pleasantly unsettling.

> The *natural* woods of the region of Vallombrosa *are* deciduous, and spread to a great extent; those near the convent are, indeed, mostly pines; but they are avenues of trees *planted* within a few steps of each other, and thus composing large tracts of wood; plots of which are periodically cut down. The appearance of those narrow avenues, upon steep slopes open to the sky, on account of the height which the trees attain by being *forced* to grow upwards, is often very impressive.[82]

The principle underlying the economic management of Vallombrosa's woodlands has its corollary in A. J. Downing's contemporaneous aesthetic-cum-moral paradigm for seeding the new world's garden. "One of the chief elements of artistical imitation in Landscape Gardening, being a difference in the materials employed in the imitation of nature from those in nature itself, nothing can be more apparent, than the necessity of introducing largely, exotic ornamental trees, shrubs and plants, instead of those of indigenous growth."[83] To paraphrase the scrupulous documentarian Errol Morris,

nothing is so unobvious as what is readily apparent.[84] While the lesson of Hyde Park, or Krum Elbow, was how to house the legacy of a president "intact," the corresponding lesson of Vallombrosa is the inevitable and perhaps necessary scattering of leaves.

"A New Birth of Freedom"

In a press release of November 5, 2008, Senator Dianne Feinstein, chair of the Joint Congressional Committee on Inaugural Ceremonies, announced the theme of the 2009 presidential inaugural: "A New Birth of Freedom." The theme was chosen to commemorate the 200th anniversary of Abraham Lincoln's birth, and it was judged to be especially fitting, Feinstein stated, "to celebrate the words of Lincoln as we prepare to inaugurate the first African-American president of the United States." Needless to say, the phrase comes from the closing passage of the Gettysburg Address, in which Lincoln, confronted with a harvest of death, called for a new birth of freedom, so that "government of the people, by the people, for the people, shall not perish from the earth." The contemporaneous reviews of Lincoln's dedicatory speech were mixed. The *Chicago Times* wrote, "Aside from the ignorant rudeness manifest in the President's exhibition of Dawdleism at Gettysburg and which was an insult at least to the memory of part of the dead ... it was a perversion of history so flagrant that the most extended charity cannot view it otherwise than willful."[85] The abolitionist Massachusetts Senator Charles Sumner offered the now more generally received opinion: "That speech, uttered at the field of Gettysburg, and now sanctified by the martyrdom of its author, is a monumental act."[86]

Before he went to the Harvard Law School, where he was the first black editor of its prestigious law review, Obama arrived in Chicago to work with the faith-based Developing Communities Project.[87] His true apprenticeship was in organizing residents of the Altgeld Gardens housing project. "Everybody in the area referred to Altgeld as 'the Gardens' for short," Obama wrote in his memoir *Dreams from My Father: A Story of Race and Inheritance*. What did Obama know of his father? In a brief article published in the *Honolulu Star-Bulletin*, upon

81   "How Chicago's Suburbs Were Planted and Named," 37.
82   William Wordsworth, Poems, *Chiefly of Early and Late Years; Including the Borders, A Tragedy* (London: Edward Moxon, 1842), poem on page 133; note on page 403. Emphasis in the original.
83   Downing, *A Treatise on the Theory and Practice of Landscape Gardening*, 35.

84   Errol Morris, *Believing Is Seeing: Observations on the Mysteries of Photography* (New York: Penguin Press, 2011), 8.
85   "The President at Gettysburg," *The Chicago Times*, November 23, 1863, 2.
86   Charles Sumner, "Promises of the Declaration of Independence, and Abraham Lincoln. Eulogy on Abraham Lincoln, before the Municipal Authorities of the City of Boston, June 1, 1865," *The Works of Charles Sumner*, vol. 9 (Boston: Lee and Shepard, 1875), 404.
87   Fox Butterfield, "First Black Elected to Head Harvard's Law Review," *New York Times*, February 6, 1990.

Barack Hussein Obama Sr.'s graduation from the University of Hawai'i, the Kenyan student scolds the school for herding visiting students into dormitories and "forcing them to attend programs designed to promote cultural understanding." Obama, the son, discovers the article "folded away among my birth certificate and old vaccination forms."[88] Visitors to the planned Barack Obama Presidential Center can and should debate how well his administration responded to the promise of "transparency and open government" articulated in a memorandum issued on January 21, 2009, the president's first full day in office. But whatever papers or other "historical materials" the center chooses to display, in the name of decency, this blasted birth certificate should never be a part of it. The vaccination forms, however, might serve as an emblem of responsible citizenship.

What did Obama learn from his education in Chicago? In the year before the municipal incorporation of its leafy suburb Hyde Park, the lustily growing, if not yet great, inland metropolis added the motto *Urbs in Horto* (City in a Garden) to its corporate seal. Obama found there his own garden to tend. He also came to appreciate "the irony of the name."[89] Conceived in 1944 to house black war workers, the housing project was named in honor of John Peter Altgeld, the German-born former governor of Illinois and conscientious voice of the Democratic Party's progressive wing. In 1895, Altgeld refused an invitation to speak at the Iroquois Club, which would have forced him to endorse the misbegotten policies of Grover Cleveland, "the slimy offspring of that unhallowed marriage between Standard Oil and Wall Street."[90] But it was in the unhallowed nature of the "gardens" in the name "Atlgeld Gardens" that Obama detected the fatal irony, "its evocation of something fresh and well tended—a sanctified earth."[91] All was mildewed, contaminated, in need of sanctification—a new birth. Obama did not come to Chicago to dedicate a burial ground, but to restore the livability of a blighted garden, a fundamental public amenity. The record is written in compassionate deeds informed by monumental speech acts. Jackson Park has been chosen as the home of the Obama presidential library. So let us take Jackson at his word, "For every tree is known by his own fruit."

88 Barack Obama, *Dreams from My Father: A Story of Race and Inheritance* (New York: Three Rivers Press, 1995), 26.
89 Ibid., 164.
90 John Peter Altgeld, "Altgeld's Plain Talk," in William Jennings Bryan, ed., *The Commoner Condensed*, vol. 3 (Lincoln, NE: Woodruff-Collins, 1904), 413.
91 Obama, *Dreams from My Father*, 164.

Edward Eigen is an architectural historian and scholar, and an Associate Professor of Architecture and Landscape Architecture at Harvard Graduate School of Design.

Civic Histories

Civic histories engage the city and its representation: marking the formal build-up of planning, legislation, and investment in the built environment, as well as aspects of social formations, civic memory, and collective production.

Several projects considered infrastructural influences on the ground and subterranean level of the city—a place that, Dominique Perrault points out, was considered the zone of engineering for many years with metros, walkways, and other underground programs developing.[1] Fiona Connor and Erin Besler researched the Chicago Pedway system that connects the towers underground, and found that the material finishes attest to a complicated story of private and public management, regulation, and maintenance (p. 82). Similarly sited, Piovene Fabi assembles a story—by recombining Pirelli rubber tiled floors and terrazzo of the 1960s Milan Metro stations—of the Italian postwar material industry and design culture (p. 132). Meanwhile, AWP address the same urban strata via an archeological drawing process that layers the foundational and infrastructural aspects of postwar city development in large-scale oblique view maps.

Dogma examines the singular room as the basic unit of domesticity, but also as a private and political space of subjective representation in the ways that

1   Perrault, Dominique. *Groundscapes: other topographies* (Orléans: HYX, 2016)

the personal is expressed via consumption and object display (p. 80). Taking famous historical and literary figures and examining their belongings, this project plays on the interior as both a psychological and spatial state to be regulated for the functioning of societies. Dogma, and other projects engaging civic histories, examine the social formations that are enmeshed in the activity of living collectively, often dealing with the nomenclature of architectural spaces (for instance, rooms) and the ways terminology has the ability to regulate lifestyle.

51N4E explicitly address the relationship of memory and identity at the civic scale (p. 36). Their project collects together narratives including Albanian artist Anri Sala's video *Intervista*, that depicts his discovery of old footage showing his mother in her activities as a leader of the Communist Youth Alliance. Entangled in this narrative are several historical sources; Sala's mother's failing personal memories; the recording technologies, which never held the soundtrack; and the recollections and interpretations of those Sala interviewed seeking further information. This video is shown by 51N4E amongst artifacts of official history, like the documents from their recently completed Skandberg Square project also in Tirana. Their project, as an ensemble, produces a temporal overlay that is personal, intimate, and also collective: a state activated by their programming including workshops and conversations during the exhibition run.

Many of these projects, including 51N4E, reveal an interest in collectivity as a productive social format for exhibition making. In their attention to the cumulative and political aspects of architectural discourse, these projects plan workshops with invited guests and visitors. Aranda\Lasch and Terrol Dew Johnson examine the collaborative working relationship and the possibility of knowledge transmission (p. 50). This is demonstrated by the repeated exchange between Johnson's own traditional knowledge of weaving and coiling and the computer modeling and scripting of Aranda\Lasch. MG&Co explicitly reference the importance and modality of publications in the distribution and regulation of architectural ideas. *Rooms for Books* amalgamates written history, wrapping each book in a standard sleeve and subsuming the diversity of cover art for the homogenous library environment (p. 125). At the same time, they provide visitors with the anachronous power of a Xerox machine to sample and recombine their own bootleg publications or histories.

Structure of Place   SHINGO MASUDA + KATSUHISA OTSUBO Architects — Tokyo, Japan

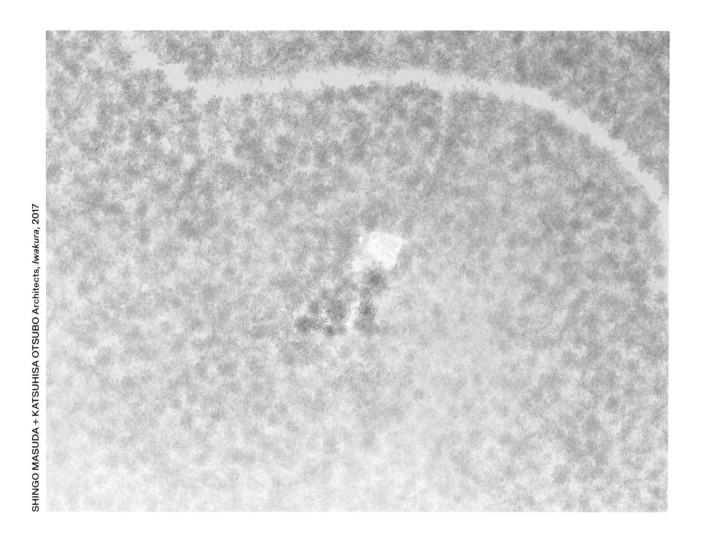

SHINGO MASUDA + KATSUHISA OTSUBO Architects, *Iwakura, 2017*

Iwakura is an early belief in the natural from old Shintoism which existed in Japan before the imported influence of Buddhism. The existence of Iwakura in ancient Japanese ethnology conceptualizes the intimate relationship between humans and place; it is a dwelling site where god settles, and it is usually in reference to natural large rocks. Important to Iwakura is the sense of place generated by the existence of rock and the surrounding environment. Mountains, forests, rocks, etc. were regarded as gods in times when there weren't any shrines. Buildings came later on in the history. One can read the landscape and find the existence of Iwakura. It was not like other spaces and, in this

difference, people naturally gathered, danced, and prayed. In other words, this concept of Iwakura, before the notion of architecture came in from the mainland, seems to be a primitive architectural mindset toward place in ancient Japanese history.

Today we see the opposite: a world overflowing with myriad options. It is a peculiar era in human history: full of things beyond necessity. By carefully reading the possibilities in the contemporary urban environment and weaving various levels of relation with minimum necessary elements and conditions to transform "sufficient spaces" to "place" is one important work which architectural design can perform in the present age.

L'air pour l'air (Air for air)   SO-IL and Ana Prvački
— New York, USA/Los Angeles, USA

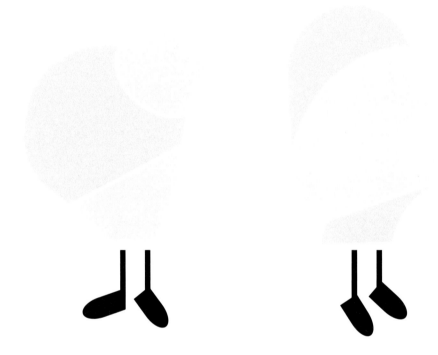

The legacy of modernism has imbued in us a desire for pristine surfaces and sleek, industrially produced forms. Beneath this polished shell, the figure still dances and the heart still beats. For the 2017 Chicago Architecture Biennial, SO-IL in collaboration with artist Ana Prvački go beyond the traditional relationship between figure, object, and nature to explore how the complex notions of purity and pollution interact with the self, architectural space, and sound.

For the Chicago Architecture Biennial, SO-IL and Prvački will produce an ensemble of enclosures constructed out of air-filtering meshes. Functioning somewhere between a mask and a shelter, the enclosures are for musicians playing wind instruments, as they clean the air that produces the music. A series of musical performances by local Chicago musicians will show the piece in use during the run of the show.

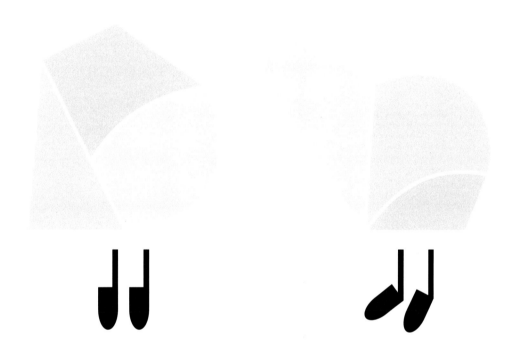

The Balloon Frame Revisited — New York, USA

Stan Allen Architect

Stan Allen Architect, Hudson River Studio, Study models for Elizaville, New York, 2015

The installation celebrates a distinctive Chicago innovation: the balloon frame as developed in 1833. A large-scale model mounted directly on the wall reveals both the tectonics of balloon frame construction and the compositional logics of part-to-whole aggregation. While the individual units are of a domestic scale and recall the archetypal house-form, the larger aggregation suggests collective functions and public assembly: a school-house, a grange hall, or a collaborative workspace. Balloon frame construction (which came to be known simply as Chicago Construction) took advantage of two nineteenth century innovations: pre-cut dimensional lumber and mass-produced nails. Unlike the heavy timber frames associated with early American construction, which required skilled joinery, these lightweight standardized elements allowed relatively unskilled builders to build rapidly and cheaply. The need to supply lumber for this new industry in turn triggered massive deforestation in Wisconsin and Northern Michigan, highlighting the intricate interconnection of technology, architecture, urbanism, and ecology.

Nail guns have replaced hammers, engineered lumber allows greater spans, and platform construction has replaced true balloon frame construction, but lightweight dimensional lumber is still the preferred technique for small-scale construction in North America. Vincent Scully has identified the taut, skin-like effect of the balloon frame as a particularly American way of building. Like the Jeffersonian grid, it is standardized and democratic yet it allows individual expression. It is above all pragmatic, tied into networks of supply and distribution, with readily available tools and techniques. We propose to reflect on this ongoing production with an expanded field of possible balloon frame constructions: to make the history of the balloon frame new again through a hypothetical project that explores aggregation, part-to-whole relationships, repetition, and field-like strategies. The project is a reflection on the logic of material histories seen in the context of regional ecologies, changing construction technology, and networks of supply and distribution.

Tower for Chicago   Studio Anne Holtrop
— Amsterdam, Netherlands/Muharraq, Bahrain

Studio Anne Holtrop, Study for *Tower for Chicago*, 2017

For the 2017 Chicago Architecture Biennial, Studio Anne Holtrop proposes a tower in the atrium of the Chicago Cultural Center that sits in proximity and dialog with the 2015 installation by Atelier Bow Wow, part of the inaugural Chicago Architecture Biennial, entitled Piranesi's Circus. Holtrop's monolithic work is a model for a tower, and might also be understood as a large column amidst the ramps, bridges, and swings of the work of Atelier Bow-Wow. The two works are in different scales, but both have a surreal aspect to them. The ground form of the tower comes from an inkblot drawing—like a Rorschach inkblot referring to nothing specifically— but, due to it sculptural form, it triggers imagination and associations.

Material Connections   Studio Gang — Chicago, USA

For millennia, materiality connected architecture to its specific place on the planet and the people who created it. Inventing ways to build with what was available and relatively nearby, including excavating the very earth beneath their feet, humans developed architectural knowledge—from establishing tectonic principles and construction and drawing techniques, to elaborating on the cultural meanings of built form.

The development of industrial processes and transportation networks transformed architecture's material relationships, radically expanding the footprint of architectural fabrications and altering the methods of their construction. To make steel a viable building material, for example, multiple means of mass production were required, such as motorized chain saws, modern railroads, more efficient blast furnaces, and the division of labor. Together, this web of technology, infrastructure, and people made the tall buildings of Chicago possible and drove the modern movement.

As older practices of material extraction become less viable due to scarcity and harmful effects on our environment and more scrutiny is given to the negative impacts of certain materials on our bodies (including the health of the workers who create and handle them), our practice has put emphasis on investigating how an expanded engagement with materiality can drive architecture in the twenty-first century. In particular, we have been exploring how the history and production of materials—understood as encompassing social, political, economic, environmental, and philosophical issues—can inform architectural form-making.

Questions about materials' origins and meanings, reducing material use, and increasing performance—as well as the potential of hybridization and the inverse of construction—are several lines of inquiry we are pursuing to move beyond inherited constraints and associations. Laying out formally generative territory, these inquiries also ground our wider exploration of the role architecture can play in a post-industrial, post-colonial, and even a post-Anthropocentric world.

When seen through material's multifaceted lens, many of the buildings we have inherited become monuments to squandered resources as well as human and environmental exploitation. How can this same lens help us redefine architecture's relationship with material today in order to move toward shaping a different future?

Studio Gang, Arcus Center for Social Justice Leadership at Kalamazoo College, Kalamazoo, Michigan, 2014

Prima Materia   Studio Mumbai — Mumbai, India

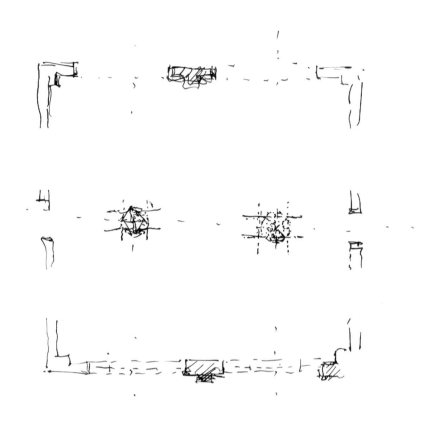

Studio Mumbai, Plan for Chicago Architecture Biennial, 2017

We are invested in the inquiry of the rudimentary and elemental.

Water
n.
A colorless, transparent, odorless, liquid which forms the seas, lakes, rivers, and rain and is the basis of the fluids of living organisms.

Air
n.
The invisible gaseous substance surrounding the earth, a mixture mainly of oxygen and nitrogen.

Light
n.
The natural agent that simulates sight and makes things visible.

Our engagement lies not in nostalgia or romanticism but in technological and scientific interest.

Lores are what allow rediscovery of appropriate technology through a rather non-linear narrative. These serendipitous discoveries are imperative in the world that is constantly changing. Lore carries tacit knowledge through past, present, and future— answers to each time lie in its appropriation. Most importantly, it is intuitive and rational: subjective and objective at the same time, essential to both survival and nourishment of mankind.

Lore
n.
A body of traditions and knowledge on a subject or held by a particular group, typically passed from person to person by word of mouth.
n.
The space between the eye and the base of the bill of a bird or between the eye andnostril of a snake.

Super Models   Sylvia Lavin with Erin Besler and Norman Kelley — Los Angeles, USA

If the call to make new history became central to architectural debates after 1965, the response was most visible in efforts to define the history of architecture as a history of ideas rather than of buildings and monuments. Conceptual architecture and histories of architectural concepts both operated to establish the field as an autonomous discipline and to loosen the once necessary association between building and architect. An initially unintended consequence of this logical structure, however, was to turn architecture into something that could be made by different kinds of producers, including the historian. To make new history, in other words, entailed not only making new historical narratives but also new kinds of historians and new historiographical methods.

In the context of this shifting terrain of historical argument, the architectural model acquired a surprising and paradoxical importance. Models could move through the world as exemplary works of conceptual art: highly authored but, nevertheless, removed from the traditionally built object of desire. Growing investment in the model as idea and a growing interest in the medium of model-making generated a jet stream of auratic things that played a significant role in speeding architecture's entry into the museum and the burgeoning art market of the 1980s. Unlike a building, models could be collected, exhibited, and traded, acquiring value and historical stature with every exchange. Architectural museums were established to collect models and, in turn, buildings were designed and constructed to appear to be models.[1] New histories became histories of models.

On the other hand, the model was also understood as a perfectly transparent representational device—an exact replica of a building without intrinsic ideational force. Because models were not typically signed but made by office staff and even outsourced to model makers as a matter of course, models could easily be cast as akin to documents: objective, factual, and anonymous.[2] These models too, however, entered the space of collecting and display as the appetite to make history led curators and historians to produce more and more so-called exhibition models: sometimes authorized by the architect, sometimes not, sometimes replicas of buildings and sometimes models after other models. Over time, the provenance and purpose of these models became murky as they inched their way into the archive shelves and museum collections of "originals" that form the repositories of historical knowledge.

As three-dimensional printing and modeling software become not only increasingly ubiquitous, but increasingly capable of further collapsing the distance between representation and buildings, models make it evident that the very distinction between concept and thing that has organized architecture for the past fifty years no longer pertains. This shift has significant implications for how we approach current historical work. Scattered throughout the very institutions we might turn to as we make new histories—including a virtually infinite stream of digital models and images— are not documents or works of architecture, but models of conceptual instability that occupy the strange space between alternative fact, forgery, and fiction. As is becoming increasingly clear, this space—where evidence is designed and fabricated—is where new history is to be made.

Super Models is presented in parallel to Exhibition Models, simultaneously on view at the Princeton University School of Architecture.

---

1   As its founder and first director, Heinrich Klotz opened the Deutsches Architekturmuseum in 1984. It was the first museum in Europe focused exclusively on architecture. The collection was initially anchored in a group of models by Frei Otto. The museum building by Oswald Mathias Ungers was designed around the concept of inserting a house model inside the shell of an existing nineteenth century villa.

2   The highly influential *Modern Architecture: International Exhibition* (better known as the *International Style*, curated by Philip Johnson and Henry R. Hitchcock) that took place the Museum of Modern Art in 1932, consisted almost exclusively of photographs and models of built work, many of which were not made by, and, indeed, never seen by, the architects.

Atelier Markgraph/Heiko Pro–fe–Bracht, publicity photo staged at the Deutsches Architekturmuseum, used for catalog cover of *Nouveaux plaisirs d'architectures* (Paris: Center Georges Pompidou, 1985)

Ghostbox   T + E + A + M — Ann Arbor, USA

T + E + A + M, Model detail of *Detroit Reassembly Plant*, 2016

"What does a jpeg of a brick want to be?"

Materials embody narratives, histories, and cultural associations—not just as physical artifacts but as a form of visual currency. We work on both material and its image to align with alternate histories and cultures. For our recent proposal to rebuild the Packard Plant, a building whose decaying concrete and brick has made it an icon of Detroit's blight, we created a new image by mixing and recasting rubble from its partial demolition onto the remaining structure. Our project, Detroit Reassembly Plant, transformed the repetitious factory building into an unfolding scenography of texture, color, and surface. In "Notes on Ruin Porn," McLain Clutter positions the "inherently mediatic quality" of Detroit Reassembly Plant; "In manipulating the aesthetics of urban decay, T + E + A + M knowingly produces a project native to the very same media culture that has afforded ruin porn its recent prominence. In this sense, we might read into the project a trajectory toward the redemption of ruin porn—an attempt to co-opt the form and redirect it away from its conventional narrative of

decline and toward narratives of urban resurgence in which Detroit's ostensible depravity is traded for a rich aesthetic abundance."[1]

Clutter identifies a possible way for architecture to extend its reach by accepting the spectacle of its mediation and leveraging its image quality toward enrolling new audiences. "In these images we can perhaps find aesthetic qualities uniquely fit to redress the representational capacities of civic architecture, consolidating a public for whom urban reality and urban mediation are complexly intertwined." In an increasingly digital world, materiality is often seen as the antidote to mediation. To us, this is not only a false opposition, but a missed opportunity. Where experimental architects in the 1960s and 1970s were working on architecture's mediation through installation, performance, and other exhibition formats, we are committed to the discursive power of building as a material practice and a mediated experience.

1   McLain Clutter, "Notes on Ruin Porn," *The Avery Review*, no. 18 (October 2016): http://www.averyreview.com/issues/18/notes-on-ruin-porn.

T + E + A + M, Model detail of *Detroit Reassembly Plant*, 2016

An American Temple The Empire with Ilaria Forti, Joseph Swerdlin, and Barbara Modolo — Verona, Italy

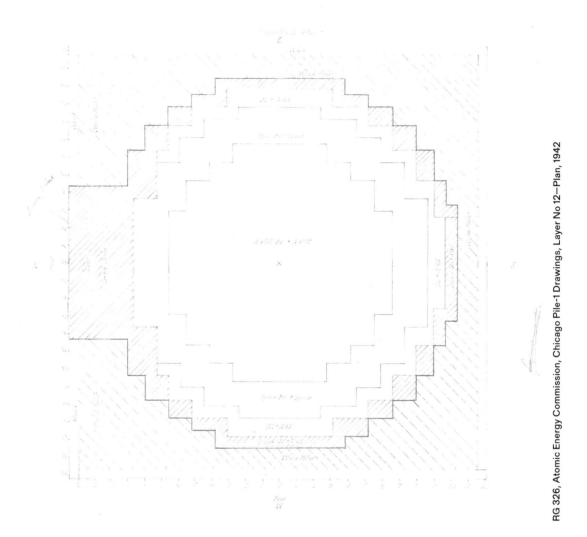

RG 326, Atomic Energy Commission, Chicago Pile-1 Drawings, Layer No 12—Plan, 1942

The first nuclear pile, Chicago Pile 1 (CP-1), does not exist anymore. Built as part of the Manhattan Project—the program promoted by the U.S. Government that brought about the development of the first atomic bomb during World War I—CP-1 allowed the initiation of the first man-made self-sustaining nuclear chain reaction. The head of the team who created it, Italian physicist Enrico Fermi, described it as "a crude pile of black bricks and wooden timbers."[1] CP-1 was built at the University of Chicago on a racquetball court located under the western stands of the former Stagg Field. The final iteration of the pile, made of AGOT graphite bricks arranged in a quasi-spherical form mounted on a cradle of timbers and enclosed within a tent made of hot-air-balloon fabric, had an approximate width of twenty-five feet across the middle, six feet at the edges, and a height of twenty feet. Over its lifetime, the pile was frequently dismantled and rebuilt just as a Japanese temple is, but for different

reasons. The proposal to create a full-scale reconstruction of the volume defined by CP-1's graphite core in the context of the CAB would yield a final iteration of this unique structure. The installation—composed by the CP-1's reconstruction, along with maps, diagrams, and archive materials—is conceived not as a celebration of war or nuclear weapons, but as a secular American temple erected in the city of Chicago, which is a key node in the network of sites connected to the Manhattan Project scattered across the country. This network constitutes a heritage that possesses tremendous relevance both for the present and for future generations. The installation will force us to reflect upon crucial questions about how we deal with landscape and nuclear energy, as well as history and collective memory.

1   Enrico Firmi, "Fermi's Own Story", in *The First Reactor,* (Oak Ridge, Tennessee: United States Atomic Energy Commission, Division of Technical Information, 1982), 24.

Alberto Sinigaglia, Graphite brick from the Chicago Pile-1, 2016

New Artist Residency in Senegal
Toshiko Mori Architect — New York, USA

Toshiko Mori Architect, Artists' Residency and Cultural Center, Sinthian, Senegal, 2015

Thatched roof construction that occurs everywhere in the world allows for an increase in size, performance, and span when combined with contemporary design tools and engineering knowledge. The primitive is in fact full of sophisticated wisdom and potential and, with accurate observation and attention, can arrive at an elegant solution using local materials and traditional techniques. Making new history, in this instance, is about breaking the divide of the architectural paradigm, classified according to divisions in society and economy that have caused the rise of false values that pertain to identity through assumptions of edifice and edification.

In our opinion, returning to study the primitive and the specific vernacular in architecture offers a pause and reflection and, at the same time, some prejudgment that we may offer to the value of culture in general. When architecture starts to invade societies without architects, inevitably one must make a new history for its community. Instead of imposing an externally perceived or borrowed identity, or resorting to nostalgia for the traditional, this effort is to excavate and rediscover latent potential through a community's authentic history while moving it towards future possibilities.

Being with History　Urbanus
— Shenzen, Beijing, China

Urbanus, Five Dragons Temple Environmental Refurbishment,Yuncheng City, China, 2016

Urbanus examine two recent projects: the environmental design for the Five Dragons Temple—the oldest Taoist temple in China located in Ruicheng County, Shanxi Province, abandoned for more than one thousand years then restored as a spiritual center and museum of ancient Chinese architecture—and the Nantou Old Town rehabilitation project to revitalize a 1730 year old town in Shenzhen, whose exacerbated urbanization has made this town a city within an urban village. Here we are tackling the complexity of balancing preservation and development in the course of a dynamic urban transition.

The solutions for the two projects are not limited to architectural measures, but also involve social forces. The Five Dragons Temple is the first national monument preservation project in China financed in partnership with private sectors through the help of the 2015 Milan Expo and crowdfunding. This initiative has sparked much public passion and debate on the preservation of national heritage sites. The Nantou Old Town project utilized the 2017 Bi-City Biennale of Urbanism/Architecture in Shenzhen and Hong Kong—co-curated by partners of Urbanus—to garner attention for the town. By exhibiting these two projects in the Chicago Architecture Biennial, Urbanus exemplifies how architects could reach beyond their traditional role to make a new history.

Art Deco Revisited   WORKac — New York, USA

At the end of Lebanon's 15 year civil war, the public-private company Solidere was formed to reconstruct downtown Beirut with the motto, "Beirut, ancient city of the future." Today, the heart of the city is at once a beautiful restoration of streets and significant buildings punctuated by contemporary architectural interventions while also being empty, with the preservation-as-editing process having turned the once buzzing, tight-knit, and layered fabric of downtown into a city of icons—old and new.

In order to preserve its history, Beirut—outside of its landmarked boundary—has displaced the pressures of development to its periphery, where historic houses have been steadily replaced with banal apartment buildings. Our project builds on this contrast to reflect on historic preservation's potentials and pitfalls. Centered on an insignificant 1930s art deco villa, it is an invitation to think radically about architectural preservation: exploring the varied contemporary political, social, and economic forces that are shaping the field through the specific context and history of Beirut.

Historic preservation is often couched within seemingly benign alibis such as the preservation of identity, heritage, or cultural specificity. Our project enlists, instead, architectural preservation's combined powerlessness and resiliency in the face of development forces to embody concepts, produce content, and shape context, as it reveals alternate archives while also constructing new productive fictions.

At a time of wrenching violence, it is important for architects to contribute a greater understanding to the historical, social, political, cultural, and economical complexities at hand, taking responsibility to articulate and engage both the real and its representation in more complex and incisive ways. To engage in that complexity is to acknowledge the renewed urgency of historical knowledge while also embracing the responsibility to project much-needed alternate futures.

WORKac, 1930s Art Deco villa, Beirut, 2017

Zago Architecture — Los Angeles, USA

Zago Architecture, Study models for Visual and Performing Arts Center, University of Illinois at Chicago, 2015

There is a joke that goes: "What's red and tastes like blue paint? Red paint." But, in fact, a different chemical produces red and blue, so they may not taste the same. Each color is, and always has been, a physically different construction, which is why there had been historically a limit to the number of colors that could be produced from available materials: there may have been three reds, two blues, etc. The wide range of vibrant colors that are available today are the product of nineteenth-century chemistry. Le Corbusier and Amédée Ozenfant discuss this aspect of color in their essay on purism in the magazine *L'Esprit Nouveau*. They declare that color is essential, but that one must not be seduced by the latest products coming out of the chemistry lab—these new colors are a distraction. Architecture is about a form; the color is there so that you can clearly see that form, its enhancement and its three-dimensionality. Color's role is to make form stronger, not weaker. Zago inverts this hierarchical distinction and examines the ways that color can produce alternative legibilities.

Make New Hutong Metabolism, Beijing
ZAO/standardarchitecture — Beijing, China

ZAO/standardarchitecture, Micro Yuan'er, Cha'er Hutong #8, Dashilar, Beijing, 2013

Conservation and revitalization in the old cities of China have always had a paradoxical relationship. Hutongs in Beijing, the traditional courtyard and alley system of urban dwelling that is the most essential part of the city, has recently been captured at the center of the battlefield between development, conservation, and renovation. After decades of development frenzy in the old city of Beijing, the hutongs are on the verge of being either completly erased to make space for office towers, apartments, and shopping malls, or disfigured by kitsch restorations that fake images of a nostalgic past.

The subtle complexity of the hutongs as authentic contemporary urban spaces has been overlooked by both advocates of *tabula rasa* redevelopment and by the defenders of historical restoration. In either case, the operation involves the relentless exodus of the hutong's traditional dwellers, resulting in the gradual disappearance of ethnic diversities in the hutong communities and a rapid diminishing of traditional cultures.

The *Make New Hutong Metabolism* installation—presenting three projects located in the hutong areas of Beijing: Micro Yuan'er Children's Library and Art Centre, Micro Hutong and Co-living Courtyard by architect Zhang Ke, and his ZAO/standardarchitecture through mockup and models—will explore alternative perspectives of looking at China's historical cities and their problems. It will consider them as living organisms, and study them both as macro-scale infrastructures and in micro scale units. It will respond to the problems with both historic and futuristic thinking, and to explore the potential of old hutongs and courtyards as generators of communal spaces and catalysts of social interaction. *Hutong Metabolism* refers also to the historical Metabolism movement in an old city background with a renewed perception.

A Love of the World
The photography of the 2017 Chicago Architectural Biennial — Jesús Vassallo

The artists gathered in *A Love of the World* present us with a kaleidoscopic view of architecture and the city where the ideas of the discipline and the artifacts of the world find new and fertile common grounds. Through their insistence on looking at architecture across the grain of its own categories and as part of a larger context, the images comprising this exhibition construct a discourse that is both a response and a companion to the main thesis of the second Chicago Architecture Biennial—Make New History. The proposal is that in order to effectively reintroduce history as a working material for architects today, we must also adopt an understanding of architecture as being, at any point in time, part of a larger material culture.

In order to support the case made by the exhibition, this essay articulates the origin of the delamination of architecture from these broader categories by examining the role of abstraction in the emergence and evolution of modern architecture. It then proposes the external vision provided by the artists in the show—which both expands and challenges our mental image of a canonic modernity—as a possible lens to reconceptualize the relative position of architecture within the built environment. The exhibition is part of an effort to undo artificial dichotomies and expand the source materials available for contemporary architectural production.

The original split between architecture and history can be located with precision in the early twentieth century, at a moment when the exhaustion of history as a foundation for architectural education was paralleled by an increasing interest in formal abstraction. After the project of historic eclecticism had run its course and attempts to perpetuate its logic of styles with movements like *Jugendstil* and *Modernisme* had failed, modern architecture finally presented itself as an anti-style, ready to represent the essence of a new era of progress and development and eager to materialize its impending footprint on the planet. Abstraction acted at this point in time as a disinfectant or an eraser, generating a new space—a void—in which modern architecture could unfold on its own terms, independent from the burden of previous local models and historic traditions.[1]

For the early moderns, however, abstraction was not a monolithic phenomenon; it had different origins and different attributes. On the one hand, it was imported to architecture from avant-garde painting and its related disciplines, which had

---

[1] Such a role is implicitly acknowledged within the framework of this biennial. In 2013, the biennial's artistic directors, Sharon Johnston and Mark Lee, made an argument sympathetic to the one in this essay when they noted that "the International Style of early modernism assumed a generic form to homogenize and sterilize the specificity of local context." Sharon Johnston and Mark Lee, "Generic Specificity, Five Points for an Architecture of Approximation," *2G* 67 (2013): 166.

already succeeded in their fight to liberate themselves from the shackles of figuration. Architecture, which had harbored at its core an interest in geometry since its inception as a differentiated profession during the Renaissance, was quick to recognize the possible synergies between abstract painting and architectural drawing. On the other hand, for architects, abstraction was also an effort to make sense of the schematic or reduced materiality of the products and artifacts of industrialization, a way to absorb and to a certain degree legitimize a series of constructions that, because of their lack of formal articulation or aesthetic precedent, had been ignored by the profession. Looking at the new objects and structures of the industrial era as possible materials was an attempt by modern architects to make sense of the violent changes already underway in their built environment, in order to be able to engage and influence their development.[2]

These two ways of understanding abstraction overlapped and coexisted with ease in the life and work of the first generation of modern architects. Walter Gropius, who staffed the Bauhaus school with abstract artists in order to generate and teach the new architecture, also famously collected and published images of rugged North and South American factories and silos, which he proposed as examples of the architecture of the future.[3] Le Corbusier, an abstract painter himself who borrowed Gropius's photographs for his own publications, shamelessly included as many industrial materials and artifacts as he could in the houses he built. The sawtooth skylights in the Ozenfant studio and the zinc bars and aluminum counters that adorn many of his domestic designs were literal fragments of the new industrial world. The architect borrowed and composed these materials—which originated outside of and without regard for architectural academia—to fabricate his proposal for an anti-bourgeois abstract architecture. Similarly, Ludwig Mies van der Rohe's involvement with the German interwar art scene is as relevant to an understanding of his work as his obsession with equalizing the value allotted to classical and industrial materials in architecture.

The two approaches to abstraction were based on the underlying belief that medium specificity—to use the term later made popular by Clement Greenberg—is the root and destiny of any form of modernism. However, while both approaches shared the mandate that any modern art form should fulfill the potential of the medium in which

it operates, they differed decisively in that one situated architectural medium specificity in the realm of geometry, while the other located it in the realm of construction. The strain of abstraction that we describe here as pictorial or geometric went beyond reacting against the heaviness of eclectic buildings to propose an architecture that would ideally tend toward immateriality. The second approach to abstraction, described here as constructive or specific, was as much an exclusion of historic models as an inclusion of previously repressed contemporary objects and urban phenomena. It signaled a shift in the consensus about what comprised the legitimate materials of architecture in an attempt to bring the discipline closer to the actuality of the built environment of its time.[4]

The happy coexistence of these diverse understandings of the role of abstraction was gradually undone through the years, as pictorial abstraction grew in prominence and led to increasing self-referentiality and disembodiment within the modern architecture project.[5] This process was fostered by the sequential translations that modern architecture underwent: first, as it was exported from Europe to the United States and then from there to the rest of the world and, second, as it crossed generations and the teaching of modern architecture became institutionalized. Geometric abstraction happened to be more portable, so to speak, and easier to teach.

It was precisely in the United States, in the 1960s, that the fragile balance between an interest in the schematic quality of the artifacts of industrialization and the geometric abstraction of avant-garde painting was definitively shattered. Exemplary instances of this development were John Hejduk's series of drawings on nine square and diamond configurations, produced under the influence of abstract painter Robert Slutzky (who was in turn channeling Piet Mondrian), and Peter Eisenman's early studies for his House Series, which instituted the idea that architecture was a mental process based on the interplay of formal and spatial relationships that could exist in total detachment from physical existence.

The historic arc of events retraced here suggests that the processes that were initially set in motion in order to disconnect modern architecture

4   The absorption of industrial construction into modern architecture as a parallel and competing influence to avant-garde pictorial composition, mostly of Russian origin, has been exposed many times in the past. For instance, it was the underlying thesis in Erich Mendelsohn's *Russland, Europa, Amerika: ein Architektonischer Querschnitt* (Berlin: Rudolf Mosse Buchverlag, 1929). However, perhaps my favorite version of the argument, for its directness, is the one provided by Alison and Peter Smithson in an obscure opinion piece of the mid-1970s. See Peter Smithson, "To Embrace the Machine," *Architectural Design* 44, no. 4 (1974): 213–16.
5   It is important to note here that this was foremost a generational phenomenon, as the main initial proponents of modern architecture, especially Le Corbusier, all circled back to an emphasis on materiality in their later careers.

2   For a parallel and much expanded version of this argument, see Pier Vittorio Aureli, "Architecture for Barbarians," *AA Files* 63 (2011): 3–18.
3   This historic episode is unpacked in Reyner Banham, *A Concrete Atlantis: U.S. Industrial Building and European Modern Architecture, 1900–1925* (Cambridge, MA: MIT Press, 1986).

from its asphyxiating historical baggage eventually took on a life of their own and ended up producing an even deeper and more systemic disconnect, this time between architectural production and the reality of our urban environments. The fact that we have somehow come to understand the discipline of architecture and the built environment as two different and even mutually exclusive categories is a testament to the decisive nature of these developments, according to which architecture abandoned its ambition to transform the world and turned its attention instead towards an increasingly intense but isolated private conversation on a few ideas, projects, and authors.

It is worth noting in the context of this text that this turn within architectural culture coincided with a pivotal moment when architecture and the arts were falling generally and dramatically out of synch. Around the mid-1960s, at the same time that North American architects retreated to a project based on pictorial abstraction, the American artists of the Pop, Minimal, and Conceptual art movements did quite the opposite, as they reinvigorated interest in the materiality of the objects around them and the cities in which they lived.[6] Ed Ruscha's photographs of cheap apartment buildings and storefronts, Dan Flavin's fluorescent light bulbs, and Donald Judd's early and rough three-dimensional works made out of pallets and other scraps found around his studio are all testaments to this changing tide, as American art abandoned the purity of abstract expressionism to investigate its own material culture as a repository of work materials. Thus, architects fully embraced the purest strain of geometric abstraction precisely in the moment in which artists abandoned it to take on a project of specific abstraction that was by all measures inspired directly by architecture and its artifacts.

It should not surprise us then to notice how, ever since this schism emerged, there have always been architects who have recursively sought out the work of visual artists, especially photographers, in order to approach the actuality of their surroundings in an attempt to appropriate them as part of their work. A famous example of this would be the obsession of Robert Venturi and Denise Scott Brown with the images of apartments and gas stations produced by Ruscha, which triggered their own attempts to appropriate commercial vernacular architecture. Closer to our day, another celebrated instance of this type of exchange is found in the collaboration of Jacques Herzog and Pierre de Meuron with the artist Thomas Ruff, whose work validates the architects' interest in

the superficiality of everyday life as a legitimate subject matter.

In scouting the world, visual artists, especially those in the tradition of documentary photography, detect and validate certain ignored or repressed fragments of reality by isolating them and including them in their production. It is precisely through this new context and valuation that architects can access them already with a first degree of abstraction that renders them as actionable items. More importantly, artists are oblivious to the idea that the elite of architectural production and the bulk of the physical reality of our cities belong in different categories. Their artworks, therefore, produce a redistribution of value among the artifacts of the world, which allows the architect to rediscover certain objects in a new light and to imagine different futures based on the actuality of the things around us.

It is precisely this capacity to operate diagonally across high and low modes of production and to resituate the core of architecture around its physical manifestations and its contributions to material culture that justifies the proposition to organize an exhibition of photographic works as a parallel thread or comment on the main thesis underlying this edition of the Chicago Architecture Biennial. Following from this idea, *A Love of the World* gathers a series of works of photography that collectively and inclusively expand the contours of architecture as a discipline and insinuate a larger field of work and responsibility for architects. In order to do so, the exhibition capitalizes on the power of the camera to alternatively elevate or demystify reality, producing in the process a reconceptualization of abstraction for architecture as a filter with which to approach the world, rather than a generative system that exists outside of it as a promise of order.

A didactic way to explain this mode of operation may be to contrast Nikolaus Pevsner's famously exclusive dictum, "A bicycle shed is a building; Lincoln Cathedral is a piece of architecture," with the effect produced by the work of a photographer like Walker Evans. Armed with a simple 35 mm camera, Evans had the capacity to present to us the humblest buildings in a light that rendered the distinction between architecture and construction as irrelevant. In a symmetrical move, photography—and we need only think of the tradition of the snapshot—also has the power to disclose even the most iconic masterpiece of modernism as just another building, an assemblage of the same steel beams and pillars as the gas station across the street, brought about by the same economic urgencies and, unavoidably, in its fragments and in any given moment, just the backdrop for the drama of someone's life.

6   See Joshua Shannon, *The Disappearance of Objects: New York Art and the Rise of the Postmodern City* (New Haven and London: Yale University Press, 2009).

All the artists included in *A Love of the World* operate somewhere in the spectrum found between the two contrasting photographic approaches described above, as they challenge the canon of modern architecture by either producing alternative accounts of its core episodes or proposing to expand its boundaries by incorporating objects and phenomena traditionally considered to lie outside of it. More important than the quantitative redistributions of value that they perform among objects or spaces are the specific qualities that they highlight and how their works allow us to imagine new and exciting alternatives to what we know already, effectively producing new worlds and new meanings through the sheer intensity of their way of looking at things.

A fitting example would be the work of Luisa Lambri, whose images of the Farnsworth House (Mies van der Rohe, 1951) appear to us as distant memories of a former inhabitant. By focusing on the house as a frame for the landscape and letting the building itself fade away in our peripheral vision, Lambri partially erases the canonical architecture and leaves us with the bits and pieces of life that get captured in its corners. Her conflation of detail and atmosphere produces a reading of the architecture that is simultaneously more disembodied and more domestic, and in doing so, her

photographs create a new architecture that departs from Mies to insinuate a contemporary understanding of inhabitation.

James Welling's colorized images document the IIT campus and the Lake Shore Drive Apartments, both also by Mies van der Rohe and closely associated with the modern movement of the 1950s. His series, succinctly titled *Chicago*, renders these two canonic works of architecture according to a series of techniques borrowed from the experimental photography scene of the 1960s. The resulting images, produced through the layering of multiple exposures and two highly idiosyncratic periods of art history, result in an anachronism that we could describe lightly as a "psychedelic Mies," an unexpected and completely new cultural construct that defamiliarizes the original work and produces instead an encounter with myriad new readings and future possibilities.

David Schalliol's series on the Chicago Housing Authority deals with the literal dismantlement of the modern legacy of Mies and his contemporaries through the demolition of the midcentury social housing projects of the city. In doing so, Schalliol shatters the aura of atemporality associated with modernism and the notion that it exists outside of history. In his careful and personal portrayal of this process, which transcends traditional documentary

Scott Fortino, *Untitled (Purple Hotel)*, 2013

photography to become its own genre, Schalliol contrasts the disassembly of the buildings with the vitality of their inhabitants. It is as if the architecture, a theatrical backdrop for daily life, becomes itself animated, putting forward the illusion that the buildings are receding into the mists of time as much as they are transforming to mark a new and uncertain beginning.

In a different part of town and with a different focus, Scott Fortino also reflects on the current life of the Miesian legacy, as he interrogates a cross section of its high-rise glass prisms. Fortino puts forward his own account of how the promise of the transparency of modern architecture has played out across the decades and how it exists today in Chicago, with its relaxed mix of high modern masterpieces and corporate replicas. As Fortino directs his gaze from the public space of the city into the interiors of these buildings, the reflections caught up in the glass curtain walls virtually turn each photograph into a double exposure, a synthesis of the experience of Chicago in which the intimacy and pathos of an almost domestic interior is overlaid with an afterimage of street life and the presence of nature in the city.

Veronika Kellndorfer similarly revises our narrow understanding of modern architecture, which has been enabled over the years by the persistence of a few period photographs and drawings. In her suite of photographs of Mies van der Rohe's Neue Nationalgalerie (New National Gallery), in Berlin, which are printed on sheets of glass, Kellndorfer exposes the gap between our mental image of the building and its actuality in the world today. Her photographs of the empty gallery at the beginning of a process of restoration focus on its raw materials; the original steel, glass, and stone coexist with the new stacks of materials waiting to be installed and with the dust and dirt of the construction site. In her documentation of a moment of change, Kellndorfer portrays the building as simultaneously unravelling and becoming.

True to his beginnings as an architectural historian, Filip Dujardin has produced a series of digital prints that focus on the interaction and interdependence between urban form, architectural type, and construction detail. His inclusive survey of high-rise construction in Chicago reveals to us the ways in which what we understand as the image of a city is constructed first and foremost through repetition and consistency. By manipulating the parameters underlying such consensus within the highly recognizable system of the Chicago grid and its architecture, Dujardin proposes a series of transfers or contaminations between different time periods, scales, and modes of architectural

David Schalliol, *Untitled (Chicago Housing Authority's Plan for Transformation)*, 2003–17

production, yielding images that contain alternative histories for the city.

Dealing with similar preoccupations, Philipp Schaerer capitalizes on the most banal and anonymous constructions to build a series of images that propose possible architectures for the city out of its very own raw matter. In his *Chicago Series*, Schaerer departs from his previous explorations of party walls—true byproducts of architectural design—and focuses instead on the roofs of the city. The artist then generates a series of digital images produced from the sampling, replication, and cropping of existing satellite photographs. The resulting constructed images are ambivalently positioned between the precious and the banal, between an emphasis on surface and a certain objecthood. Schaerer's dual mastery of the languages of architectural drawing and documentary photography allows him to pitch these two media against each other, in a perfect demonstration of a new and reconciled approach to the problem of abstraction as proposed in this essay.

Similarly, Daniel Everett's digital images, grouped under the name *Marker*, focus on urban space through reading the traces left by change in the literal surfaces of the city. His systematic recording of the ground plane as the site of the programming and reprogramming of collective behavior and public life is a testament to the way

that architecture and urbanism become a pervasive and almost subconscious presence in our daily routines. For Everett, modernism and its legacy exist simultaneously—although not without conflict—as a utopia and as the actual normative space of mass-produced architectures that form the backdrop of life in the developed world. Through the ambiguity and nuance of his visual technique, he walks us seamlessly through a series of scales in the city of Chicago, focusing on the tension between order and imperfection that defines the substrate of collective space in our contemporary condition.

Finally, Marianne Mueller turns her attention to the architecture of the venue, in this case the Chicago Cultural Center, in order to focus on the moments when the different stages of its life enter into contact with each other. Through her hunter-gatherer approach, which is rooted in the photographic tradition of the snapshot, and her deep understanding of architecture as being made up of a series of elements that are in essence democratic, Mueller captures the clashes between the noble architecture of the center's nineteenth-century building and the contemporary generic materials of the additions and partitions that enable its many functions today. Her blown up prints of fragments of the building interiors, installed in the vitrines at

Daniel Everett, *Untitled (from Marker)*, 2017

the G.A.R. Hall in the Chicago Cultural Center, open up a meta dialog about the representational role of architecture and its interiors. In doing so, Mueller's work becomes a testament to our changing notions of public space and public institutions and, more critically, to the resilience and the capacity of architecture to survive and renew itself through time—to traverse history and speak the different languages of its present.

A sense of *presentness* is perhaps what all the artists gathered in *A Love of the World* share, and it is the defining trait of a project that tries to instill in architecture an urgency to work with the materials of the here and now. As we traverse the mosaic of images produced by these nine artists, which are laid out across and in conversation with the different exhibits in the architecture biennial, we gain a sense of how our idea of architecture is embedded in a much larger field. Within this field—physical but also cultural—architecture is nonetheless a powerful actor. By creating a new context in which the myth of modern architecture's exceptionality is challenged through its confrontation with the evidence found in our built environment, the exhibition insinuates new modes of authorship for architects, but also a renewed responsibility, as it elicits an invitation to consider once again our duty to touch the lives of the many.

This exhibition is an attempt to enrich and expand the materials available to architects today. It poses an opportunity to rethink the different intensities at which architecture can operate and what its scope should be, in an effort to imagine new registers and modes of cultural production that would result in an increased role for architecture in public discourse and the construction of a shared material culture. Nowhere as in Chicago, a place where the myth of modernity and the building stock of the city become almost one and the same thing, can we find better reasons to put forward an informed argument for engaging the material world in all its breadth— an optimistic proposal for the future.

Jesús Vassallo is an architect and writer, currently an assistant professor at Rice University.

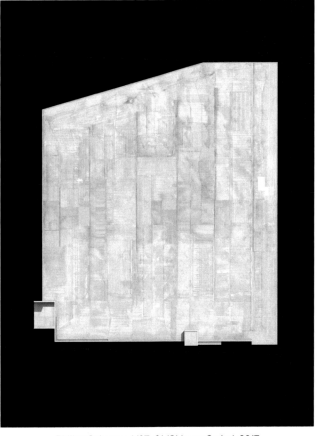

Philipp Schaerer, *V07–01 (Chicago Series)*, 2017

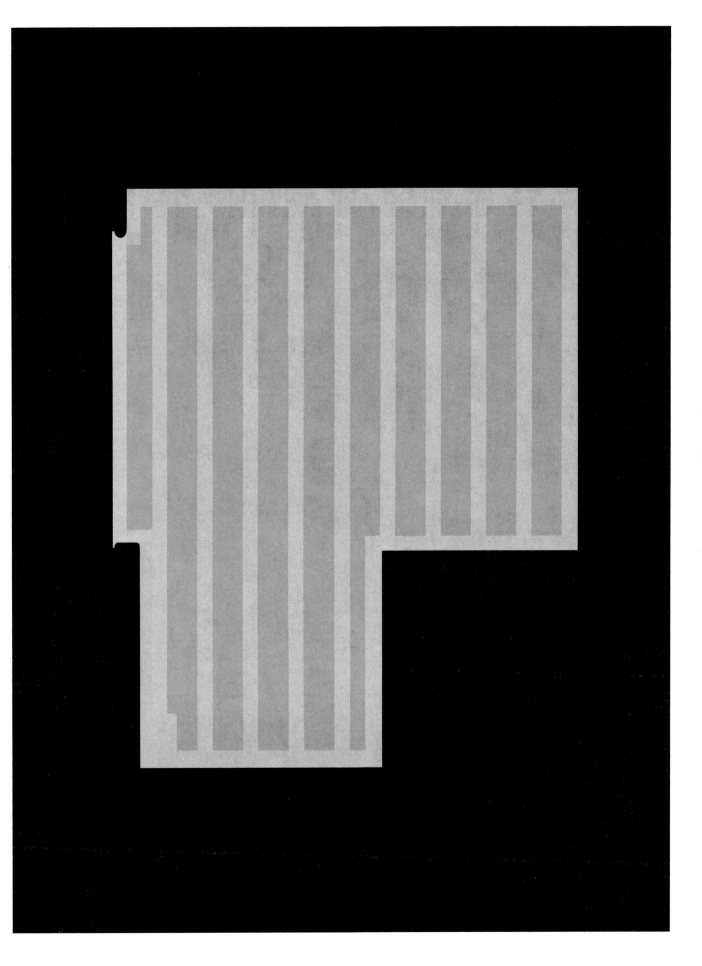

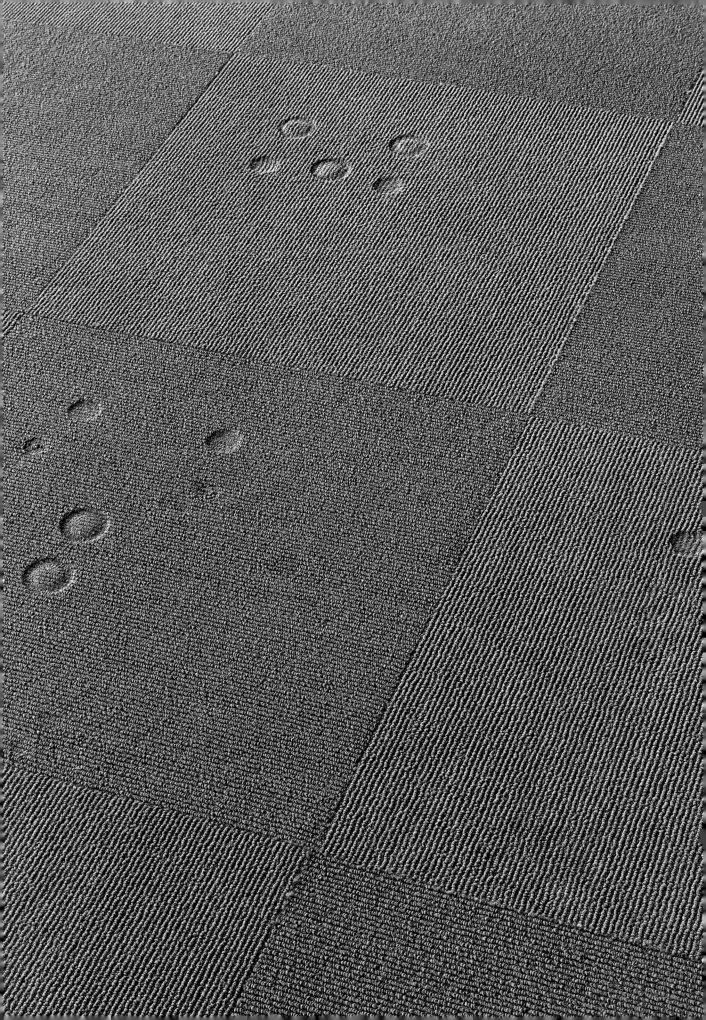

Image Histories

Projects that examine image histories are primarily concerned with the world of visual culture and architecture's relationship to it. One might consider these projects alongside the relaxing of the visual canon from the disciplinary and historical images of buildings to the stunning array of "non-pedigreed," everyday material and pop infiltration that marks postmodernity. More than simply a problem of studying the ways that architects produce visual likenesses, these projects are concerned with images as reference points, image production and display, and architecture photography as its own discipline.

Organizational and formatting problems may not be self-evident in the projects in the biennial, but they underwrite the renewed interest as well as increased visibility and mobility of historical content in our contemporary image world. The cut and paste culture of architectural drafting—stencils, blocks, and repeatable drawing elements born out of efficiency—also drives today's drawing sensibilities. The Internet's endless supply of electronic images, CAD referencing options, and architectural representations increasingly incorporates a smoother version of the early twentieth century montage logic: what British architect and participant Sam Jacob calls post-digital drawings (p. 242).[1] Projects based around the organization of images or information are trafficking in a sensibility of collecting and assembling that often links platforms of display with those of storage, finding new questions in the interruption and adjacency of two or more images.

Participant baukuh, in collaboration with photographer Stefano Graziani, look at the Renaissance cartoon drawing that held information scaleable and transferrable from paper to the wall as a means of exploring the technological histories of image production (p. 68). Their study for a chapel looks at the contentless format, taking the narrative portals of Giotto's Scrovegni Chapel in Padua, Italy and replacing them with empty stage sets for a fictitious encounter between the Queen of Sheba and Italian oil magnate Enrico Fermi: two figures that lived eras apart. In this work, baukuh celebrates the discordance, rather than a smooth encounter of image-based worlds such as those described above.

The disciplinary interest in the production of architectural ideas is considered by Bak Gordon (p. 64) and Caruso St John (p. 72). Bak Gordon's sketches follow a long lineage of drawing understood as the carrier of the expressive impulses of the architect; his large scale sketches do not carry the careful finish of the render, and their looseness attests to their immediacy. On the other hand, Caruso St John's project takes on the production of the office through a collection of references images, image-like models, and photographs of finished buildings that relate to a mix of realized and unrealized building designs. Represented in solid, blockish, and flat painted models and collected on a table in the form of a city block, this project speaks of the architect's output in the most uniform sense; their assembly suggests the passage of imagery and ideas between references, models and buildings.

Image histories are also produced out of the contemporary collaborative efforts of architects and photographers. Jesús Vassallo's curated exhibition *A Love of the World* (p. 183), organised as a discrete collection of works distributed through the cultural center, features art photographers like James Welling and Luisa Lambri whose photographs are captured in canonical sites of modernist architecture. Other photographers in the biennial work more actively alongside the architects whose work they shoot, like Filip Dujardin and Stefano Graziani. These myriad photographic practices that form between building, image production, and reproduction suggest that architectural design and building is changing to increasingly consider potential imageability; buildings stand to become the object of visual interpretation of many different types.

1   In his article and titling of "Post-Digital Drawing," Jacob infers that definitions that once held between media and technique are subsumed into the smoothed category of the image. He prioritizes software platforms at work in the screen environments that produce merging potential for photographic material, alongside what might have been considered graphic.

Vertical City
Collective Projects 2017

Vertical City brings together 16 architects to reconsider the 1922 brief for the design of a tower to house the Chicago Tribune newspaper company. The original competition attracted 263 entries from the US and around the world—each including a rendered perspective from the same vantage—later published as a report alongside a touring exhibition of drawings that stopped at various educational and cultural institutions in the United States. The collusion of print media, exhibition, and architecture, in this instance, effectively sealed the imagery of individual towers shown as a collection; and the influence and reach of this particular project drove many responses and copies. The most famous of these was an exhibition of late entry drawings organized in 1980 by the Chicago Seven, led by Stanley Tigerman, that gathered a contemporaneous cross section of architectural ideas and influences. The Chicago Seven's version of the competition was decidedly paper-oriented. Problems of language and ornament—that were, in 1922, occupied with building production—in 1980 relocated to drawing production, which was more characteristic of the period.

The 2017 Chicago Architecture Biennial eschews drawings for the exhibition format. Each tower design is represented as a scaled model, 16 feet high.

Collected together, these enormous, slender forms appear as a Hypostyle Hall stage set. The designs are at once a tower and a column.

Two replica towers from the original competition—Viennese architect Adolf Loos's overscaled column and German Ludwig Hilberseimer's rationalized block—are set up like poles in the *Vertical City* and establish the backdrop for the current designs. Loos's design was an image that, during the 1970s, captured the attention of a generation of architects who were interested in formal models of communication. Hilberseimer's austere and flat gridded scheme, though never officially submitted in 1922, slowly made its way into the official accounts and, more recently, reignited architectural interest in the economies of ornament and labor. Elements and impulses of these two towers can be recognized in the 2017 Tribune submissions. Today, the towers reflect formal explorations of the tower type, exquisite corpses, as-found objects with new scales and material tests.

The Brief

Program:	The tower provides office space for *The Chicago Tribune Company*.
Building Dimensions:	H 400' - Base 100' × 100'
Model Scale:	Imperial Scale 1/2"=1'-0" (1:24 metric)
Mandatory:	Maximum height 16.6' Base dimension 4.16' × 4.16' (Keep in mind: the structures are self-standing, no fixing to the floor or to the ceiling, so account for steady construction.)
Model Construction:	Solid body, single material construction with apertures.

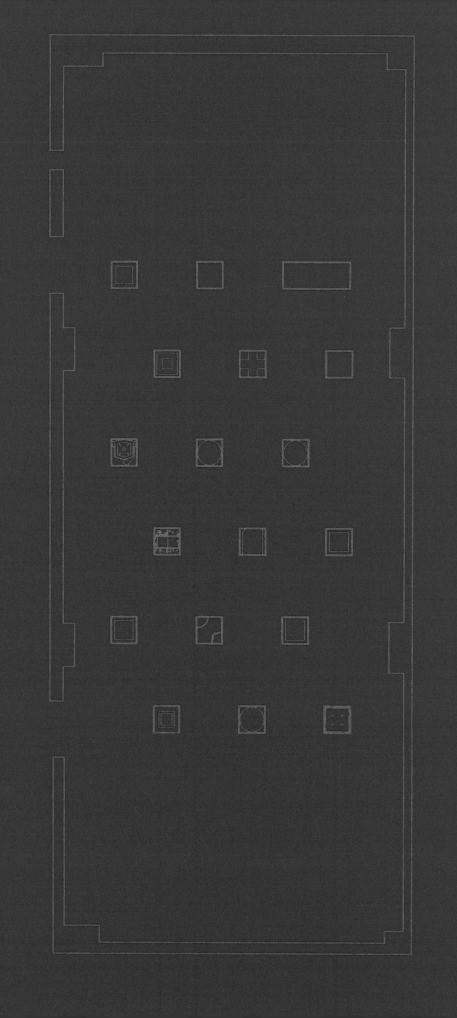

Vertical City

6a architects
Barbas Lopes
Barozzi Veiga
Christ & Gantenbein
Ensamble Studio
Éric Lapierre Architecture
Go Hasegawa
Kéré Architecture
Kuehn Malvezzi

MOS
OFFICE KGDvS with
    Peter Wächtler and
    Michaël Van den Abeele
PRODUCTORA
Sam Jacob Studio
Sergison Bates
Serie Architects
Tatiana Bilbao Estudio

Georgian Room installed at the Art Institute of Chicago. English, c. 1750.

As the European entries to the Chicago Tribune Tower competition were being unloaded from a New York freight train, another architectural consignment was also ending its transatlantic journey. The content of crates originating in Berlin, Vienna, Paris, and other centers of the avant-garde would set the revolutionary spirit of modernism in the aftermath the First World War. In the other crates, a room of eighteenth century wooden panels delicately carved in fine rococo patterns arrived as a new *Period Room* exhibit for the Art Institute Chicago. The Georgian Room, as it became known in Chicago, played its traditional role of presenting a declining European culture (and empire) being rapidly overtaken by Chicago and rest of the US. Sometime after the second World War, it was repacked and stored away. By the 1980s, it had returned to England where it stayed in a barn in Essex until 2008, when 6a architects were designing the extension to the two Georgian houses in

Spitalfields, East London, for a contemporary art center. Archives revealed the whereabouts of the nomadic room, which—detached from the walls of one of these houses almost ninety years earlier— was reinstalled as if staying in one place immobile the whole time.

Architecture is the subject of more change, more violence, and jeopardy than in the unlikely world tour of this interior. The rise and fall and rise again of the modern city passed through every room of the two East London buildings as the legacy of the Chicago Tribune Tower competition conveyed the architecture of the century. The tower presented here reconstitutes, in a model and in documents, the architecture of a room that has existed in London and Chicago over two and half centuries and seen the making of new histories in the coincidences and accidents of the city, which unfold alongside the polemical landmarks of architectural discourse.

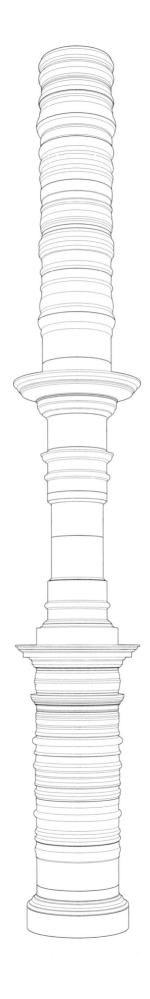

Barbas Lopes Arquitectos — Lisbon, Portugal

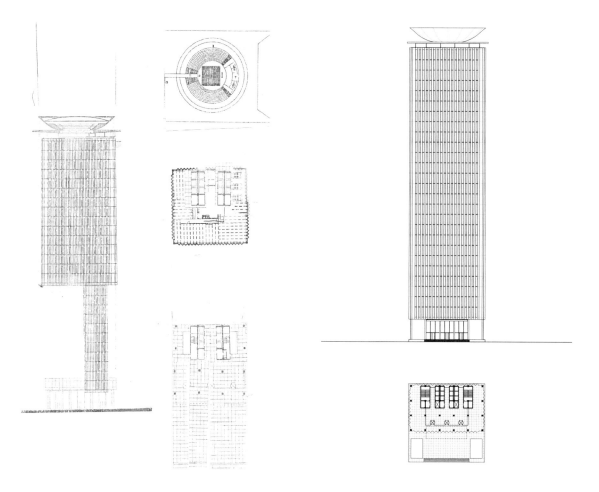

Barbas Lopes Arquitectos, Sketch and study for *Vertical City*, 2017

We will not hesitate to redo Loos's Doric column with our own reference findings: showing what, for us, is "the most beautiful and distinctive office building in the world."[1] In a time where information goes around so fast and truth is increasingly unclear, a newspaper such as the *Chicago Tribune* must have a combined austerity and abstraction. Architecture must be without time: modernist in form but classicist in principle. Loos's column provides a model of proportion and objectiveness, and our aim is to work with its principle structure: base, shaft, and capital. From that starting point, we will proceed with the improbable juxtaposition of three disparate references, collected from our beloved twentieth century architecture and from our own ongoing practice. This exercise of

historical imagination brings together the representation of significant features in our contemporary society: the first referring to the progressive alienation of capitalistic economy; the second responding to technical constraints and overwhelming design regulations; and the third to emphasize the need for a heroic belief that a newspaper is a house to build information, opening it to wider debate within our society. We want to emphasize and share the American newspaper slogan campaign, "the truth is more important now than ever."[2]

1   Staney Tigerman et al., *Chicago Tribune Tower Competition / Late Entries*, vol. I (London: Academy Editions, 1980), 3.
2   "The New York Times," print ad, *New York Times*, no. 57.520, February 26, 2017.

Chicago   Barozzi Veiga — Barcelona, Spain

Barozzi Viega, *Chicago*, elevation, 2017

We always work with what we find in a place. Our main interest is to discover the specificity of the different contexts. We are interested in architecture that strikes a balance between the specificity and authenticity of the site and the autonomy of form. We always seek an architecture that aspires to confer dignity, identity, and a sense of belonging to places of civic community life through an autonomous, primal approach that can transcend the point in time at which it emerges. It would establish a temporal link between past, present, and future. Our proposal for the Chicago Tribune Tower aspires to establish an intimate relationship with the context in which the building is to be integrated. The project formulates an intersection between different periods of time, techniques, and visions of the specific place. It is a piece of architecture that is simultaneously specific and autonomous: capable of preserving and reviving the richness of Chicago's tradition and history.

Inspired by the terra cotta style, the project is a pure cuboid form, which is characterized by a static structural geometric grid that becomes a dynamic continuous ornament.

The repetitive character of the structure creates a clear modular organization in order to maintain integrity of all parts of the project, thereby underlining its autonomy. The project is a certain intimate reflection that absorbs all of the small aspects of the surrounding context, keeping its own independence and purity. From this intention rises a simple, pure building which proposes continuity and transformation of the tradition that has marked the identity of Chicago.

227

Monumental Objet Trouvé
Christ & Gantenbein — Basel, Switzerland

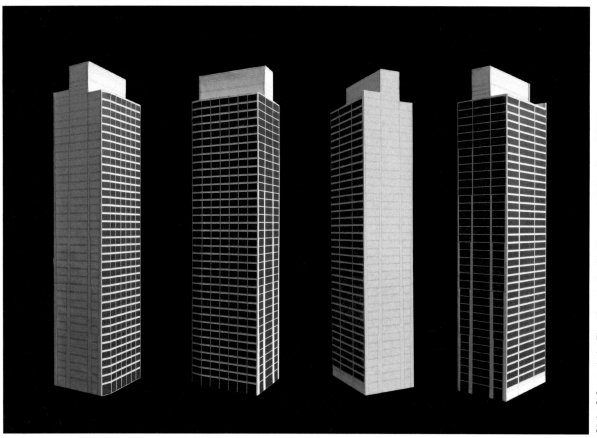

Christ & Gantenbein, Elevation studies for *Monumental Objet Trouvé*, 2017

One of the architect's roles is to introduce memory and recognize our profession as rooted in tradition. In a society where most processes are engaged with now, we architects represent a minority who still acknowledges yesterday through the simple fact that buildings can, or at least could, last hundreds of years. Thus, architecture has always dealt in strategies of appropriation. This is why, by elaborating our designs, we always look at precedents. Our design for the Tribune Tower shall depict a building as part of a typological collection of urban anonymous architecture. These buildings express tectonics, materiality, but most of all, they represent our interest in typological precision: where pragmatic rules condition architecture. Our Doric Column of the twenty-first century— a contemporary counterpart to Adolf Loos's 1922 proposal—is the pristine architecture of pure tectonics embedded in an automatic garage tower. The realization of an architectural dream, this exercise in fundamental tectonics—expressed in the most honest structure and in a denial to design—reaches classical beauty. However, beyond its pragmatic rules, it becomes an ideal design in its tension with the context. We would like to celebrate this caricature of a perfect high-rise—statics, tectonics, infill, and lift—as a monument to architectural perfection. Our act of design is simply to declare this *objet trouvé* as part of the legacy of historical architecture. The chosen model is an existing garage tower in São Paulo. Built in 1964 by Abelardo de Souza and Bernardo Vaisman, the Garagem Roosevelt conveys the classical beauty of technical objects; its concrete structural grid becomes thinner towards the top and bricks and concrete fill its gaps. Its four facades are different. A concrete party wall alternates with two facades of different structural rhythms, while a corner is subtly chamfered and grounds the prism in its site: the wild topography of central São Paulo.

Big Bang Tower: A Column of Columns for The Chicago Tribune   Ensamble Studio — Madrid, Spain/Cambridge, USA

Ensamble Studio, Detail photograph of study model, 2017

In our contemporary culture, working spaces can no longer be understood as the fixed cubicles where the worker spends the entirety of her day immersed in her own particular task, progressively accumulating piles of paper that will require ample amounts of physical storage. A shift of paradigm is happening, enabled by information technologies, that opens new avenues to reimagine the meaning of space. An office can be a cubicle and also an open co-working area, a cafe, a lounge, a lab, a multipurpose room, virtual substance in the cloud, a room in your house, and much more. This diversification—and enrichment—of the meaning of "office" provides the opportunity to think about architecture in renewed urban terms, especially when the structure that supports such expanded function is a tower with a big physical presence.

Big Bang Tower embraces the scale of the city and the need for transformation of its programs. By dividing the typical central core of a conventional high-rise building and locating the fragmented parts in the envelope, access to the stacked floors is multiplied. The thick asymmetric columns adapt

to the requirement of the server spaces to resolve at once vertical structure and infrastructure: everything the space needs to enable the activity. The rest is open space: open to the requirements of an increasingly diverse program, open to the transformation of these requirements over time, open to exciting connections with the public realm of the city. The convenient shell and core concept developed for modern office buildings is here given new spatial scale and quality. The horizontal structures that tie the perimeter columns together contribute to this purpose by varying their position, area, and height, so the activity is not contained identically in level. Manifold ways of framing the city and connecting interior spaces are provoked.

This column of columns, that learns from history and reframes the context of the Chicago Tribune Competition, is not dismissive of the competition goal to design "the world's most beautiful office building" and looks for this beauty in the revision of the typology and its relation to the urban context.

365 Student Housing
Éric Lapierre Architecture — Paris, France

Éric Lapierre, Pier in construction for the 365 Student Residences, 2007–17

We did not design this column for the purpose of the 2017 Chicago Architecture Biennial. We borrowed the column form from an earlier project of our office, the 365 Student Housing building in Paris. The original column is made of poured-in-site concrete. Various constraints influenced the geometry of the 365 building. The housing plans are very thin (eight feet) and deep (twenty-six feet), so they are fully glazed to allow light to flow in completely. The zigzag profile of the facade comes from avoiding flat glazing that would make the building appear as if an office. French fire regulation drove the ornamental concrete slab edge that prevents fires from jumping floor levels. The column is designed with this same slab edge profile. The columns are

formally rationalized to work under compression. The smallest one is about two-and-a-half feet and the largest one is thirty feet. All of them are poured in one pour with no joints or holes, as genuine monolithic columns are. Thus, the whole building is texturized in the same proportion and form in all its parts, bringing to it a strong formal coherence.

Our proposal for the *Chicago Tribune* is to build a new column form in reflecting steel as a sculptural object. Up close, this polished surface will be engraved to suggest a curtain wall transforming the whole column into the scale tower model. The model produces an ambiguity between the polished steel in which it is built and the glass it represents.

The Glass Tower   Go Hasegawa — Tokyo, Japan

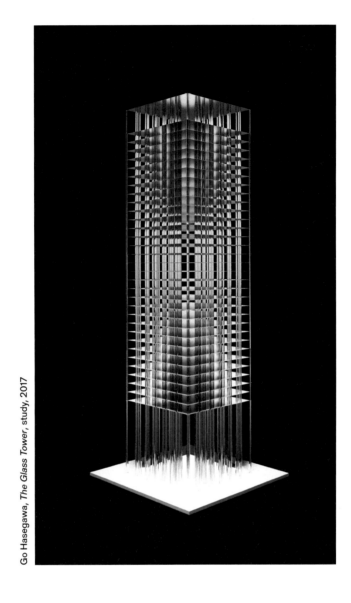

Go Hasegawa, *The Glass Tower*, study, 2017

Within a decade after the Great Chicago Fire in 1871, the value of the land in the city soared, and the introduction of the skeleton frame favored the perfection of the skyscraper typology to efficiently use the valuable space. The architects of the First Chicago School, in fact, replaced the traditional exterior load-bearing walls with larger expanses of glass, and the thin curtain walls hung from the frame allowed for more interior space. This research surfaced again with Ludwig Mies van der Rohe and his disciples of the Second Chicago School, whose style focused on the metal cage and undecorated frame of the building, regarding the structure in the abstract as the most important objective of architecture. *The Glass Tower* explores the relationship between structure and skin. It does so by creating a dialogue between the curtain wall, a major interest of the two Chicago Schools, and towers: the archetypical expression of the desire of men to reach higher using pure structures. The structure moves itself into a perimetrical wall made by the repetition of enormous columns of massive glass. This combines structure and facade in one single gesture and fills the massiveness and enclosure of traditional towers with a new meaning of transparency. Each floor is thus freed from any load-bearing component, and organized only by the four inner columns hosting the circulation systems. Because of the use of the round element of the column, the tower loses the aesthetic of the sharp, right angle characteristic of Chicago Schools' buildings, only to gain a feeling of solid sinuosity. Then, the optical effect given by the massiveness of the glass columns renders the interior a special environment: blurring the edges between inside and outside, between container and content.

Kéré Architecture — Berlin, Germany

"Come, let us build ourselves a city, and a tower whose top is in the heavens; let us make a name for ourselves, lest we be scattered abroad over the face of the whole earth."

— King James Bible

As the Tower of Babel represents a powerful symbol of human ability and strength when united in a common goal and language, Kéré's reimagined Tribune Tower also embraces communication and community as driving forces for the design. The proposal anticipates multiple aspects of modern life existing within the same building footprint such as housing, workplace, commerce, and recreation. To accommodate these activities, the tower is composed of segmented blocks each with a central void. As opposed to a conventional skyscraper design with a technical core running through the center, all structural and technical aspects of Kéré's design exist in three separate cores pushed to the exterior, freeing up the interior for a variety of dynamic amenities, communal functions, or constructed landscapes. Each block has the potential to host a different program in relation to the vertical proximity to the city at the ground level. For example, the crown of the tower may contain private apartments while the base holds a cultural center. In alignment with current trends, the design forecasts that people will value a balanced work and life ratio while retaining real and meaningful connections with each other and with the places that they live.

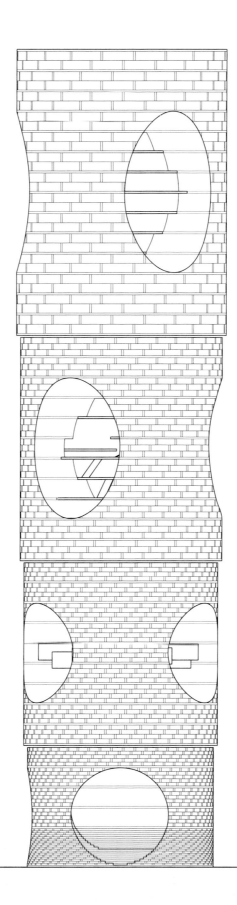

Kéré Architecture, Elevation for Tribune Tower, 2017

If Raymond Hood's Chicago Tribune Tower epito-mizes the tall office building beyond prairie heroism, then Loos's 1922 competition entry projects the corporate tower beyond European modernism. Today, the transatlantic realists Hood and Loos will finally meet. Their encounter takes place at the historical site of the original competition, witnessed by the real Chicago context and influenced by two ideal European counterparts who haven't seen the light of day.

Around 1922, the European modernists, except for Loos, conceived of the high-rise as a typology that was key to redesigning the city as a different space, acting as decisive urban elements to replace the nineteenth century urban block. In contrast, Hood's tower and Loos's column do not pretend to make urban space in the first place. Rather, they provide iconic objects to grow from the extant reality of a generic urban block.

Meeting in 2017, the heterogeneous Europeans set the stage for a new confrontation with the Chicago site. It results in an unlikely turn. A bastard is going to be generated from the urban block and its reversal, cross-breeding the longing for iconic buildings with the claim for urban space.

Turning the volume inside out, what used to be the space in-between the high-rises becomes building mass and will house the offices of the *Chicago Tribune*. The building shells instead turn into highly defined voids that act as urban squares, their facades being reversed. Figure becomes ground, solitary objects turn into spaces, and vice versa. The result is a novel urban fabric that intro-duces the commons into the commercial block. Where there used to be facades along the block perimeter, now there are sectional cuts, whereas inside the block we encounter the historical facades oriented towards the articulated urban spaces enclosed by them. The existing Tribune Tower by Raymond Hood will not be substituted but revisited and transformed.

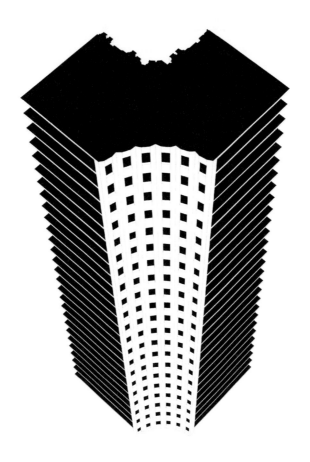

& Another (Chicago Tribune Tower)
MOS — New York, USA

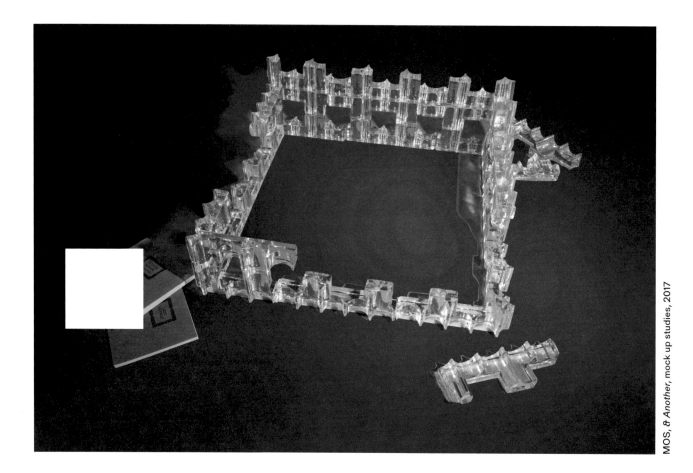

MOS, *& Another*, mock up studies, 2017

Whatever this is, it is on the verge of nothing-in-particular. It is a ghostly figment of something, constructed out of structural, cast glass blocks. It is an average. It is a technical marvel. Maybe it is a knowing wink and nod toward quote-unquote history. Maybe not. It couldn't care less or more.

MOS, *& Another*, 2017

The competition for the Chicago Tribune Tower is one of these events whose aftereffect in the realm of architecture culture was probably bigger than the impact of the actual event at the actual time. In a fashion not unlike the postmortem fame of say, the Velvet Underground—"All the people that bought the original record started a band," as the famous saying goes—the Loos-Hilberseimer duality is one of historical appropriation. Still, we need to ask ourselves: does the duality help us think about the urban tower as a problem? Is the space opened by the monumental dialogue between these two rather unresolved totems of architectural discourse a fertile one? As imposing as each of the projects might be—beautiful and somehow consistent in their own right—neither one is a proper tower, in the Chicagoan sense: not in 1922 and not today. In many respects, both buildings are the vehicle of an argument only vaguely connected to the problem of the tall and urban project. In hindsight, both seem rather the result of savvy cultural posturing, projected from overseas.

When Mies van der Rohe built his Seagram tower, he was an American architect. Mies's office was Chicagoan, but his architecture found its real form in a confrontation with McKim, Mead & White's enlarged palazzo of the Racquet and Tennis Club in a direction spatial opposition on Park Avenue. Perhaps it was there that the real themes of building tall and building urban were tackled: a perpetual negotiation between palace and tower, structure and facade.

Our tower is conceived as an ambiguous repetition of the same window. Always according to a set proportion system, the incremental multiplication works against perspective (in favor of floor surface) in height. The structure stacks a family of palazzi pregnant in self-expression. Their presence consciously acknowledges the only European building type that Americans could successfully enlarge and multiply, without losing its defining principles to build their own version of the city: one tower, many palazzi. If, indeed, the problem of building tall is only reduced to multiplication (But, then again, the multiplication of what?) we have to accept that the negotiation with tectonics—the unresolved dance around expression, thus the desire to be forever close and far away—takes center stage. Mies understood that right away—his buildings are their own expression. In our complex dance with Peter Wächtler's art, we merely achieve an approximation—as an upside down obelisk.

Two Towers   PRODUCTORA
— Mexico City, Mexico

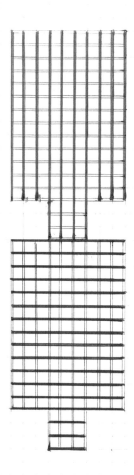

Carlos Bedoya, *Two Towers*, sketch, 2017

The project for the *Vertical City* at the Chicago Cultural Center is based on two earlier projects of the studio. The first one is the design for the open international competition for the Bauhaus Museum in Weimar, a collaboration with Derek Dellekamp Architects from 2011. In this project two similar volumes with different materiality are stacked one on top of the other in order to reduce the perceived overall height of the building. This compositional strategy was repeated again in PRODUCTORA's competition entry for a private developer, in the city of Queretaro, a year later. In both cases the stacked volumes create a totemic urban composition, with half the volume dedicated to terraces. The simple bic drawings by Carlos Bedoya became an important reference to represent this design strategy at the Chicago Architecture Biennial. By rendering the large MDF model in blue and red bic, we play with the ambiguity of the commission. Are these columns conceived as scale models of a possible tower proposal? Are they just a sculptural prism in dialogue with fifteen other participants in the Yates hall? Are they a miniature version of a tower, an upscaled drawing, or an enlarged sketch?

Sam Jacob Studio — London, UK

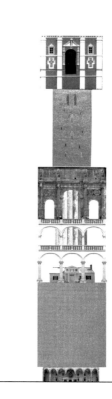

Sam Jacob Studio, *Tribune Tower Studies 3, 4, 5, 2017*

The installation is a proposal for a tower that comes loaded with multiple, pre-existing forms of architecture. The first form is the imagined Tribune Tower—Adolf Loos's cyclopean Doric column architecture. Loos's Tribune is an object out of place and out of scale as if a piece had become a whole, as if an object had become a building. The second form is the actual Tribune Tower on Michigan Avenue that unwittingly pays tribute to Loos's tactic of appropriation and decontextualization. One hundred and fifty fragments of other buildings—architectural relics of historic or curious significance—are embedded in the facade of the building. Our tower deploys Loos's tactic of appropriating existing architectural form while using the Tribune's fragments as a generator; series of architectural pieces, each referring to one of the fragments, are arranged in a vertical stack like an architectural version of the surrealist exquisite corpse. It functions like the Pasticcio in the courtyard of the Soane Museum—a totem pole-like assemblage of stylistically diverse architectural fragments of reclaimed buildings.

Here in the Chicago tower, pieces of history are removed from their geographical or chronological context and assembled into a new whole. Varied architectural references are fused together into a new singular tower-like form. It shifts mode, acting in part as a model (of the original references, of a large scale model of a tower) and as a thing itself (an actual tower, a column). These historical antecedents are used to generate an alternative tower typology. It suggests that architectural possibility exists in acts of appropriation, assembly, and remaking. And that architecture is not something that we create but something that already exists, just waiting for us to discover it. This is an architecture that acknowledges the multiplicity of origins that underwrites the field. The tower suggests that architecture is as much knowledge as material, and that it is always a model even when it's built.

Re-imagining the tower   Sergison Bates
— London, UK/Zurich, Switzerland

Sergison Bates, Sketch study for tower, 2017

Our contribution to this third iteration of the 1922 Chicago Tribune Competition is a pencil tower of such slender form and great height that it resembles a column. Inspired by the column drums of ancient classical architecture which were stacked and pegged together to form majestic structures, our pencil tower is constructed by stacking sections: one on top of the other, creating a sense of weight and solidity.

The tower has eight sides and is divided into three distinct parts: the base, the middle, and the top. Each of these sections is expressed by making an angled cut into the form that lends the building a sculpted appearance and emphasizes the classical tripartite order. This combination of slenderness and solidity results in a robust beauty that evokes the ancient buildings we love. The weight of the tower is transferred to the ground through columns that form a plinth-like base scaled to match an imaginary city block structure. The upper sections, which step and chamfer on different sides as the building rises above the city, are adjusted to create a rotational movement that releases the building from the geometries of the imagined city structure it is grounded in.

We imagine the building with a brick facade that lends it a powerful materiality and a miniature scale in counterpoint to the overall height of the building. Horizontal bands of fine, precast concrete emphasize a secondary horizontal proportion with large structural openings between brick piers.

Internally, the vertical pegs that form the interlocking structure represent the cores of an imaginary office environment of open work space. The thickness of the external walls is exaggerated to contain a sequence of niches and windows with deep reveals from which the city outside can be viewed and contemplated.

Sergison Bates, Visualisation of tower in Yates Hall, 2C17

Serie Architects, *Other Histories*, stacked table pavilions frame events in the tower, 2017

To make new history, we need to look at other histories. If the primary source of derivation for modern architecture is classicism, what would an architecture that is derived from a non-Western historical tradition be? This proposal for the new Chicago Tribune Far East Asian Headquarters explores a possible answer. Its design is grounded in principals of ancient Chinese architecture with the aim of locating a contemporary architectural vocabulary in an eastern formal and philosophical basis. The source of a Chinese architectural language can be found in the architecture of all its imperial cities, where the irreducible part is the pavilion. When stacked vertically, pavilions form a pagoda: a structure without the hierarchal and tripartite relationships of Western classicism, that instead embody more pliable organizational possibilities. The building is a tower of pavilions, an accumulation of parts, each subtly differentiated. It is a vertical city where meaning is embodied in the relation between elements. Within the conventional logic of high-rise, it rejects the extruded floor plate to create a tower of volumes, each with its own autonomy and status in the vertical axis. Pavilions spill over from one to the other, the table tops defining spatial limits but not limits of influence. The spaces of this new vertical city are attuned to the nature of the knowledge economy and the contemporary media environment where performance dominates, flexibility sets value and well-being is the ultimate cause. Pavilions frame theaters, meeting zones, restful landscapes, and hedonistic gardens: the true productive spaces for today's media workers. This is architecture with a language not rooted in Western thought and with a history outside of the narratives of modernism. It is a tower for a media with global reach and capital based offshore. It makes new histories for a polyglot and multi-centered architectural culture.

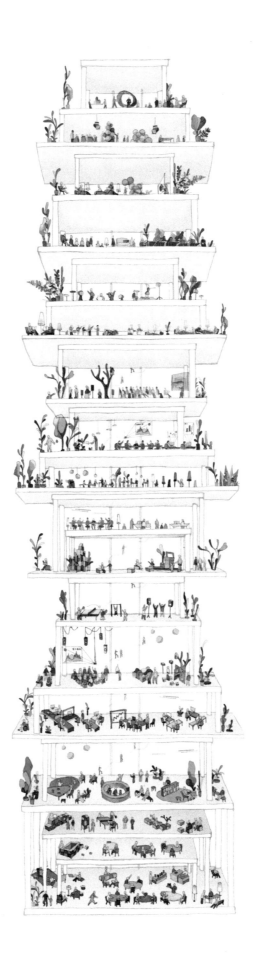

(Not) Another Tower   Tatiana Bilbao Estudio
— Mexico City, Mexico

Ever since the Chicago Home Insurance building was unveiled in 1885 creating a new typology—the skyscraper—human imagination has been fascinated by the promise inherent in these structures. Skyscrapers were both the product of necessity—housing a growing metropolitan population—and desire, as architects sought to explore the latent possibilities delivered by technological advances.

Today, with an increasing majority of people worldwide living in cities, the future is urban. As land becomes increasingly scarce, communities will economize space by going vertical. Advancements in construction and technology continue to expand the limit of how high we can build. In the relentless craze to reach towering heights—driven by exploding real estate prices, resulting from decreasing land availability and bragging rights over who can make the tallest building—we have overlooked one question: should we? As buildings tower upwards, the social fabric of a community is stretched ever

thinner, effectively enclosing people within vertical suburbs. Thus, the question for developers, builders, and architects should not be "Can we build higher?" but rather, "How can space be manipulated, worked, and connected to create truly vertical communities?"

Tatiana Bilbao Estudio's proposal attempts to reconcile vertical urbanization within a tower typology that can host a city's civic character. Since cities are not the products of a singular vision, but patchworks of spatial historical layers, the project attempts to emulate this process by subdividing the tower into 192 plots and collaborating with fifteen studios—each responsible for designing their own plot while maintaining a connection to neighboring sections. Each collaborator puts forth a vision for the design of the tower, the construction of the city, helping create not merely a vertical sculptural mass but realize a three-dimensional matrix of possibilities.

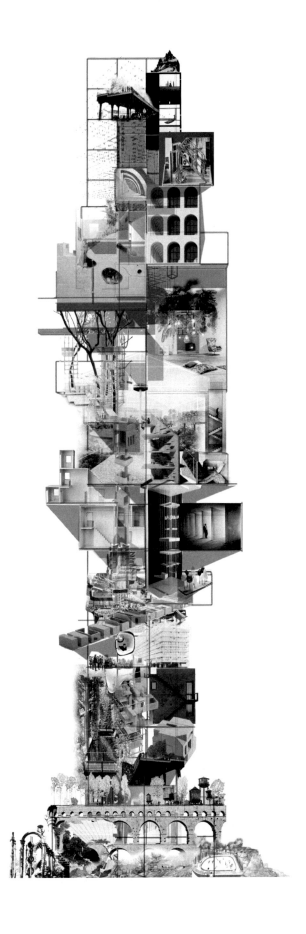

Horizontal City
Collective Projects 2017

For the second collective project of the 2017 Chicago Architecture Biennial, *Horizontal City*, 24 architects were invited to reconsider the status of the architectural interior. The exercise foregrounds the rich history of representation and its role in the "emergence"[1] of the interior as a model of sociability, from the domestic to the communal scale. The architects referenced a photograph of a canonical interior, from any time period, and considered the ways that their selection might extrapolate out from the cropped photographic frame into a spatial and lifestyle construction across a larger, horizontal site.

The 24 models are laid out on a field of plinths. The size and location of the model and its plinth relate to the footprint of the 1947 Mies van der Rohe plan for the IIT Campus: a very familiar figure and ground that operates like a collective afterimage in the GAR Hall gallery.

1   Charles Rice, *The Emergence of the Interior: Architecture, Modernity, Domesticity* (London: Routledge, 2008).

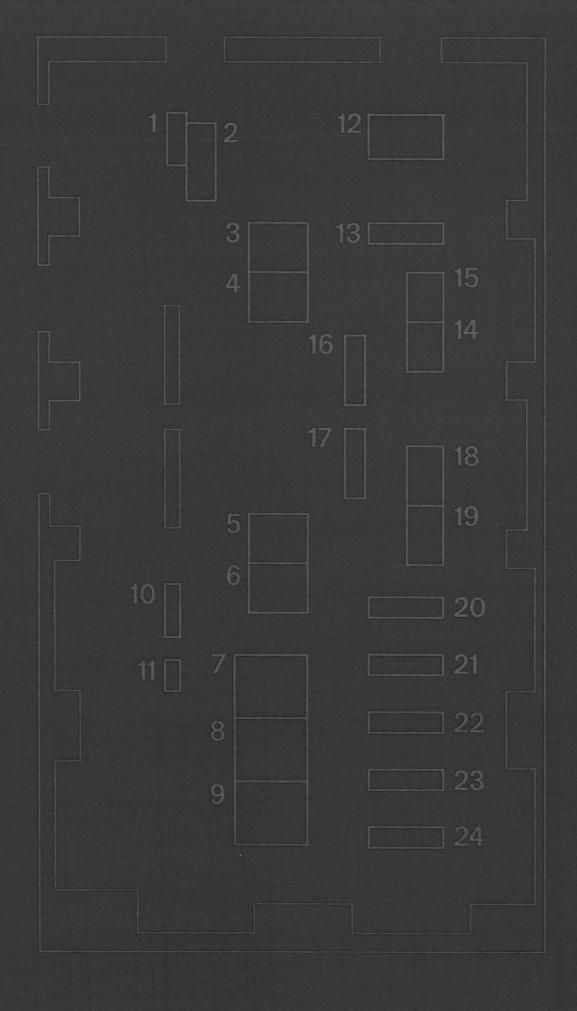

Horizontal City

Infinitely Intimate   Karamuk * Kuo Architects
— Cambridge, USA/Zurich, Switzerland

Karamuk * Kuo Architects, Model view, 2017

Adolf Loos's American Bar in Vienna seems to us apt for a revisit on the occasion of the biennial, particularly within the current social and political context. Perhaps the smallest big space in the modern architectural canon, it was designed after his visit to Chicago where he was profoundly moved by the works of Louis Sullivan. The bar's role as the watering hole of the intellectual and cultural milieu of Vienna, with the likes of Egon Schiele, Sigmund Freud, and Arnold Schoenberg, cemented its standing as a cultural icon and as a haven of free exchange, debate, and social conviviality. At a time of political upheaval in Europe, the American Bar became the symbol of a safe place, the star spangled banner a shining beacon of modernity. Since then, replicas of it have spawned in Dublin and Manhattan and who knows where else—exports of the initial export—extending its global significance not only as a product of cross-border exchanges, but also as a space of culture and openness that

seems as universal as it is specific. It is a space not only disseminated through its photographic representation in the media but through life-size reproductions, each time quietly holding a mirror to its context. Defined by its dualisms, the American Bar is intimate yet expansive, simple yet opulent, introverted yet interconnected: a hidden world nested into a foreign context. In particular, we're interested in its simple use of the (illusory) grid and its paradoxical role in underscoring the intimacy of the space through the lens of its infinite extension. We'd like to imagine an intensified version of this experience that plays up the two ends of the spectrum, following Loos's lead in taking the grid beyond an ordering device towards a space of specificity and contemplation. What if Loos was able to reflect the infinite space of the interconnected world beyond, showing both the fragility of the bar as well as its anchoring to a place?

Adolf Loos, American Bar, Karntner Passage, Vienna, Austria, 1908

A Room Enclosed by Hills and Mountains
UrbanLab — Chicago, USA

To escape the "hegemonic grip"[1] of classical—and conventional—architecture in the city (individual boxes further subdivided into small rooms), Superstudio transformed the rules underlying site-specific design. Rather than design buildings that provide functional necessities to meet societal expectations, which in turn perpetuate unjust social inequities, Superstudio's architecture shaped a "single continuous environment, the world rendered uniform by technology, culture, and all the other inevitable forms of imperialism."[2] At once a surface and envelope, Superstudio's 'grid' promotes a truly democratic human existence: because every point on the grid is more-or-less equivalent, no one 'room'—however mega-scaled—is more important than the next. However, in retrospect, a few of Superstudio's grids do produce structure, hierarchy, and site-specific—i.e. divisible—space. In the photo-collage "Fundamental Acts, Life" from Superstudio's Supersurface—The Encampment project of 1971, mountains frame the grid to produce a valley-scaled 'interior' room. Our project for *Horizontal City* re-interprets and re-examines the meaning underlying this canonical interior. We deploy Superstudio's technique of extension and multiplication—of grids across the landscape—to create "a space infinitely reflected."[3] Our project is a series of small cubic spaces made of mirrors on four (or more) sides. Looking into and through these cubes, one sees spaces infinitely reflected. For Superstudio, these types of spaces symbolize benign environments: looking up one sees sky, looking down one sees a continuous gridded infrastructure. Emerging from the infrastructure plane, one sees a series of life-supporting atmospheres like air, heat, and water. This endless environment is divested of all but a few essential elements in order to re-examine, as Superstudio did, what is the essence of architecture and the environment.

1   Lang, Peter, and William Menking. *Superstudio: Life Without Objects* (Milano: Skira Editore S.p.A., 2003), 14.
2   Ibid., 69
3   Emilio Ambasz. *Italy: The New Domestic Landscape* [Press release]. Museum of Modern Art, New York, NY. September 11, 1972. 1.

Superstudio (A. Natalini, C. Toraldo di Francia, R. Magris, G. P. Frassinelli, A. Magris, A. Poli [1970–72]), *Life, Education, Ceremony, Love, The Encampment, The Fundamental Acts*, 1971–72

UrbanLab, Interior render view, 2017

The Grand Interior   MAIO — Barcelona, Spain

MAIO, Model study detail, 2017

In his introduction to *The Architecture of the Well-Tempered Environment*, Reyner Banham highlights the extent to which architectural history had excluded almost entirely some crucial aspects (such as mechanical services) from historiographical discussion, at least to the date the book was written. But beyond structures and mechanical services, a third layer could be added to this form of historiographical oblivion: its interiors. It's not difficult to realize the extent to which the canonical books of architecture of the twentieth century have not dealt in depth with interiors and their objects, regardless of the importance given to them by architects and designers in the definition of their habitats. It's a fact that preservation's scope has often included just architecture as a built form, neglecting the world of objects that defines the inner space of the built environment. Thus, objects and interior spaces remain the most fragile part of architecture: excluded from it while gaining at the same time their own autonomy. New technologies have radically transformed the domestic sphere: blurring or subverting the traditional limits between public and private, between production and consumption, highlighting its renewed importance. This interconnection of infinite interiors makes it possible to think of the world as a "grand interior," which Sloterdijk defines as an endless domestic landscape defined by objects and technology. Different attempts such as the *Whole Earth Catalogue*, Archizoom's *No-stop City*, Quickborner's Bürolandschaft, or Ambasz's 1972 *Italy: The New Domestic Landscape* exhibition at the Museum of Modern Art, New York, can be seen from the present as pioneer preludes to actual conditions, but also as an intent to stress the importance of objects and technologies as anchors amidst this endless continuity.

In 1927, Duchamp built in his Parisian apartment at Rue Larrey 11 a device with the aspect of a door provided with two frames, so that the door was paradoxically open and closed at the same time. Ironically, Duchamp was stressing both the continuity and discontinuity of space by means of design. Taking Duchamp's door as a trigger, *The Grand Interior* aims to show the new condition of this endless domestic sphere represented by interconnected, canonical, and popular domestic spaces, by means of proposing an interior made of interiors where massiveness of architecture has been removed and rebalanced toward objects, furniture, appliances, and technology as a primary—and often neglected—layer of architecture.

Marcel Duchamp, 11 Rue Larrey Paris, France, 1927

259

Josephine, Strawberry, and Wilson
First Office — Los Angeles, USA

We came across a photograph of a modern interior, its walls covered in a mural of a mountain range. The Swiss house, also known as La Vedette, turned out to be the final home of the nineteenth century French architect Eugène-Emmanuel Viollet-le-Duc during his work on the restoration of the Lausanne Cathedral. The highest mountain peak frames one of the doors, its center aligned to the opening. Another lower peak rises barely over the public entry; its profile just misses the left corner of the trim surrounding the jam. A third peak hovers above the fireplace. But unlike the others, it reveals a tree-scattered scree, which seems to rest on top of the mantle, as if producing a clearing for the fire to be set into the perspective of the landscape image. The rocks increase in size and populate the foreground as the painting approaches the floor. They are depicted in increasing resolution until they become deeply textured, nearly real, and finally get cut off by the chair rail. But this is not the end of the image, just the limit of the paint. Beneath the chair rail, the room is encircled in a stone base. This is real stone, composed of uneven slabs that seem to have broken out of the flattened image and entered the room as a thin layer of cladding. And while the chair rail implies a border, it is in fact an architectural transition: a bond between representation and material reality. Looking up above the mural, we find another such transition. While the chair rail, door trim, and baseboard are all treated in a dark finish, the crown molding is painted in a color that merges with the tone of the sky in the panoramic image. The edge of the room seems to break open and the ceiling joists appear to hover, as they too are painted in matching tones.

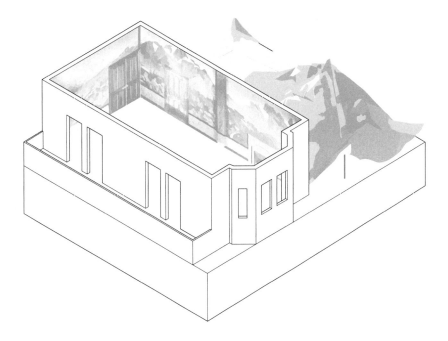

A. Room interior with panorama.   B. Mountain.

Sonsbeek Readymade — Basel, Switzerland   Sauter von Moos

The canonical interior we chose as the basis for our intervention stems from the Sonsbeek Sculpture Pavilion in Arnhem. Built by Aldo van Eyck in 1966 (rebuilt in the garden of the Kröller-Müller Museum, Otterlo, in 2006), it stands at the climax of the Dutch architect's tendency to interiorize the exterior. The work consists of a sequence of labyrinthine interstitial spaces resulting from the layered assemblage of six parallel, partly fragmented walls with changing circular recesses. Situated on a grander circular concrete plinth, the simple shelter is covered by a light, semi-translucent roof. Ambiguously, the space is both open and closed at the same time, and, as a ruin-in-reverse, reminds one with its prehistoric aura of places such as Stonehenge. The building's bare construction in concrete bricks underlines that the worth of architecture is not to be found in the materials used, but rather in the expression of their ordered tectonics to delineate and harbor a series of finely calibrated spaces. Creating a complex matrix of large and small rooms with close and wide views, a myriad of situations reveal themselves for the intimate encounter with the sculptures that are placed on individually designed plinths. On these occasions man, art, and the world directly meet. In our scaled reinterpretation of this built manifesto of the in-between-space, we intend to utilize white Styrofoam with incised brick patterns as basic building material for the architectural structure. Cheap and easy to build, it should add enhanced lightness to van Eyck's Pavilion without diminishing its spatial richness through the interplay of light, form, and openings.

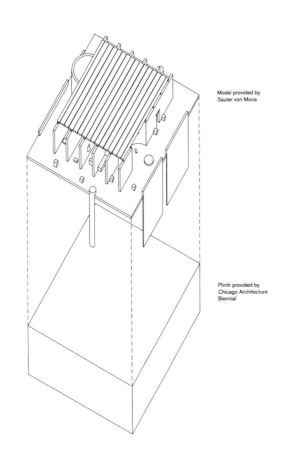

Model provided by
Sauter von Moos

Plinth provided by
Chicago Architecture
Biennial

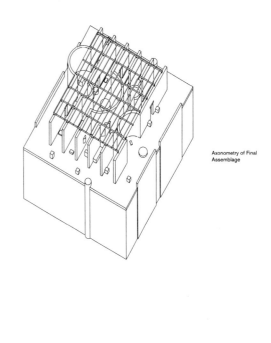

Axonometry of Final
Assemblage

Sauter von Moos, *Sonsbeek Readymade*, diagram, 2017

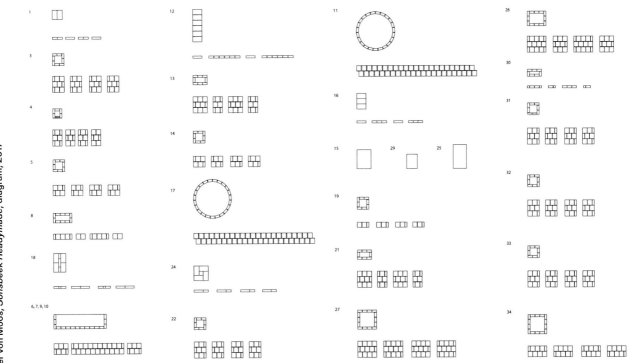

Nine Symbolic Spaces   fala atelier
— Porto, Portugal

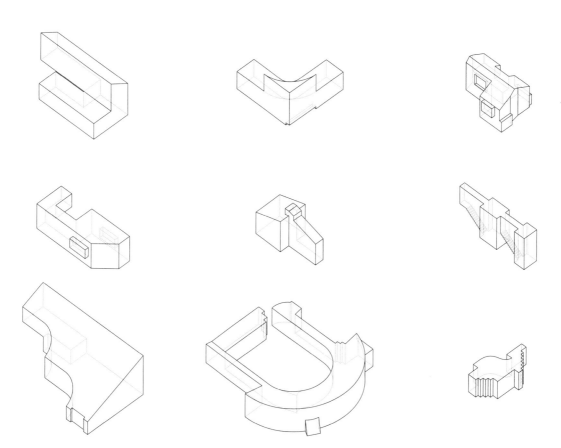

fala atelier, *Nine Symbolic Spaces*, axonometric views, 2017

This proposal is based on the work of four Japanese architects, Kazuo Shinohara, Itsuko Hasegawa, Toyo Ito, and Kazunari Sakamoto, during the period of 1969 to 1977. It is comprised of nine projects that make sense as a collection of old and remote buildings existing here and now: nine photographs capturing a fragment of the space, nine photographs with precise and very well defined compositions, simple and carefully calculated gestures. Nine, not one, we couldn't limit ourselves with just one image, because we love them too much to choose and we value the energy of the moment even more than the authorship of a single architect. We think of photography as the true zenith of architecture production. It idealizes the project and fixes it in time. When the project is built and photographed, it's considered to be finished. Photography is a proof of existence, but also an act of portraiture, ultimately aiming to disconnect you from reality, to mislead you, but

in a very intellectual way. The selected photographs have undeniable similarities. The nine spaces are intentionally abstract: they show whiteness, even a certain dryness, a feeling of emptiness. Imposing an absolute order, they are trying to be perfect in creating these fictitious interiors: a synthesis of the monumental and the casual. Is there anything else architecture could aspire to?

These images go backwards almost, back to the project via photography to rediscover the spatial entities with their complexities and discontinuities: nine houses that could almost be one house; nine rooms or nine living spaces that could be parts of one building; nine houses that share traits, perhaps even a language; and four architects and nine houses that somehow made sense together, as if parts of a single, untold project. It is a coherent selection of spatial ideas: a very alive study on an almost forgotten golden age.

Toyo Ito, House in Kamiwada, Okazaki, Japan, 1976

Pantheon   DRDH Architects — London, UK

Thomas Struth, *Pantheon, Rome*, 1990

Photography has had a profound effect on the understanding of architecture and its spaces, appearing able to define both the image and the idea of a building or interior in ways that can seem more powerful and memorable than actual, individual experience. The photographer takes on an almost authorial role: through the framing of a precise spatial composition, in the rendering of a particular quality of light, or the capturing of a moment of inhabitation. Contemporary photographic practice goes further, critiquing the understanding of photography as objective witness and reconceiving it as an agent, enhanced with digital tools that enable it to move beyond representation, through processes of manipulation, erasure, and image reconstruction.

As a practice we have long been fascinated by the work of the generation of German photographers known as the Düsseldorf School and taught by Bernd and Hilla Becher. The sustained, laconic observations of city streets, the unconscious places discovered in the work of Thomas Struth have had a particular influence on our own understanding of the role and experience of architecture in the city, which is reflected in the ways that the buildings we make respond to their urban situations and are attuned to their cultural circumstances. The absence of people in these photographs offers them an inherent latency. In counterpoint, his photographs of public interiors seem to dwell upon their representational character as part of an inhabited scene, which, on occasion, he makes evident through their deliberate staging. Struth's photograph of the Pantheon frames a section of its platonic interior volume, the curvature of the lens flattening its geometries. Within the model, his reading of this archetypal space will be reconstructed as a stage set: a singular image seen from the same viewpoint as the photographer's lens and with reference to our own work on historic and contemporary theatre spaces.

Charlap Hyman & Herrero — New York, USA

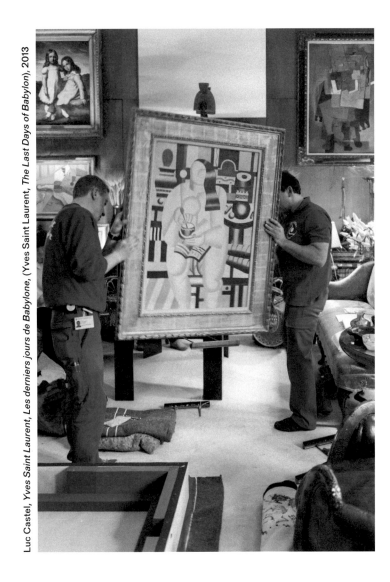

Luc Castel, *Yves Saint Laurent, Les derniers jours de Babylone*, (Yves Saint Laurent, *The Last Days of Babylon*), 2013

Our model depicts the salon of Yves Saint Laurent's and Pierre Bergé's Rue de Babylone apartment in flux. Inspired by Luc Castel's photograph of two art handlers lifting Fernand Léger's *La Tasse de thé*, we have reconstructed the room, not as it was shown to guests nor as it was pictured in numerous publications, but rather in the process of being disassembled shortly after Saint Laurent's passing. The room is no longer the Proustian ensemble of art and design that the couple amassed over time into this pharaoh's tomb of sorts, and not yet the individual works for auction in what Christie's would call the "sale of the century." Like the photograph, our model portrays a liminal space of objects as they pass from the deceased to the living, from kin to the rest of the world.

Though Saint Laurent and Bergé would leave the architecture of the art deco apartment much as they found it in 1970 with interior designer Jacques Grange, in it the couple developed a formidable collection of art and design by old masters and modernists alike. Eileen Gray's *Dragon Chair*, Goya's portrait of an exquisitely dressed young noble, and the wooden Brancusi sculpture that once belonged to Leger, to name a few, represent the accumulation of various stylistic, historical, and literary explorations that Saint Laurent and Bergé made together over time. Not a single piece of the Rue de Babylone collection was sold until St. Laurent's death; Bergé felt it should be auctioned in its entirety, refusing to hold onto what he saw as elements of an indivisible whole. At once, the apartment, and particularly its salon as displayed in our model, embody decades of collecting, centuries of art and design, a continuing inspiration for aesthetes, and, yet, a mere moment in the life of a room and its contents.

A Bar at the Folies-Bergère
June14 Meyer-Grohbrügge & Chermayeff
— New York, USA/Berlin, Germany

Édouard Manet, A Bar at the Folies-Bergère, 1882

She stands indifferent in a crowded room. She works as a waitress at the bar of the most famous palace of pleasure in Europe, the Folies-Bergère, whose name refers to the latin term *folia*, used during the eighteenth century to denote a country house hidden by leaves where it was possible to dedicate freely to diverse occupations. Only the large mirror behind her tells us where we are, but at the same time, the only solid realities are the marble bar top and the objects placed on it—crème de menthe, champagne, beer, a bowl of oranges, and a vase with two flowers. The perspective and optic rules are off, creating an inconsistency to the relationship between the reflections in the mirror and possible realities. The reflected interior is composed by different parts of the building that are, in reality, not together. Édouard Manet, unlike his contemporaries, was not interested in classical antiquity but sought to objectively describe the trivial reality of his time. We intend to look to the past to inform the present as we look ourselves in the mirror, building a one-to-one model of the real elements of the painting, the bar surface, and the objects. The model creates the scene using Manet's mirror strategy, reducing the marble materiality to a surface without thickness or weight. It sits oblique on the plinth recreating the painting's perspective. The interior of the GAR Hall becomes the reinterpretation of the interior of the painting, and the audience of the 2017 Chicago Architecture Biennial repopulates it and its pleasures.

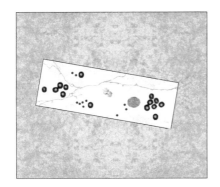

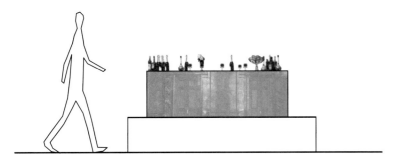

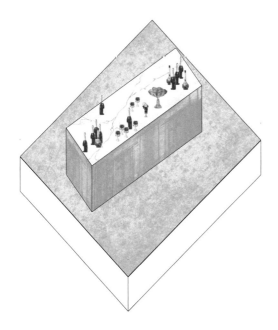

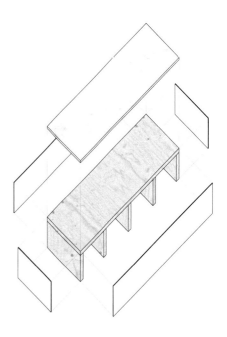

Another Raumplan BUREAU SPECTACULAR
— Los Angeles, USA

Adolf Loos, Villa Müller, Prague, Former Czechoslovakia, 1930

Bureau Spectacular speculates on the relationship between photography and architectural desires with a model based on the ubiquitous photography of the Adolf Loos's Villa Müller interior. As Beatriz Colomina argued in her book *Sexuality and Space* (1992) the villa organized spaces based on the construct of viewer and viewed. A photograph of the interior documents the power of architecture to be a viewing mechanism and producer of subjectivity.

One could argue that Villa Müller was built to facilitate voyeurism and construct a spatial relationship between the viewers who hold the power over the actions of the subject. These ideas materialize in a viewing machine; the reexamination of Villa Müller's constructed and framed views might shed new light on the relationships between interiority and exteriority to produce an ungendered interpretation of Loos.

Morning Cleaning, Mies van der Rohe Foundation, Barcelona (1999), View from Above (2017)
Norman Kelley — Chicago/New York USA

Norman Kelley proposes to reference Jeff Wall's monumental photograph *Morning Cleaning, Mies van der Rohe Foundation, Barcelona* (1999). In the spring of 1999, the Vancouver-based photographer Jeff Wall spent two weeks staging and digitally arresting a man (Alejandro) cleaning glass inside of the German pavilion designed by Mies van der Rohe and Lilly Reich for the Exposición Internacional of Barcelona in 1929. The cool image, along with its coolly observed architecture, is at odds with itself. Foremost, Alejandro is cleaning the glass of a replica of the original pavilion (built in 1986)—a double effort to "repair" history per art historian Michael Fried. Also, Wall's signature near-documentary tableau illuminates how commonplace themes might appear in a building that is anything but common. Alejandro's actions are inadvertently severed from the pavilion's modern plan, its dissonant structure, and the now faded analogies to a new German Republic that would ultimately fall to National

Socialism. To oversimplify: the architecture is heavy yet inauthentic, while the image is seemingly light but disarming. Together, the two mediums—architecture and photography—illustrate the complexity that arises when trying to establish what constitutes the identity of an aesthetic work and its contemplation. We are presented with a building reconstructed in 1986 and a photograph imagined in 1999. Each iteration relocates the identity of the original and moves it elsewhere. To reveal that which unifies, or further separates, Wall's absorptive image from the modern pavilion itself, our proposal will reconsider several ways of looking disinterestedly. Wall initiates this way of looking, in which the subject is unaware of being observed, through his stagecraft, while the pavilion does so in terms of its relationship to modernism. By reconstructing the pavilion in Wall's image, the architecture will continue to resist a single theme, a single author, a single origin story, towards the accumulation of new meanings.

Glass House   REAL Foundation — London, UK

When Freddy Mercury burst into the squalid sitting room of a British terrace—dressed as a housewife and singing "I Want to Break Free", he was protesting the intrinsic oppression embedded in domestic interiors. The music video depicts a working class woman struggling to escape labor relations and gender roles prescribed by her home and its objects. The Latin word *domus* is often translated as "home," but means "dominion" or "place of domination." Here, the patriarch has total control over the life and death of his dependents. He trains them to obey his will through actions and the design of the interior in a process called domestication. A free interior produces a free family and society. That was certainly what many modernists believed; though, by conflating open plans with indeterminacy they failed to understand the impossibility of separating functionality from economic rationalism. *Glass House* is a proposal for a collectively owned housing block in London. It is an experiment in layered interiority. The external frame is a simple steel grid of louvered windows, its volume produced by real estate value engineering. This rational, abstract, inhuman aesthetic continues the history of the British terrace house as a mechanism for social formation. In the high-rise typology each floor is a contained household, with many possibilities for gradients of privacy and temporal use. The inner façade wanders as it articulates spaces disconnected from possible use. At the scale of the apartment, glass bathrooms replace frigid spaces of sanitation. Their green sculptural form stems from the movement of the body, while also directing and dividing space. In negotiating the relationship between the city, the collective, and the individual, *Glass House* asks, "What is the role of the individual in the home? And what is the role of the household in the state? How is sovereignty different from freedom, and where are the two located in communal inhabitation?"

272

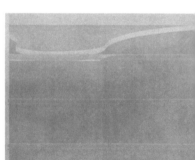

Formlessfinder Dept. of the Interior:
The Domestic Landscape of Casa das Canoas
formlessfinder — New York, USA

One would be hard pressed to find a more arche-typal example of modernism than the Casa das Canoas that Oscar Niemeyer designed for himself outside of Rio de Janeiro in 1953. The building's dramatically cantilevered roof slab, its thin steel columns, and above all, its elegantly undulating glass walls all speak the language of modern archi-tecture with the fluency that established Niemeyer as one the masters of the idiom. The house, like the many iconic modernist residences realized in the same decade, also played an important role in the normalization—indeed, the domestication—of modern architecture. If the prewar years saw modernism emerge as a radically avant-garde style, in the postwar era it became mainstream. Architectural photography played a key role in this process, as iconic images of modernist houses were widely disseminated in the popular press and shaped the public understanding of the style. The images produced by Dmitri Kessell in his photo shoot of the Casa das Canoas for *Life* magazine in 1959 exemplify photography's role in this process. Niemeyer and his family are shown elegantly ensconced in their home, their casual poses helping to familiarize the new features of the architecture behind them: for example, the vast expanses of glass that seem almost to bring the lush jungle vegetation of the site into the house. The most radical dimension of the house normalized by these images is the huge granite boulder that protrudes into the living room. In one of the photo-graphs, Niemeyer lounges on it as if it was just another piece of built-in furniture; yet, this boulder is actually a profound moment of exception. While the blurring of interior and exterior space in modernist domestic architecture has been much discussed, nature was typically brought into the domestic interior in the form of a backdrop, safely on the other side of the transparent glass walls that became a signature feature of the modernist house. This is the relationship between architecture and environment captured in most iconic photos of such buildings, perhaps most memorably in Julius Schulman's famous photos of the Case Study Houses and the Kauffman house. The boulder, in contrast, represents a physical penetration of the environment into the house interior.

formlessfinder, *Formlessfinder Dept. of the Interior: The Domestic Landscape of Casa das Canoas*, plan, 2017

Oscar Niemeyer and family photographed at their home, Casa das Canoas in 1959 for *LIFE Magazine*

Proposal for Collective Living II
(Homage to Sir John Soane)
Andrew Kovacs — Los Angeles, USA

We propose to rethink the iconic section and the subsequent interior of Sir John Soane's London home and museum as a proposal for collective living for the twenty-first century. We view the material that creates Soane's universe and assemblage as the impetus to make architecture from architecture. If architecture organizes the world around us, making architecture from architecture is about reorganizing what exists in the world for new architectural purposes. We propose a new contemporary collection of architectural matter to make architecture from architecture—each meticulously documented, flattened, and valued equally as parts. Our collection consists of wholes and parts, totalities and fragments, as well as unities and bits. As an assemblage, this new collection of architectural matter conceptually turns Soane's house inside out and fully covers and encases the provided plinth in the room of plinths. As such, this new sum is the result of the collection, contiguity, and composition of pieces, parts, and fragments that form a horizontal composite speculating on a new possibility for human habitation. Our proposal for collective living for the twenty-first century rethinks Soane's interior as exterior. This project recontextualizes Soane's home as a city. It also repositions Soane's museum as not strictly devoted to an individual but rather to a new collective. Finally, it reimagines Soane's collection of objects that are meant to be viewed as objects that are meant to be inhabited.

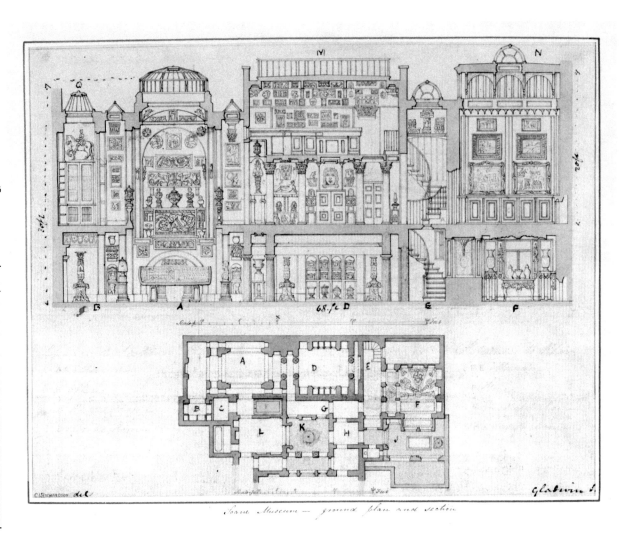

Soane Museum — ground plan and section

Asam Basilica in Altenmarkt, Osterhofen, Germany, c. 1262 and renovation c. 1725

There is nothing remarkable about the entrance to the Basilica of Saint Margaret at Osterhofen Abbey. It is an everyday passage through a series of nouns. On a two-lane street with no sidewalk, up a short flight of stairs, and through a gate in the perimeter wall, across the lawn of a small cemetery, behind an oak door, there is … what exactly? The grossest imaginable dilation of the building envelope. Whereas, from the outside, the church has one of those run-of-the-mill barn-ish roofs that all German churches seem to have, on the inside there is something different and much, much larger.

On the surface of the shallow handkerchief vault there is painted: a giant hole in the ceiling, nearly one-third of the entire nave, above which— stacked along the rim of a gold frame—is the busy courtyard of some municipal building. A bit further into the nave, above the crossing, are rays of light bearing an angel who is either flying up into or falling down out of a second, slightly smaller hole

in the ceiling through which another scene is visible from below: this time, a gathering underneath a monumental dome.

Stacked above the interior of Osterhofen are entire worlds of interiors. We propose to model them.

Our model is a section cut down the middle of the Osterhofen nave. It does not show the entire nave, just that part above decorative banding that separates the occupiable space of the church from the zone of decoration and painting on the ceiling. In other words, it is a model of the zone that separates baroque heaven and earth—or, in this case, rococo heaven and earth. As the model transitions from one zone to another, the material and architectural palette shifts as well: from the familiar elements of architecture, to an expanded repertoire that incorporates modeled drapery and clouds as structural elements entangled with the conventional stuff of buildings.

Reframing Can Lis   Diego Arraigada Arquitectos
— Rosario, Argentina

The main living area of Can Lis is a significantly renowned architectural interior designed by the late Danish architect Jørn Utzon, but it was also his own home in Mallorca in the 1970s. Spatially, the room has formally interesting characteristics: in particular the relationship of the interior with the exterior landscape. This relationship is mediated by windows as sculptural viewing devices that focus on perspectival framing, detached from any structural elements. The views provided are not the sweeping panorama of an all-glazed facade, but rather several fragmented viewing experiences.

The purity of the space and the importance of its contemplating function is enhanced by using a single material on every surface and object in the room. And, at the same time, the use of stone is a statement about local construction techniques and its rusticity that establishes an ambiguous relationship between interior and exterior. Finally, the role of furniture becomes vital for the space and the way of experiencing it; by means of a built-in semi-circular sofa and coffee table, the furniture and overall interior architecture is rendered as one indivisible thing.

Jørn Utzon, Can Lis, Mallorca, Spain, 1972

The Great Hypostyle at Karnak
Angela Deuber Architect — Chur, Switzerland

Angela Deuber Architect, *The Great Hypostyle at Karnak*, study, 2017

Depicting the implied space between four columns of the Great Hypostyle at Karnak, Angela Deuber casts and inverts negative space. In the picture the columns are strongly present. However, the Egyptians did not imagine the interior as enclosed:

"Aversion to interior space–Great Hypostyle, Karnak: Columns of the side aisles of the great hypostyle, whose 134 colossal papyrus columns fill the void of the hall so that no interior space can develop. This was strengthened by offsetting the column centers in alternate row."[1]

And they didn't imagine a roof, which means the columns directly support the sky:

"The great hypostyle halls with their forests of papyrus–columns, blue-painted ceilings, and dim lightning were not conceived as enclosed interior spaces. This is everywhere apparent from their tectonic treatment... the Egyptians, like the Babylonians, considered the temple ceiling as a heavenly vault."[2]

1   Siegfried Giedion, *The Eternal Present: A Contribution on Consistency and Change*, vol. 1 (New York: Pantheon Books, 1962–64), 508.
2   Ibid., 509.

The Great Hypostyle Hall at Karnak, Egypt, c. 1290–1224 BC

Lindenstraße 34–35   Thomas Baecker
Bettina Kraus — Berlin, Germany

We view the Galeriehaus at Lindenstraße 34–35 in Berlin-Kreuzberg as an object of spatial hypothesis. The building sits at the overlap of different historical conditions; regarding both its own insides as well as the surrounding inner city as interior contexts. Biographically, the buildings were host to various programs and functions due to their convertible spatial qualities inside the structural concrete skeletons. Together with another historical block, the twin house was integrated as a war ruin into a newly built residential development during the IBA rebuilding efforts of 1987.

As a fragment of a now landmarked building ensemble, the former department store and commercial lost its representative facade and steeply pitched roof. Over time and in parallel to the changing hierarchical structure of society, the facade's address changed from vertical to horizontal.

The proposal converts the interiority of the historical roof into a contemporary construction by opening it up from a previous storage space to allow transparent public function. An essential prerequisite in this transformation is the ability to recall internalized images based on past experiences. Our design arises out of the superimposition of a recalled and fictive image.

Adhering to the spirit of critical reconstruction, the restored block edge and courtyard structure take their cue from prewar Berlin's permitted building height, which forms the speculative basis in the proposed project for a type of city plinth typical in Berlin. In the discourse on urban growth and the spatial possibilities of increasing density, dealing with this city plinth forms the starting point for a multitude of projects, of which the proposal for a contemporary interpretation of a historic roofline is one.

Tham & Videgård Arkitekter
— Stockholm, Sweden

Tham & Videgård Arkitekter, House, Lagnö, Sweden, 2012

Long rows of boat houses, standing side by side with gabled roofs, are still a common sight in the Stockholm archipelago. They remind us of a time when this vast aquatic landscape, and its several tens of thousands of islands, was the home and work environment of farmers and fishermen. Construction was in wood throughout, locally sourced on the small forested islands. Timber, being a lightweight material, made it possible for two men to carry each building part from the boats to the site. As the houses were lightly placed directly onto the characteristic polished granite bedrock and on plinths of found stones, they could easily be dismantled and moved to another location. This also meant nature was left untouched if the houses disappeared. The archaic character of these vernacular constructions is the result of making maximum use of scarce local resources in the most

direct and efficient way one could imagine. Still, these primal architectural spaces now represent a typology loaded with sensuous qualities: the solid wood detailing, a filtered light, and an intimate scale in sharp contrast to the bright daylight and open, often rough, waters outside. Over time, some of the boathouses have been interconnected and form an interior sequence of spaces that vary in scale depending on the width and height, as well as the pitched roof angle, of each unit. House Lagnö borrows its fundamental spatial organization from this configuration, but with a completely new and different logic to its construction. Entirely made in exposed in-situ-cast concrete, it appears as hollowed out from the grey bedrock. The main space consists of a number of transverse gable roofs, reminiscent of the row of boathouses connected to each other with a pleated interior section.

I see Paris, I see France — Los Angeles, USA   WELCOMEPROJECTS

Le Corbusier, De Beistegui Apartment in Paris, France, 1929–31

The De Beistegui Apartment in Paris was a rooftop penthouse designed and completed in 1931 by Le Corbusier for local playboy Charles de Beistegui. One of Le Corbusier's lesser known projects, it is often touted as either his flirtation with surrealism or a work in which his client pressured the modernist into the costume of the surrealist. In planning, the penthouse placed a minimalist white box atop a Haussmann-style apartment building on the Champs-Élysées. While in some ways a feat of modernism in the sky, the space itself was designed with several strange characteristics. First, it was not wired for any electrical lighting leaving only candles for illumination. Second, it included a built-in periscope with which to view the city. Third, a series of hedges as well as interior walls were designed to slide and reposition using electrical motors. And fourth, the highest point of the rooftop garden was a small, square walled room with wall

heights that hid what would have been an unobstructed view of the Parisian skyline. The apartment no longer exists. Left behind are only a handful of images. It is this status—a ghost captured in a photograph—that makes this work of architecture simultaneously real and imaginary. The limited photography and the oblique views that are captured of the space leave the De Beistegui Apartment a palimpsest onto which new architectural narratives can be written. The blankness and height of the garden room walls suggest an amnesia to the reality of Paris beyond them. The framing of the view, rather than specific to reality, allows for multiple fictions about what remains unseen. The walls transform the distant monuments of the Arc de Triumph and the Eiffel Tower into small objects. A magic scale shift occurs, and beyond the walls of the garden room the city is transformed into an urbanity of objects.

Enjoy Your Deck :) Besler & Sons LLC — Los Angeles, USA

Craig Heffernan, *How to Build an 8 × 10 Deck for Beginners*, 2013

Inscribed with a uniquely domestic focus, how-to home improvement videos activate the residential backyard as a space of public and private display. It is here that aspiration, leisure, and performance are engaged through simultaneously productive and recreative tasks, such as chores, projects, pastimes, and parties. Requiring little more than basic building materials, some power tools and a weekend, the construction of a backyard deck exemplifies the genre of online how-to videos. Besler and Sons reframe online video sharing platforms as a category of media that circulates architectural imagery, while simultaneously generating an attendant set of language, media, data, and associations. This is the language of comment sections, view count statistics, recommendations for related viewing, popup advertisements for local lumber yards, closed captions, and various options for sharing with friends and across social media. The decks in these videos are surprisingly versatile forms. Their complexity, size, and architectural style are made to fit the site; they often stick to a simple plan. The online instructional video provides an opportunity to rethink the differentiations that are typically perceived between expert and amateur practices in architecture, building and design, and their increasing inadequacy for models of production. Self-made, self-composed, and often self-narrated, the video tutorials that the DIY aspirant records and uploads today on YouTube are short, narrative clips that depict construction and building practices as media imagery—engaging issues of labor, competency, and discourse.

Capsule Dreams The Living — New York, USA

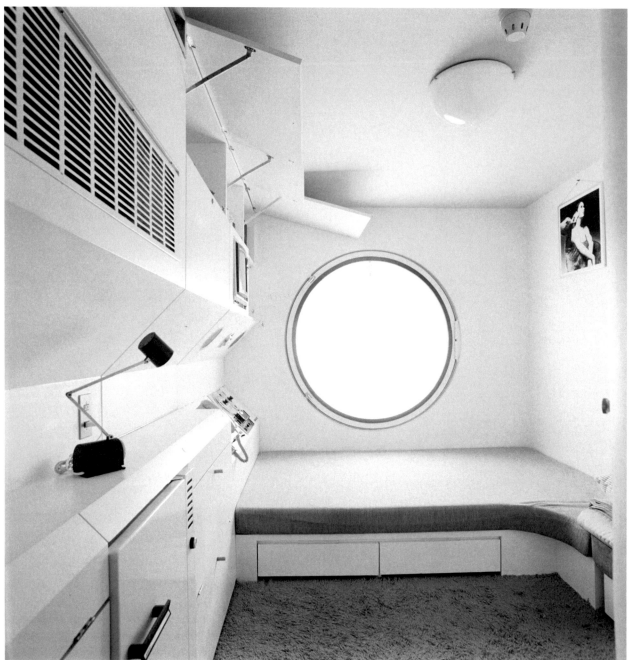

Kisho Kurokawa, Nakagin Capsule Tower, Tokyo, Japan, 1972

As a hallmark of the Metabolism movement, the Nakagin Capsule Tower, designed by Kisho Kurokawa and constructed in 1972, was intended to denote human society and to continually evolve. This reinterpretation starts from a historic photo of the interior of one apartment—which is notably devoid of people or personal touches—and creates a model that reactivates the project through layers of human occupation and passing time. Depicting the interior of two units, the model also allows views into eight alternate units through the circular window. Each of these eight units will offer a portal into a different past, present, or future version of occupation. The Living offer speculation on alternative futures for the Metabolism movement.

From Mixed Use to Different Use
Adamo-Faiden — Buenos Aires, Argentina

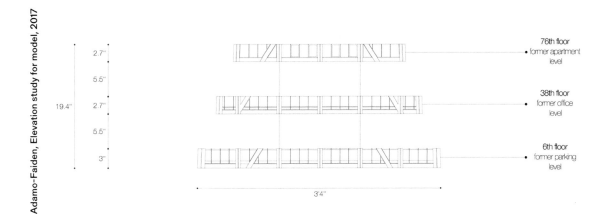

Adamo-Faiden, Elevation study for model, 2017

2.7"

5.5"

19.4"   2.7"

5.5"

3"

3'4"

76th floor
former apartment
level

38th floor
former office
level

6th floor
former parking
level

SOM, John Hancock Center, Chicago, USA, 1965–69

Skidmore, Owings & Merrill's John Hancock Center offers one interior space, one hundred times repeated. This single module displays a progressive alteration in two of its variables: the distance between the core and the façade, and the clearance height between floor and ceiling slabs. Ezra Stoller's photographs portray the tower interior where the same interior location is shown associated with three different programs: car park, offices, and dwellings. Adamo-Faiden noticed the importance of the objects occupying the space, and the way that they revealed the conflict of housing conventional programs in a non-conventional structure.

Adamo-Faiden's model tests the relationship of homogeneous planning with specific usage by reoccupying three levels of the tower and obliterating the functional categories they were designed for.

A Day at the Beach
Lütjens Padmanabhan Architekten
— Zurich, Switzerland

The Lieb Beach House has always been one of our favorite Venturi buildings. "Small in size, but not small in character" it exudes the essence of casual life.[1] Like any of Venturi's buildings, the Lieb Beach House is the result of a wonderful transformation of the normal into the particular. It is small and delicate with a number of sturdy large-scale architectural elements. It is architecture that looks at history as a cultural reference, yet its sensibility is pop. Few photographs of Lieb Beach House have ever been published. The famous set by Stephen Hill depicts the building with its inhabitants, in its immediate context. Only one image has been taken from inside. The Lieb Beach House was moved from New Jersey to Glen Cove in 2009. Recent images that can be found on the Internet have nothing of the magic and seductiveness of the original black and white pictures. Vulgar wide-angle photographs show a house that not only lost its context, but also its charm: like a mysterious nightly lover seen in plain daylight. With our model, we would like to revive the spirit of the original quality of Lieb Beach House. The model features a portion of the upper floor interior, the radio loudspeaker window, and a slice of the context including the car.

1   Pilar Viladas, "Domesticities | Lieb House, Saved," *The New York Times*, February 08, 2012, http://tmagazine.blogs.nytimes.com/2012/02/08/domesticities-lieb-house-saved/?_r=1.

Venturi, Scott Brown, and Associates, Inc., Lieb House, Long Beach Island, New Jersey, 1969

The Urban Unconscious and the Visual Archive: On Architectural Image Culture — Martino Stierli

I.

Recent years have seen a great deal of interest in the meaning, agency, and use of images in contemporary architecture culture. Mainly triggered by the notion that words are increasingly superseded by images in the digital age, a lot of thinking has been devoted to critically assessing this assumption by historicizing it.[1] Architectural thinking and production have been dependent on "images" at least since the Renaissance, but they have done so differently under changing historical circumstances. The theoretical scrutiny of the architectural image has gained momentum since the late 1980s, when questions of representation and the role of the spectator came to dominate art historical discourse, and the "iconic turn" was proclaimed.[2] Architecture has resisted this paradigm shift to some degree and has become increasingly disconnected from dominant discourses in visual culture. Yet the term of the "iconic building" nevertheless continues to be a prevalent—if by now largely exhausted—catchphrase.

As Alina Payne points out in an insightful and fundamental contribution on the relationship of architecture and images—and on the iconicity of buildings in particular—the icon "carries the implication...as sacred, ritualistic, and worshipped object, with all its rich implications of the icon of mystery, 'presence' and 'aura' that absorbs the gaze in its power to attract and hold."[3] "Iconicity," in other words, relies on the material, auratic presence of the singular, physically manifest object vis-à-vis the beholder. The icon is essentially corporeal, three-dimensional, and invested with cultic power.[4] When we reference "iconic buildings," however, this term usually refers to a building's "imageability"—its ability to produce a memorable image.[5] Such images are usually photographic, and, in the digital age, they have become fleeting, immaterial impressions that somehow seem to prevail in the endless and rapidly multiplying ocean of images of our contemporary condition. These images are anything but "present," "corporeal," or three-dimensional. Rather, they are representations located at the diffuse boundary between the

1   Conversely, Mario Carpo has recently argued that in the digital age, two-dimensional images are increasingly superseded by virtual spaces in the representation of architecture. See Mario Carpo, "Space Odyssey: The Rise of 3-D Technology," *Artforum* (March 2017), 230–37.
2   I owe this observation to Alina Payne, "Architecture: Image, Icon or Kunst der Zerstreuung?" in Andreas Beyer, Matteo Burioni, and Johannes Grave, eds., *Das Auge der Architektur: Zur Frage der Bildlichkeit in der Baukunst* (Munich: Fink, 2011), 59.

3   See Payne, "Architecture: Image, Icon or Kunst der Zerstreuung?" 59.
4   For a discussion of the visuality and presence of icons, see Hans Belting, *Likeness and Presence: A History of the Image before the Era of Art*, trans. Edmund Jephcott (Chicago: University of Chicago Press, 1993).
5   I am using the term introduced by Kevin Lynch in his seminal study, *The Image of the City* (Cambridge, MA: MIT Press, 1960).

physical object and the perceiving subject, and they seem to borrow their iconicity precisely from their ability to multiply infinitely while at the same time retaining their memorability. (We will return to the notions of memory and memorability later.)

The weight accorded architecture's photographic image has in many instances come at the price of a building's functionality and aesthetic quality as a three-dimensional, inhabitable object, and this doubtlessly has contributed to the present weariness of "iconic architecture." In *The Art-Architecture Complex*, Hal Foster discusses the commodification, in the society of the spectacle, of architecture *as* image.[6] If the rhetoric of the iconic building has thus come to an intellectual impasse, in what other ways can the relationship of architecture and the image be reconsidered? Art history has a long tradition of thinking of architecture in terms of images. Two main strands of this debate may be discerned.[7] The first is the understanding of the image as a semiotic system, that is, essentially, as an entity charged with specific symbolic meanings. This conception is prevalent in the history and theory of Baroque architecture, and was perhaps most prominently advocated by Hans Sedlmayr. As exhibited in the title of Charles Jencks's seminal *The Language of Post-Modern Architecture* (1977), a semiotic understanding of the visuality of architecture underlies postmodernist thinking as well.[8] The second major way art history has theorized architecture in terms of images is in considering buildings as architectural "frames" of flat(tened) surfaces—in the sense of the tableau. While such architecturally framed images may appear on the facades of buildings themselves, the German art historian Dagobert Frey has argued that the viewer selects a point of view that allows him or her to reduce a spatial, three-dimensional phenomenon into a two-dimensional, picturesque (*malerisch*) entity.[9]

If, however, we consider architecture as the art of making and shaping of *space*, the two cardinal ways of coming to terms with architectural visuality briefly outlined here seem insufficient. Architecture, at least in our modern understanding, is an art of three dimensions, and any attempt of capturing it and reducing it to two dimensions will ultimately not do it justice. However, the antagonistic relationship between architecture as space versus architecture

as image may be a false dichotomy. The conception of architecture as the art of space is relatively new and can be dated to the late nineteenth century, when psychology and theories of perception and empathy became driving forces in art history. In 1893, the German art historian August Schmarsow was among the first to define architecture as the "art of space" and the "creatress of space."[10] Schmarsow's phenomenological approach defined the physical body of the observer as the "meridian" of three-dimensional space and thus related to the corporeality of visual perception and, ultimately, the creation of space. Even for Schmarsow, though, architectural space was ultimately a visual phenomenon produced by physical movement through that space—a sequence of images of a procession through space stored in the mind of the observer. At the same time, visual perception not grounded in corporeal experience was, for him, unthinkable. To some degree, Schmarsow promoted a proto-cinematic approach to the perception of space; and it is perhaps more than coincidental that this kind of theorization took place at the same historical moment that photographic images became mobile. In an important essay published posthumously (in 1989), the Soviet filmmaker Sergei Eisenstein characterized architecture as the forerunner of cinema in that it relies on sequential perception of space in time.[11]

The invocation of bodily perception presents problems for understanding the visuality of architecture. Considering architecture and architectural space as predicated on a bodily experience leads us into the realm of "atmospheres" or even "immersion." Architect Peter Zumthor and philosophers Gernot Böhme and Peter Sloterdijk have all argued along these lines recently.[12] Immersion, in the sense of a physical experience of architectural space, is predicated on the dissolution of distance between the perceiving subject and the perceived object. But this very distance is an essential precondition for the perception of a visual entity as image (as outlined above). It would seem, then, that the physical experience of a space would disturb or even inhibit its perception as an image. This, however, is only true in so far as we adhere to a static conception of the image in the sense of a tableau. Space presupposes movement, as does the cinema. While in the latter the moving image unfolds

6   See Hal Foster, *The Art-Architecture Complex* (London: Verso, 2013). What is often not taken into account adequately in these discussions is the fact that "iconicity" does not necessarily need to be in opposition to program and functional needs.
7   I am borrowing this critical distinction from Andreas Beyer, Matteo Burioni, and Johannes Grave, "Einleitung: Zum Erscheinen von Architektur als Bild," in *Das Auge der Architektur*, 12–15.
8   See Charles Jencks, *The Language of Post-Modern Architecture* (New York: Rizzoli, 1977).
9   See Dagobert Frey, *Kunstwissenschaftliche Grundfragen. Prolegomena zu einer Kunstphilosophie* (Vienna: Rohrer, 1946).
10 See August Schmarsow, "Das Wesen der architektonischen Schöpfung. Antrittsvorlesung gehalten in der Aula der K. Universität Leipzig am, 8. November, 1893," http://www.cloud-cuckoo.net/openarchive/Autoren/Schmarsow/Schmarsow1894.htm.
11 See Sergei Eisenstein, "Montage and Architecture," *Assemblage* 10 (1989), 110–31. In this regard, see also Giuliana Bruno, *Atlas of Emotion: Journeys in Art, Architecture, and Film* (New York: Verso, 2002).
12 See Gernot Böhme, *Architektur und Atmosphäre* (Munich: Fink, 2006); Peter Zumthor, *Atmospheres: Architectural Environments— Surrounding Objects* (Basel: Birkhäuser, 2006); and Peter Sloterdijk, "Architecture as the Art of Immersion," *Interstices* 12 (2006), 105–9.

in a sequence in front of an immobile spectator, in the former, a mobile spectator's movement allows for a chaining of visual impressions into a coherent (or disjunctive) sequence. Modern architects from Le Corbusier to Rem Koolhaas, Bernard Tschumi, and Jean Nouvel have been aware of this elective affinity between the two media, and it is fruitful to further explore the unlikely kinship between the two artistic media anew.[13]

II.

A reflection on the iconic/visual dimension of buildings is one way to address the intersection between architecture and images. Another would be to look into how images have informed architectural discourse beyond the realm of the built. In doing so, we consider not so much the "medium" dimension of architecture (as an intermediary between its user and the outside world) but its "media" quality, that is, how architecture is reproduced and represented by means of images. I would like to address this question with regard to architecture culture of the

1960s and 1970s, which in many ways marked a turning point for how architects dealt with images, as a consequence of the increasing reproducibility and ready availability of photographic images in a consumer-oriented society. Analyzing artistic culture of the 1960s, Benjamin H. D. Buchloh has famously identified, in the work of artists such as Gerhard Richter, Bernd and Hilla Becher, and Marcel Broodthaers, a predilection toward the accumulation of found or intentionally produced photographs in grid formations.[14] (figs. 1, 2) Richter's *Atlas* stands out in particular: Originally conceived from the mid 1960s onward as a collection of personal and press photographs, newspaper clippings, and sketches, the artist later started to arrange these materials on loose sheets of paper. Referencing the historical precedent of Aby Warburg's *Mnemosyne Atlas*, this new typology of the atlas has, according to Buchloh, adopted "photography's innate structural order (its condition as archive) in conjunction with its seemingly infinite multiplicity, capacity for serialization, and aspiration toward comprehensive totality."[15] In all of these aspects, it shares a structural affinity with

13 See Martino Stierli, *Montage and the Metropolis: Studies on the Conception and Representation of Space in Modernity* (New Haven, CT: Yale University Press, 2018) (forthcoming).

14 Benjamin H. D. Buchloh, "Gerhard Richter's Atlas: The Anomic Archive," *October* 88 (Spring 1999), 117–45.

15 Ibid., 118.

Fig. 1, Gerhard Richter, *Atlas, Tafel 5*, 1962–66

Fig. 2, Bernd and Hilla Becher, *Fabrikhallen*, 1967–92

the totalizing bureaucracy of the military-industrial complex of the postwar period. For Buchloh, the quintessential significance of these works (and in particular in the case of Gerhard Richter's *Atlas*) lies in their mnemonic dimension, that is, their implicit critique of the culture of memory loss and collective amnesia in postwar Germany, and, more broadly, Western Europe.

Can we apply Buchloh's observations on "atlases of remembrance against a massive apparatus of repression" (of historical memory) in postwar German Art to architecture culture of the same period? It is noteworthy that the procedure of " systematically organiz[ing] knowledge as didactic models of display or as mnemonic devices,"[16] as described by Buchloh, can be found as well in one of the seminal attempts at organizing architectural knowledge based on a systematic collection of photographic images in the 1960s—architects Robert Venturi, Denise Scott Brown, and Steven Izenour's "Learning from Las Vegas" research project. At the core of this endeavor was a course taught at the Yale University School of Architecture in the fall of 1968.[17] One of the principal objectives

of this "research studio" was to collect, together with a group of students, a large number of photographic images and film footage in order to document the Las Vegas Strip as an archetypal manifestation of a newly emerging form of the contemporary American city. (fig. 3) This visual data was then organized into visual charts, diagrammatic representations, and atlas-like configurations in order to analyze the underlying structural principles of this urban form and the architectural typologies that define it. (fig. 4) In Venturi and Scott Brown's understanding, the photographic archive and its organization according to conceptual categories served to uncover the hidden structures of contemporary urbanism. Despite the formal correspondences, this architectural/urban research project served an entirely different purpose and produced a fundamentally different meaning from the more or less contemporary artistic (primarily European) projects discussed by Buchloh. Nevertheless, in retrospect, "Learning from Las Vegas" took on a comparable mnemonic dimension, in that it charted the emerging suburban form of 1960s Las Vegas precisely at the moment when it was about to vanish and be superseded by a different and ultimately more conventionally dense urban model.

16   Ibid.
17   For a detailed history of the project, see Martino Stierli, *Las Vegas in the Rearview Mirror: The City in Theory, Photography and Film* (Los Angeles: Getty Research Institute, 2013).

Fig. 3, Learning from Las Vegas Research Studio, Preparations for film shoot on Fremont Street, Las Vegas, 1968

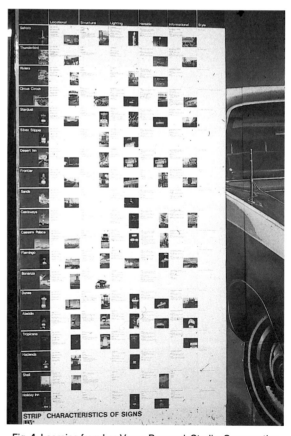

Fig. 4, Learning from Las Vegas Research Studio, Comparative chart of signs along the Las Vegas Strip, 1968

The methodology of systematically charting an urban landscape by means of photography produced a new paradigm of architectural and urban research. Although novel for architecture, the use of photography (and film) as epistemological tools was first established by visual anthropology and the social sciences in 1942, with the publication of Gregory Bateson and Margaret Mead's seminal *Balinese Character: A Photographic Analysis*, which is generally considered the starting point for implementing a methodically sound image-based approach.[18] This research project was decisive for defining the relationship between photography and science insofar as Bateson and Mead not only used photography and film for illustrating their theses, but also applied them as investigative tools in the framework of a systematic study. In many ways, 1960s conceptual photography methodologically echoed the premises first established in these disciplines, initiating a fruitful transfer of methodology

from science to art.[19] During this period, a number of photographers, such as William Eggleston, Ed Ruscha, and the members of the New Topographics group practiced photography as a kind of visual research that focused on the everyday urban environment. (fig. 5) These artists worked toward an aesthetic that de-mystified the American landscape by photographing post-industrial, para-urban, and suburban buildings and spaces. By creating an archive, by establishing encyclopedic series, and through their "documentary style," these photographers implicitly or explicitly mimicked strategies of objectivization and classification developed in the context of empirical social and cultural sciences, above all (visual) anthropology, ethnology, and sociology. The photographic work of one of the protagonists of this genre, the Los Angeles-based Ruscha, served as a direct conceptual and methodological model for Venturi's and Scott Brown's visual approach, and the group of architectural researchers visited the artist in his studio on their field trip, in October of

18   See Gregory Bateson and Margaret Mead, *Balinese Character: A Photographic Analysis* (New York: New York Academy of Sciences, 1942).

19   For these exchanges between the social sciences and 1960s conceptual photography and its impact on *Learning from Las Vegas*, see Martino Stierli, "Photographic Field Research in 1960s' Art and Architecture," in Ákos Moravánszky and Albert Kirchengast, eds., *Experiments: Architecture Between Sciences and the Arts* 2 (Berlin: Jovis, 2011), 54–91.

Fig. 5, Ed Ruscha, Double-page spread from *Thirtyfour Parking Lots in Los Angeles* (Los Angeles: Blair Litho, 1967)

1968.[20] In particular, Ruscha's self-published artist's books on architectural typologies characteristic for the contemporary city—among them *Twentysix Gasoline Stations* (1963), *Thirtyfour Parking Lots in Los Angeles* (1967, printed in 1974), and *Some Los Angeles Apartments* (1965)—as well as his accordion foldout *Every Building in the Sunset Strip* (1966)—were of great interest to these architects, with *Every Building* serving as a direct model for one of their own visual representations of the Las Vegas Strip. Setting out to visually document the contemporary urban sprawl of the American West, Venturi, Scott Brown, Izenour, and their students appropriated epistemological tools first developed by anthropologists and taken up by contemporary photographers, thus introducing a transdisciplinary perspective to architectural research and education. The resulting book, *Learning from Las Vegas* (1972), was heavily critiqued for being socially irrelevant or even cynical.[21] However, as Venturi's and Scott Brown's methodological approach underscores, the project sought to combine formal research with social concern and to demonstrate that these two seemingly disparate fields could be dialectically interrelated.

Documenting the urban landscape by means of photography through the disciplinary lens of architecture amounted to an epistemologically different undertaking than an artistic assessment of that landscape—or an ethnographic charting of inhabited spaces, for that matter. For Venturi and Scott Brown, photographing the contemporary urban landscape, for which they thought Las Vegas was the most emblematic and archetypal, meant establishing a body of visual evidence that would allow them to analyze and represent urban form and its underlying structures. This analytical approach is evidenced in *Learning from Las Vegas* through a large number of analytical charts, maps, and drawings on a wide array of different topics,

20   For an in-depth discussion of the significance of the work of Ed Ruscha for Venturi and Scott Brown, see Stierli, *Las Vegas in the Rearview Mirror*, 132–40; see also Alexandra Schwartz, *Ed Ruscha's Los Angeles* (Cambridge, MA: MIT Press, 2010).

21   See in particular Tomás Maldonado, *Design, Nature, and Revolution: Toward a Critical Ecology* (1970), trans. Mario Domandi (New York: Harper & Row, 1972), and Kenneth Frampton, "America 1960–1970: Notes on Urban Images and Theory," *Casabella* 35, no. 359–60 (1971), 25–37. For Denise Scott Brown's reply, see "Reply to Frampton," *Casabella* 35, no. 359–60 (1971), 41–46; see also Denise Scott Brown, "On Architectural Formalism and Social Concern: A Discourse for Social Planners and Radical Chic Architects," *Oppositions* 5 (1976), 100–12.

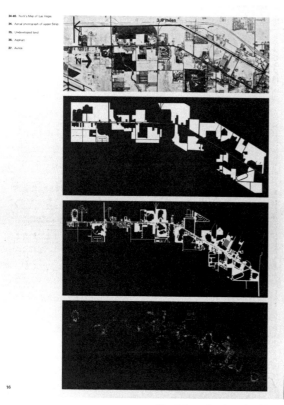
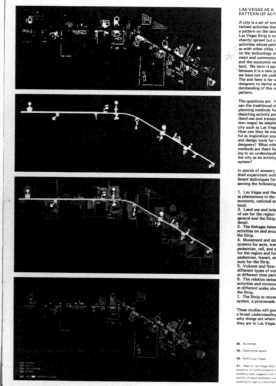

Fig. 6, Learning from Las Vegas Research Studio, Cartographic representations of the Las Vegas Strip, from Robert Venturi, Denise Scott Brown, and Steven Izenour, *Learning from Las Vegas* (Cambridge, MA: MIT Press, 1972), pp. 16–17

ranging from the light intensity along the Strip to the distribution of public vs. private space. (fig. 6) In this sense, the photographic archive accumulated during their research must be seen primarily as the visual repository of an empirical investigation, and as the basis for a critical inquiry into contemporary urban form. Nevertheless, the way in which Venturi and Scott Brown viewed the city cannot be reduced to purely documenting their research. Many of their photographs display an aesthetically motivated gaze that is informed by artistic representations of contemporary American urban form and its specific roadside typologies. They treated photographic images mainly as sources of information and as the base for the production of architectural knowledge, but they also appreciated their ability to invoke a specific aesthetic of an urban landscape that had entered the American collective consciousness by means of the visual arts.

Another seminal contribution to the period's architectural discourse that was based on the establishment of a visual archive was Rem Koolhaas's *Delirious New York* (1978). Although Koolhaas's discourse was less overtly visual than *Learning from Las Vegas*, his treatise was predicated on an archive of found images. When they moved to Ithaca, in the early 1970s, Koolhaas and

his wife Madelon Vriesendorp began to gather what became a vast collection of postcards dedicated to the city of New York. (fig. 7) Even though Koolhaas also used other types of illustrations to build his argument visually, reproductions of picture postcards were fundamental in establishing the aesthetic and the argument of *Delirious New York*. (fig. 8) While Vriesendorp's collecting interest extended to many kinds of Americana, in particular its strange, almost surreal instances, Koolhaas focused primarily on the visualization of a real or imagined Manhattan.[22] Their joint efforts led to a collection of several thousand postcards, which were meticulously filed under a number of typological categories. Both the Americana and the Manhattan postcard groups were stored in suitcases—one metallic, the other tanned leather— emphasizing the intrinsic relationship of the postcard to tourism. In a 1973 letter to the Italian architect Adolfo Natalini, who was a founding member of Superstudio, Koolhaas described the postcard collection as a remedy against the boredom and lack of intellectual challenge in rural upstate New York, calling it "stupid research into

22 See Shumon Basar and Charlie Koolhaas, "Disasters, Babies, Glass Bricks: Postcard Archaeology," in Shuman Basar and Stephan Trüby, eds., *The World of Madelon Vriesendorp: Paintings/Postcards/ Objects/Games* (London: AA Publications, 2008), 74–81.

Fig. 7, Suitcase with Rem Koolhaas and Madelon Vriesndorp's Americana postcard collection

Fig. 8, Reproductions of historical postcards of the Rockefeller Center, from Rem Koolhaas, *Delirious New York: A Retroactive Manifesto for Manhattan* (New York: Monacelli Press, 1978)

postcards, Americana, provincial movie-palaces, diners."[23] Apparently, he had not yet realized the significance this project would have for his book, published five years later.

In an interview twelve years later, Koolhaas acknowledged the impact of the "postcards and other tourist ephemera from New York": "I discovered that one must look beyond institutional paths to find the true meaning of this architecture."[24] In *Delirious New York,* Koolhaas arranged the postcards into series of montages, producing a visual urban history. The "unconscious" history of the city, the book seems to argue, unfolds in the realm of popular imagery, and this imagery is the key to urban history. This understanding is similar to Venturi and Scott Brown's from a few years earlier. The "retroactive" stance taken by Koolhaas, by which his urban theory was produced after the fact based on a large body of built and imaginary evidence, is fundamentally grounded on mass-produced images, for they are both the starting point and the evidence of the argument.

The collecting and assembling of mass-reproduced popular images as a cultural activity was anticipated, among other things, by the British pop scene of the 1950s, in particular the Independent Group, which formed around the photographer Nigel Henderson, artists Eduardo Paolozzi and John McHale, art critic Lawrence Alloway, architectural theoretician Reyner Banham, and architects Alison and Peter Smithson. In architectural discourse, the method of using postcards for a historical account was first proposed by Alvin Boyarsky, in his photo-essay "Chicago à la Carte," published in *Architectural Design* in 1970.[25] (fig. 9) Koolhaas not only studied with Boyarsky at the Architectural Association School of Architecture in London, he also chaired a conference on his Berlin

23 Rem Koolhaas, letter to Adolfo Natalini, August 1973, quoted in Roberto Gargiani, *Rem Koolhaas/OMA: The Construction of Merveilles* (Lausanne: EPFL Press, 2008), 20.
24 Rem Koolhaas, "La deuxième chance de l'architecture modern ... Entretien avec Rem Koolhaas," *L'Architecture d'aujourd'hui* 238, 3. Translated by the author.
25 See Alvin Boyarsky, "Chicago à la Carte: The City as an Energy System," *Architectural Design* 40, no. 12 (1970), 595–622; 631–40. On Boyarsky and the postcard, see Igor Marjanović, "Wish You Were Here: Alvin Boyarsky's Chicago Postcards," in Charles Waldheim and Katerina Rüedi Ray, eds., *Chicago Architecture: Histories, Revisions, Alternatives* (Chicago and London: University of Chicago Press, 2005), 207–25, and Igor Marjanović, "Alvin Boyarsky's Chicago," *AA Files* 60 (2010), 45–52. For Boyarsky's pedagogy in general, see Irene Sunwoo, "Pedagogy's Progress: Alvin Boyarsky's International Institute of Design," *Grey Room* 34 (2009), 28–57. On Koolhaas's use of postcards with a view to the context of postmodern pictorial theory, see Martino Stierli, "The Architect as Ghostwriter: Rem Koolhaas and Image-Based Urbanism," in *Postmodernism: Style and Subversion,* Glenn Adamson and Jane Pavitt, eds. (London: V&A Publishing, 2011), 136–39.

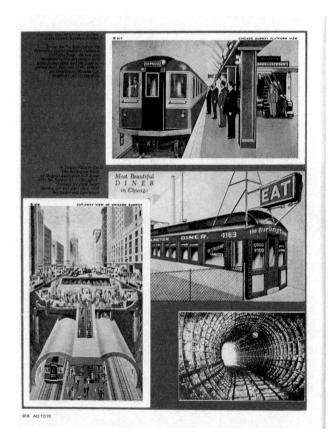

Fig. 9, Alvin Boyarsky, "Chicago à la Carte", from *Architectural Design* (December 1970), pp. 618–19

Wall research in the framework of a summer session on the topic of Manhattan that was organized by Boyarsky's International Institute of Design. "Chicago à la Carte" depended almost entirely on the reproduction of postcards with lengthy captions that held the narrative together. By contrast, *Delirious New York* is structured mainly as a text, with images serving a generally secondary, illustrative purpose. The significant role that the postcards played in the genesis of Koolhaas's argument is therefore largely hidden, while Boyarsky's strategy is ostentatiously displayed.

Collecting postcards was a preferred form of artistic research into modernity's anonymous traditions throughout the twentieth century. The American photographer Walker Evans collected some 9,000 picture postcards throughout his lifetime. He published a number of pictorial essays based on his collection and lectured repeatedly on the subject. Like Koolhaas and Vriesendorp, Evans aimed to compile a visual encyclopedia of the built environment as represented in mass-reproduced photographic images. He ordered his collection according to categories such as "railroad stations," "hotels," "factories," "American architecture," "Flatiron," "city views," "American street scenes," and "skyscrapers." The last group included many of the same postcards that Koolhaas reproduced in *Delirious New York*. Jeff Rosenheim has argued that picture postcards offered Evans "precisely the anonymous, anti-aesthetic, documentary quality that he sought to achieve in his own work."[26] For Koolhaas, conversely, they formed the base from which to reconstruct the history of the modern metropolis as it had come into being almost unconsciously, that is, without the prior existence of an urban theory or manifesto.

For Venturi and Scott Brown, on the one hand, and Koolhaas and Vriesendorp, on the other, archives of images became the foundation for an investigation into the underlying structural logic of the contemporary or, respectively, modern city. While Venturi and Scott Brown's photographic archive of images amounted to an instant archaeology of a very recent but rapidly vanishing contemporary suburban form, Koolhaas and Vriesendorp in turn treated popular image postcards as a visual repository of the collective unconscious of the modern metropolitan condition. Even photographs of commercial streetscapes or mass-reproduced popular imagery are invested with hidden meaning. In postwar consumer culture, architects took on the task of making sense of it.

26   See Jeff L. Rosenheim, *Walker Evans and the Picture Postcard* (Göttingen: Steidl, 2009), 19.

Martino Stierli is The Philip Johnson Chief Curator of Architecture and Design at The Museum of Modern Art.

Why would an institution make such an effort to collect and hold archives of architects, and historians and critics of architecture? [5]

Well, at least for the CCA,[1] the answer is quite simple: research.

But what do you mean, research?

A way to constantly examine,[3] understand, and challenge what architecture is, was, and will be.[4]

But if this is the case, then architects should definitely be spending time in the archive. [2]

The Architect, the Archive, the Researcher, and Their Institution — Giovanna Borasi

1.

The Canadian Centre for Architecture (CCA) was founded by Phyllis Lambert in Montreal at the end of the seventies, and it was not the only one of its kind. The Deutsches Architekturmuseum (DAM) in Frankfurt (1979), the Getty Research Institute in Los Angeles (1984), and the Netherlands Architecture Institute (NAi) in Rotterdam (1988) were also part of a new generation of institutions devoted to the study of architecture.

All started with a very similar set of principles testifying to a renewed interest in the discipline. For the CCA, these principles—that collecting is not merely preserving, that studying architecture's ideas involves using the past and present as tools to envision the future, that exhibiting architecture means projecting critical ideas for society, that architectural scholarship can further a public understanding of the field—directly informed the institution's breadth of activity. For the CCA and other institutions like it, defining the right balance between museum, research, archive, collection, and public engagement components became a significant (and continuing) challenge.

This new phenomenon—the realization that a new modus operandi was needed for a new institutional type—lived alongside the fact that many other existing institutions already engaged with architecture. The International Confederation of Architecture Museums (ICAM) was created in 1979 as a forum where members from both new and older institutions could share aims and practices, even with the recognition that these agendas were also shaped by diverse organizational identities related to specific contexts and resources.

All of this took place in a time and a cultural context where the history of architecture was fundamental again—for historians, but also for architects. Through the history of architecture, historians, critics, and architects found themselves in a new productive and dialectical relationship. In the wake of the modern period—a moment when architecture tried to free itself from the weight of the past, developing values and language that relied on trust in the future and the promise of technology—history came back, both as a way to create a new theoretical foundation for architecture and to feed a language that evoked past architectural forms, shapes, styles, and decorative elements. This shift was pervasive. The first Venice Biennale of Architecture (1980), titled *The Presence of the Past* and organized by Paolo Portoghesi, with Vincent Scully, Charles Jencks, and Christian Norberg-Schulz, was a manifesto for this postmodern approach. Its *Strada Nuovissima*, a streetscape of facades designed by invited architects, was tangible evidence of this presence of history in the discourse, and of architects' desires to build architecture and the city with a strong connection to historical models.

In this context, architects' drawings became fundamental. The drawing revealed the inevitable disjunction between the idea of architecture and the ultimate construction of a building. No longer directed only at the built result, the architect's attention moved from the labor of construction to the intellectual work of the project; from the design process with its contextual constraints to an idea of architecture. As a result, interest turned toward the author of the drawing, introducing a more "humanistic" approach to the history of the discipline.

Another important change soon took place in the formation of the CCA collection, with consequences for how researchers encounter and understand these holdings. The CCA has collected archives along with individual drawings since its earliest years; the institution acquired the archives of the Montreal architect Ernest Cormier (AP001) in 1981. By the mid-nineties, however, the CCA began actively to reinforce the presence of archives in its collection, shifting its acquisition strategy from key drawings, or exemplary and exceptional artifacts, to the whole archives of key figures such as Peter Eisenman, James Stirling, Aldo Rossi, Cedric Price, and Gordon Matta-Clark. The archive provides the opportunity to study the full body of work of an architect, to capture how the architect's ideas evolved in different contexts, and to trace which ideas and positions are still relevant in architectural debate. As accumulations of historical records, documents, drawings, and writings, archives allow researchers to uncover ideas, but they also become physical proof of these ideas.

Studying these holdings makes them relevant, and, by proxy, the ideas they carry. It is in the hidden connections between the many objects, in the apparent and inevitable redundancy, or in the impression that "the" archive of a figure should hold something essential about the work that an interesting space for investigation exists. And the possible and many interpretations of these holdings is what the institution has been always interested in.

Out of the box: price rossi stirling + matta-clark,
installation view, Canadian Centre for Architecture, 2004

2.

This careful and systematic work of studying and producing new meaning from an archive has traditionally been the field of operations of scholars and historians, who carried it out mainly through writing. In the last decade, the CCA has decided to modify its strategy, by introducing the idea that the findings of such study might assume different formats—an exhibition (a kind of three-dimensional statement), a seminar, or a publication—and enlarging this open field to others.

One of the specific vehicles for this broader attitude toward archival holdings is titled "Out of the Box," a program in which the CCA actively exposes archival material to research and discovery while the archive is still being organized and catalogued. Generally, institutional collecting procedures are linear: acquisition, followed by cataloguing, research, exhibition, and publication. With this strategy, the CCA works on all these activities in parallel; acquisition, research, and exhibition occur simultaneously. This temporal shift produces a series of constructive and unexpected changes in the activities themselves. Research is present throughout, and in particular the exhibition becomes a research tool, establishing arguments and drawing provisional conclusions.

The CCA initiated this approach to archiving and research with the 2003 exhibition *out of the box: price rossi stirling + matta-clark*, curated by Mirko Zardini; Mark Wigley, Marco De Michelis, Anthony Vidler, and Philip Ursprung acted as co-curators, respectively, of the section on each architect. The intention was to bring the ideas of these four pivotal figures of the 1970s into open dialogue through a group of archives that had recently entered the CCA collection. The exhibition reflected the idea of being the first step of inquiry in these archives; the four curators and others involved in this research—students and visitors included—engaged in a continuing task of adjustment and correction. The installation was designed to reflect this "instability," so that it would be ready to accept new materials, rearrangements, and changes of heart. The assumption was that the exhibition should not be a conclusive reading.

More recently, coinciding with the arrival of several archives of contemporary practices (such as Ábalos&Herreros [2012], Foreign Office Architects [2013], and Álvaro Siza [2015]), the CCA has reworked this method to strengthen the connection between archival material, research, and public presentation of the collection. In this version, the invited researchers are groups of architects, who invest time in the archive studying the body

Industrial Architecture: Ábalos&Herreros, selected by OFFICE Kersten Geers David Van Severen,
installation view, Canadian Centre for Architecture, 2015

of work of another architect that might be relevant to their own. These architects all look simultaneously at the same archive, at the same architect's body of work. The idea of introducing multiple and simultaneous lines of investigation from the beginning prompts different forms of research and diverse readings of the architects' work while challenging the idea of monography, understood as the work of a single researcher on a single subject.

This model is only possible with a particular understanding of what the archive ultimately is—a tool. In this framework, the CCA sees the archive as a means to initiate a fruitful debate and an intellectual conversation between two architects or practices: one the subject of the study, the other studying. But this also offers the institution a new *raison d'etre*. Dialogue between architects isn't new; from the seventies until around 2000, it was realized especially through the dialectic work of architectural magazines, which would invite architects to analyze, explain, and maybe criticize the building or a work of peer, publicly, on paper. Architectural magazines are less and less present in this type of debate, as discourse has moved into the diffuse environment of the internet. An institution with the ultimate goal to engage in debate, and willing to take on the responsibility of facilitating these conversations, can occupy the space left behind.

Through this approach and the resulting series of exhibitions, lectures, and publications, the CCA's intention, then, is to develop a critical discourse concerning contemporary archives and active architectural practices at the same time. The strategy is an attempt to reintroduce theoretical research and critical thinking into the practice of architecture.

The CCA began work on the first of these continued "Out of the Box" initiatives in 2013, focusing on the archive of Ábalos&Herreros (AP164). The archive—which documents over 150 projects dating from 1986 to 2006—is mainly comprised of sketches, drawings in both print and digital form, collages, textual documents, slides, and models. In the case of Ábalos&Herreros specifically, the archive holdings vividly illustrate their professional work—built projects as well as unrealized ideas for competitions—along with their research, writing, curating, and teaching. Many architects and critics observed, studied, and commented on the work of Ábalos&Herreros while the firm was active, but these readings were mainly based on their realized work and their ongoing research activities. The arrival of the archive at

Landscapes of the Hyperreal: Ábalos&Herreros, selected by SO-IL,
installation view, Canadian Centre for Architecture, 2015

the CCA presented a new opportunity for observation and discovery based on materials related to process rather than to the final built projects.

In this case, the selected architect/researchers—Kersten Geers and David Van Severen of OFFICE Kersten Geers David Van Severen (Brussels), Juan José Castellón González of ETH Zurich, and Florian Idenburg and Jing Liu of SO–IL (New York)—were invited for residencies in the vaults, designed as focused immersions in the Ábalos&Herreros archive. Each group determined a precise line of investigation and articulated a way of reading the archive and the architects' work. Geers and Van Severen, who studied under Ábalos &Herreros in Madrid, investigated the architects' fascination with an industrial approach to architecture. Castellón, who worked with Ábalos&Herreros between 2003 and 2007, was interested in their capacity to construct a hybrid materiality while avoiding any manifestation of building technology as a language. Idenburg and Liu, who have taught in the same schools as both Ábalos and Herreros, focused on their approach to inhabiting a site and their visions for new landscapes. These critical arguments, paths of investigation, and opposing points of view generated a series of seminars, and ultimately three "Out of the Box" exhibitions (*Industrial Architecture*, *Jai Tech*, and *Landscapes of the Hyperreal*) held in the CCA's Octagonal Gallery in 2015. Ideas, writings, and discussions developed during the program are now collected in a publication.

Applied to architects who are still active in the field, the program allows for a different approach to archival research in the field of the history of architecture: Ábalos and Herreros themselves, as subjects of study, also played an active role as respondents to the different proposed readings and research, and their voices are present in annotations and reactions in the book. This enhances the debate, but it also creates an immediate oral history.

It is also important to acknowledge an additional intention of the project: as no research is innocent, the specific readings by Geers and Van Severen, by Castellón, and by Idenburg and Liu say just as much about the work and the interests of this new generation of architects as they do about the work of Ábalos&Herreros. For the researchers, this immersion in the vaults was like looking in a mirror.

Besides, History: Go Hasegawa, Kersten Geers, David Van Severen,
installation view, Canadian Centre for Architecture, 2017

3.

"You travel to see new things, but paradoxically, you see them only because in them you recognize something you have known before" (Bas Princen, "Ringroad Houston," in *The Construction of an Image* [London: Bedford Press, 2017], 49).

4.

"We do not live in a society, but in a collective. When we are in a collective, it is because we collect things. A major aspect of the history of our so-called modern world, especially the scientific modern world, is to have invented collections. Why? When you are building up a collection, you survey a lot of elements simultaneously, and you can make a lot of comparisons.... To have all the projects in the same space allows to make connections. This is what a collection facilitates: collecting elements allow people to 'collect their thoughts'" (Bruno Latour quoted in Armin Linke, *The Appearance of That Which Cannot Be Seen* [Milan: Silvana Editore, 2017], 168–75).

As an institution that wants to be contemporary, the CCA continues to interrogate how we understand today and yesterday, the past century

and the next one. But it is especially curious about how we relate to architects and their current ideas, to the architects whose archives it holds (and the ones it doesn't), and even to the researchers that are looking at all this work, both archived and happening out in the world.

When Heinrich Klotz began to acquire the collection for the DAM, the special character of his approach came from the fact that he was gathering material directly from visits to architects' offices. In doing so, he also established interviews and "file reports" as common practice for the documentation of relevant knowledge for the archive and the work it contains. But another result was that the DAM's collection was necessarily a contemporary collection, coming together at the same time the architects produced and reflected on their work. There was no mediation; the drawings went from the architects' tables to the museum vaults.

"Out of the Box" challenges where the contemporary aspect of an institution resides and how it asserts itself. To be contemporary is no longer only about having a contemporary collection, through acquiring contemporary practices and projects. Rather, it is based on the premise that the institution in itself might be the generator of a reflective space for contemporary architects to produce new knowledge. The institution is not

View of collection storage, Canadian Centre for Architecture, 2007

just the repository of concepts in archives; inviting architects to looking into other architects' work becomes a new way to collect architectural thinking and capture architects' current ideas.

In this sense, "Out of the Box" runs parallel to another series of CCA exhibitions that brings together contemporary architectural practices to generate conversations, both about their work and around a given topic with current relevance; these include *Environment: Approaches to Tomorrow* (Gilles Clément and Philippe Rahm, 2006); *Some Ideas on Living in London and Tokyo by Stephen Taylor and Ryue Nishizawa* (2009); *Other Space Odysseys: Greg Lynn, Michael Maltzan, Alessandro Poli* (2010); *Rooms You May Have Missed: Umberto Riva, Bijoy Jain* (2014); and, most recently, *Besides, History: Go Hasegawa, Kersten Geers, David Van Severen* (2017). Exhibitions become a format to state an approach toward architecture, a manifesto for architects' thinking, which then also makes its way into the CCA collection.

5.

The CCA has also been actively acquiring the archives of historians and critics. The donation of the archive of Kenneth Frampton (AP197) is the most recent example. The intention is somehow to further deepen and complexify—in the best sense— the possible research and understanding not only of this one archive, but also other holdings in the CCA collection as a whole. Many of the architects Frampton studied and wrote about have archives at the CCA—Álvaro Siza, Arthur Erickson, and Shim-Sutcliffe, among others. A new network of possible and relevant links could be constructed between their work and the historian and critic's readings, and even his way of working.

More importantly, though, if the CCA's current goal is to build a critical voice in architectural debate, the possibility of directly investigating what other critical voices have said about key works or historical shifts and paradigms becomes extremely relevant to the intellectual growth of the institution— and, ultimately, to its ability to continue to play a provoking role.

The CCA sees this as its contribution to a fruitful and inevitable long-term intellectual commitment, entered into with the architect, the architectural archive, and the researcher.

Giovanna Borasi is the Chief Curator at The Canadian Center for Architecture in Montreal, Canada.

Mood, Matter, Manner, Mode
Curated by Robert Somol

Johnston Marklee asked the 2017 Chicago Architecture Biennial participants to submit three reference images that informed their contribution to the exhibition. From this collective reference pool, Robert Somol selected and assembled four readings of the field: mood, matter, manner, and mode.

Mood

From *melancholic* to *manic*, the affect of the project as directed by its mise-en-scene of relative anxiety or ecstasy. How does the project conspire to reduce or magnify a style of life, for the one or the many?

1   Alvaro Siza, House Maria Margarida Aguda, Porto, Portugal, 1979–87

2   Alvaro Siza, Maison Van Middelem-Dupont, Oudenburg, Belgium, c. 1997

3   Le Corbusier, Petite maison au bord du lac Léman, Corseaux, Switzerland, 1923

4   Edward Hopper, *Western Motel*, 1957

5   Adolf Loos, Kärntner Bar (American Bar), Vienna, Austria, 1908

6   Baldassare Peruzzi, Perspective Hall, Villa Farnesina, Rome, Italy, 1510

7   Édouard Manet, *A Bar at the Folies-Bergère*, 1882

8   Itsuko Hasegawa, House in Kakio, Kanagawa, Japan, 1977

9   Le Corbusier, De Beistegui Apartment, Paris, France, 1929–31

13   Piero della Francesca, *The Meeting of Solomon and the Queen of Sheba*, Basilica of San Francesco, Arezzo, Italy, c. 1453

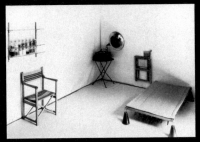

10   Hannes Meyer, Co-op Zimmer, Basel, Switzerland, 1926

14   Archizoom, No-Stop City. Paesaggio interno (interior landscape), 1971. Pictured for: Domus, March 1971

11   Mies van der Rohe and Lilly Reich, *Die Wohnung*, Exhibition Hall 4 Glassraum, Stuttgart, Germany, 1927.

15   Oscar Niemeyer and family in photo shoot at the Casa das Canoas, *LIFE Magazine*, 1959

12   Great hall of the house La Vedette, in Lausanne, where Eugène-Emmanuel Viollet-le-Duc passed away in 1879

16   Kevin Roche and John Dinkeloo, Ford Foundation, New York, USA, 1968

18 Gathering in the undercroft of Lina Bo Bardi's São Paulo
    Museum of Art (MASP), São Paulo, Brasil, year unknown

19 Master of Anthony of Burgundy, *Scene of a
    Bathhouse*, Berlin, Staatsbibliothek, c. 1470

21 Charles and Ray Eames, Case Study House No. 8, Pacific Palisades,
    USA, 1949

Manner

From *repetition* to *visitation*, the logic of the project, whether bottom-up/serial or top-down/imposed. Does the project attempt to deviate the given or naturalize the alien?

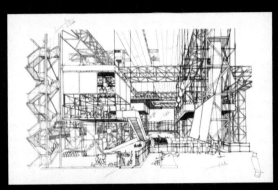

22   Cedric Price, Fun Palace: interior perspective, c. 1960–64

24   Renzo Piano, Richard Rogers, and Gianfranco Franchini, Centre Pompidou Southeast, Paris, France, 1972–77

23   SITE (James Wines), Highrise of Homes, 1981

25   Le Corbusier, Model photo of Unité d'Habitation, Marseille, France, 1947

26   Robert Duchesnay, Buckminster Fuller's US Expo '67 pavilion, Île Sainte-Hélène, Montreal, 1990

27 Matté Trucco, Lingotto Factory, Turin, Italy, 1923

30 Chicago Transit Authority, Lake Street Elevated (completed 1910), 2009

28 Mies van der Rohe, Lake Shore Drive Apartments, Chicago, USA, 1949–51

31 AA School of Architecture, One-to-One Dom-ino, Venice Biennale, 2014

29 Anonymous, Balloon framing, Chicago, USA, c. 1860

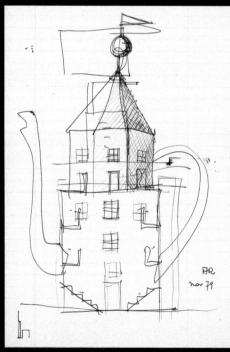

32 Aldo Rossi, Teatro del Mondo (*senza titolo*), (Theater of the world [*untitled*]), 1979

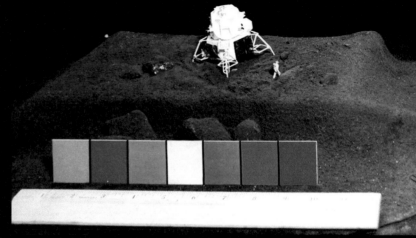

33 Gerhard Richter, Verkündigung nach Tizian (Annunciation after Titian), 1973

34 Sam Russell, RCA Rover TV Project Engineer, in *Apollo 15 Rover Television Camera*, Spacecraft Films, 1971

35 Hans Hollein, Aircraft Carrier City in Landscape, Project, Exterior Perspective, 1964

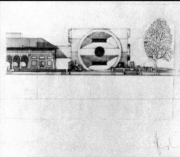

36 Diego Velázquez, *The Surrender of Breda*, 1634–35

38 Frank Lloyd Wright, Taliesin West, Scottsdale, USA, 1950

40 Claes Oldenburg, *Giant Three-Way Plug*, Allen Memorial Art Museum, Oberlin College, Ohio, 1977

39 Michelangelo Merisi da Caravaggio, *The Incredulity of Saint Thomas*, 1602

37 Kitchen of the Cistercian Monastery of Alcobaça (séc. XIII–XIV)

41 André Breton, Max Morise, Jeannette Ducrocq Tanguy, Pierre Naville, Benjamin Péret, Yves Tanguy, and Jacques Prévert, *Cadavre Exquis* (Exquisite corpse), 1928

Matter

From *geologic* to *infologic*, the substance of the project as made of stones or signs. Is the project materialized through the phenomenal/perceptual or the virtual/conceptual?

46 Brassai (Gyula Halász), *La Maison que j'habite* (The house I live in), 1934

42 Maker unknown, Ancient Egyptian brick, c. 2500 BC

47 Stone quarry pavilion

43 Rock in Hampi, India

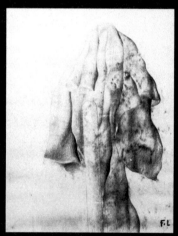

48 Fernand Léger, *Drapery*, c. 1930

44 Builder unknown, Great Mosque of Djenné, Mali. The original mosque was built in 1200; it was rebuilt in 1906, and has been reconstructed every year since.

45 Stonehenge, Salisbury, UK, c. 3100 BC

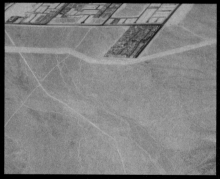

49 Benjamin Aranda, City edge, Las Vegas, USA, 2012

50 Ludwig Mies van der Rohe, Barcelona Pavilion, Spain, 1931/1983–86

51 Pieter Bruegel the Elder, *Tower of Babel*, 1563

52 Richard Wentworth, image from series *Making Do & Getting By*, 1971–2007

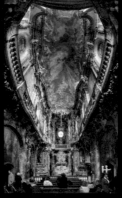

53 Egid Quirin and Cosmas Damien Asam, Asamkirche, Munich, Germany, 1733–46

54 John Baldessari, *Two Voided Books*, 1990

55 Paul Casaer, *Landscape of my personal belongings*, 2001

56 Aerial View of Beijing, 1943

57 Mies van der Rohe, Lake Shore Drive Apartments, Chicago, USA, 1949–51

58 Jürgen Mayer H., Data-protection patterns, 2011

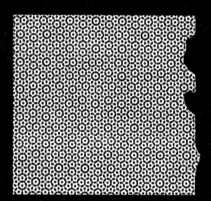

59 Jürgen Mayer H., Data-protection patterns, 2011

60 León Ferrari, Bairro (Barrio), 1980

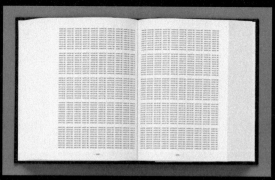

61 On Kawara, *One Million Years*, 1999

62 Mies van der Rohe, Federal Center, Chicago, USA, 1974

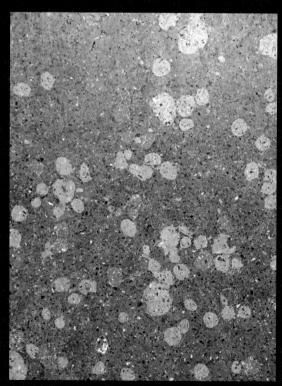

63 Franco Albini, San Babila Metro Station (1964), detail view, 2017

322

Mode

From *abstraction* to *convention*, the expression of the project, conveyed through geometric wholes or figural parts. Does the project attend to gestalt form or articulated element?

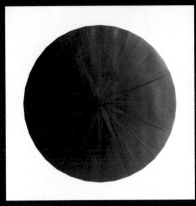

64 Mohammed Qasim Ashfaq, Black Hole III, 2014

66 Cover of Forum, no. 12 (1959–60), edited by Aldo van Eyck

70 Taj Mahal Mosque, Mughal architecture, Agra, India, 1632 AD–1648 AD

65 Kazimir Malevich, *White on White*, 1918

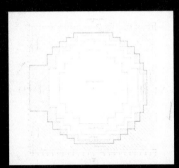

67 RG 326, Atomic Energy Commission, Chicago Pile-1. Core Plan-1 Drawings. Layer No12—Plan, 1942

71 Adolph Gottlieb, *Mist*, 1961

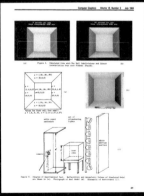

68 Page from the original publication describing the Cornell Box experiment in the SIGGRAPH Proceedings

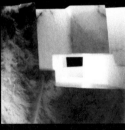

72 Eduardo Chillida, *Elogio de la Luz (Eulogy of the light)*, 1973

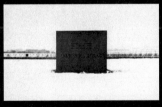

73 Piero Manzoni, *Socle du monde (Cradle of the world)*, 1961

69 Karl Glazebrook and Ivan Baldry, *The Average Color of the Universe*, 2002

74 Bas Princen, *Ringroad Houston*, 2005

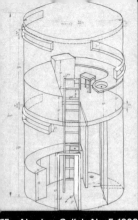

75 Absalon, *Cellule No. 5*, 1992

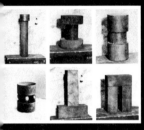

76 Carl Andre, *Found Steel Sculptures*, 1960–61

77 Albert Kahn, View of the principal and lateral façades of the addition to Boiler House No. 103, Half-Ton Truck Plant, Chrysler Corporation, Dodge Division, Mound and Eight Mile Roads, Detroit, Michigan, 1945–46.

78 Duchamp, *Comb*, 1916

79 Herzog & de Meuron, Sammlung Goetz, Munich, Germany, 1992

80 Peter Wächtler, *I*, 2015

81 Karl Wenke, Baumspenden-Gedenkstein (Memorial stone for tree donations), Grosser Tiergarten, Berlin, Germany, 1952

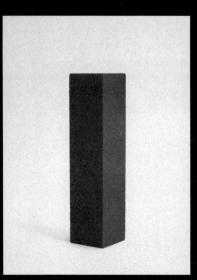

82 Atomic Energy Commission, Graphite brick from Chicago Pile-1, date unknown

83 Mies Van der Rohe, Chicago Federal Center, Chicago, USA, 1964

84 Luis Barragán and Mathias Goeritz, Torres de Satélite (Satellite towers), Ciudad Satélite (Satellite City), Mexico, 1958

Robert Somol is the Director of the
School of Architecture at University
of Illinois, Chicago.

Full Participant List

51N4E
6a architects
Ábalos + Sentkiewicz and Armin Linke
Adamo-Faiden
addenda architects with Joachim
 Brohm and Moritz Küng
AGENdA - agencia de arquitectura
Aires Mateus
An Te Liu
Andrew Kovacs
Angela Deuber Architect
Ania Jaworska
Aranda\Lasch and Terrol Dew Johnson
Archi-Union Architects
architecten de vylder vinck taillieu
Architecture of the VII Day
Atelier Manferdini
AWP office for territorial
 reconfiguration
Bak Gordon Arquitectos
Barbas Lopes Arquitectos
Barkow Leibinger
Barozzi Veiga
Baukuh and Stefano Graziani
Besler & Sons LLC
BLESS
Brandlhuber+ and Christopher Roth
BUREAU SPECTACULAR
Cameron Wu
Caruso St John with Thomas Demand
 and Hélène Binet
Charlap Hyman & Herrero
Charles Waldheim with Office
 for Urbanization Harvard Graduate
 School of Design and Siena Scarff
 Design
Christ & Gantenbein
Christian Kerez
Daniel Everett
David Schalliol
Dellekamp Arquitectos
Design With Company
Diego Arraigada Arquitectos
Dogma
Dominique Perrault Architecture
DRDH Architects
Ensamble Studio
Éric Lapierre Architecture
Fake Industries Architectural
 Agonisms and Aixopluc
fala atelier
Filip Dujardin
Fiona Connor and Erin Besler
First Office
formlessfinder
Fosbury Architecture
Francois Perrin
Frida Escobedo
Gerard & Kelly
Go Hasegawa
HHF Architects
IIT College of Architecture + SANAA
Iñigo Manglano-Ovalle
J. MAYER H. und Partner, Architekten
 and Philip Ursprung
James Welling
Jesús Vassallo
Jorge Otero-Pailos
June14 Meyer-Grohbrügge
 & Chermayeff
junya ishigami+associates
Karamuk * Kuo Architects
Katharina Gaenssler
Keith Krumwiede
Kéré Architecture

Khoury Levit Fong
Kuehn Malvezzi
LAN with Franck Boutté and project
 produced by Pavilion de l'Arsenal
l'AUC as l'AUC
Luca Galofaro
Luisa Lambri
Lütjens Padmanabhan Architekten
Machine Project
Made in
MAIO
MALL
Marianne Mueller
Marshall Brown
Matilde Cassani
MG&Co.
Michelle Chang
Monadnock
MOS
Norman Kelley
Nuno Brandão Costa with
 André Cepeda
OFFICE Kersten Geers David Van
 Severen with Peter Wächtler and
 Michaël Van den Abeele
Pascal Flammer
Paul Andersen and Paul Preissner
Pezo von Ellrichshausen Arquitectos
Philipp Schaerer
Philippe Rahm architectes
Piovene Fabi and Giovanna Silva
Point Supreme
PRODUCTORA
REAL Foundation
Robert Somol
SADAR+VUGA
Sam Jacob Studio
SAMI-arquitectos and Paulo Catrica
Sauter von Moos
Scott Fortino
Sergison Bates
Serie Architects
SHINGO MASUDA + KATSUHISA
 OTSUBO Architects
SO-IL and Ana Prvački
Stan Allen Architect
Studio Anne Holtrop
Studio Gang
Studio Mumbai
Sylvia Lavin with Erin Besler
 and Norman Kelley
T + E + A + M
Tatiana Bilbao Estudio
Tham & Videgård Arkitekter
The Empire with Ilaria Forti, Joseph
 Swerdlin, and Barbara Modolo
The Living
The LADG
Theaster Gates
Thomas Baecker Bettina Kraus
Tigerman McCurry Architects
Toshiko Mori Architect
UrbanLab
Urbanus
Veronika Kellndorfer
WELCOMEPROJECTS
WORKac
Zago Architecture
ZAO/standardarchitecture

51N4E

51N4E is an international, Brussels based practice—founded in 2000—that aspires to contribute through means of design to social and urban transformation. 51N4E is led by Johan Anrys and Freek Persyn, and is 30 people strong at present. 51N4E envisions transformations in society through the production of space by rethinking built environments and outdated urban systems, but also by reimagining how we use those environments in all their complexity. 51N4E uses the tools of architecture and design to construct dialogue settings around each project, thereby increasing collective intelligence and creating projects with a broader impact on society.

6a architects

6a architects was founded by Tom Emerson and Stephanie Macdonald in 2001 after meeting at the Royal College of Art. They won a RIBA award in 2011 and was nominated for the Stirling prize, both for their Raven Row contemporary art gallery in Spitalfields, East London. The Fashion Galleries at the V&A opened in May 2012 and were nominated for the European Union Prize for Contemporary Architecture – the Mies van der Rohe Award, 2013. The following year, the practice collaborated with fashion designer Paul Smith to design a cast iron façade in Mayfair, London which has been nominated for the Design Museum's Design of the Year Award 2014 and received a Civic Trust Award, 2014. The practice has won several major architectural competitions and international awards including the redevelopment of a large industrial complex in Oval for the London Development Agency and a housing development in Savigny-le-Temple, France. In 2012, the practice was awarded the Eric Schelling Medal for Architecture.

Ábalos + Sentkiewicz

Ábalos + Sentkiewicz is an international architecture office based in Madrid, Spain; Cambridge, U.S; Shanghai, China. It is directed by Iñaki Ábalos and Renata Sentkiewicz. The directors have taught in prestigious universities such as ETSAM, Harvard University Graduate School of Design, Architectural Association, Columbia, Cornell, and Princeton, thereby combining academic, professional, and research activities. Iñaki Ábalos is a Chaired Professor at ETSAM Spain as well as Professor in Residence and Ex-Chair of the Department of Architecture at Harvard University Graduate School of Design.

The work of Ábalos + Sentkiewicz is internationally recognized, having been the subject of fifteen individual exhibitions and many collective exhibitions in some of the most prestigious centers such as AA, London; Pavillon de l'Arsenale, Paris; MoMA, New York City; and the Biennale of Architecture of Venice. This prestige also reflects in the 40 awards received in architecture competitions. Another forty-five awards have been given to different research and design activities, eighteen of them to built works by the firm.

Adamo-Faiden

Sebastian Adamo and Marcelo Faiden are architects and co-founders of Buenos Aires based practice adamo-faiden architects. Both graduated from the Universidad de Buenos Aires in 2002. Marcelo Faiden obtained a PhD from Escuela Técnica Superior de Arquitectura de Barcelona in 2016. They have collaborated since 2005 and, in parallel to their professional activity, they have developed a solid role within academia, having taught in Universidad de Buenos Aires and Universidad Torcuato di Tella. They are currently professors of the department of postgraduate studies at Universidad de Buenos Aires. Their work has been exhibited in the Guggenheim Museum, the Venice Biennale of Architecture, LIGA, and The Storefront for Art & Architecture. There are three monographs about their work: 1:100, Buenos Aires; 2G, Barcelona; and Ediciones ARQ, Santiago, Chile. Adamo-Faiden was awarded in the XII Bienal Internacional de Arquitectura de Buenos Aires and in the Bienal Internacional de Arquitectura de Argentina.

AGENdA – agencia de arquitectura

AGENdA – agencia de arquitectura is located in Medellin, Colombia. AGENdA searches for possible architectures, no matter the scale or location. AGENdA articulates dialogues, projects, and questions regarding architecture disciplinary issues and architecture practice from a condition of crossroad between tropic conditions, history, and disciplinary matters—with special attention to uncertain conditions—as a response to specific realities and context. AGENdA was founded by Camilo Restrepo Ochoa in 2010. Camilo Restrepo Ochoa is a graduate of Universidad Pontificia Bolivariana in Medellin. He has been a guest lecturer at Harvard Graduate School of Design since 2014. Camilo was nominated for the 2014 MCHAP prize, the 2014 BSi Prize, and was one of the three finalists for the 2012 Rolex Protégé.

Aires Mateus

Francisco Aires Mateus and Manuel Aires Mateus studied architecture at the Universidade Técnica in Lisbon, where they graduated in 1987 and 1986, respectively. After some years of collaboration with Gonçalo Byrne, they opened the office Aires Mateus. They have been professors at the Accademia di Architettura, Mendrisio, Switzerland since 2001, and at the Universidade Autónoma, Lisbon, since 1998, as well as visiting professors at I.E. Universidad, Segovia in 2012; at Oslo School of Architecture, Norway in 2009; and the Graduate School of Design, Harvard University, U.S. in 2005.

Ania Jaworska

Ania Jaworska is an architect and educator. She currently is a visiting assistant Professor at the University of Illinois at Chicago, School of Architecture. She holds a master's degree in architecture from the Cracow University of Technology in Poland as well as the Cranbrook Academy of Art in Michigan. Her practice focuses on exploring the connection between art and architecture, and her work explores bold simple forms, humor, and commentary as well as conceptual, historic, and cultural references. Jaworska's work was exhibited in numerous exhibitions, notably, at the 13th Venice Biennale, Chicago Architecture Biennial 2015, Chicago Cultural Center, Chicago Architecture Foundation, and Storefront for Art and Architecture. She recently had a solo exhibition titled BMO Harris Bank Chicago Works: Ania Jaworska at the Museum of Contemporary Art Chicago and SET at Volume Gallery in Chicago. She designed a bookstore for the Graham Foundation and was a 2017 MoMA PS1 Young Architects Program Finalist.

Andrew Kovacs

Andrew Kovacs is a lecturer at UCLA Architecture & Urban Design. Kovacs studied architecture at Syracuse University, the Architecture Association in London, and Princeton University. From 2012 to 2013, Kovacs was the inaugural UCLA Teaching Fellow for which he produced GOODS USED: AN ARCHITECTURAL YARD SALE at Jai and Jai Gallery in Los Angeles. Kovacs' work on architecture and urbanism has been published widely in publications such as Pidgin, Project, Perspecta, Manifest, Metropolis, Clog, Domus, and Fulcrum. Kovacs is the creator and curator of Archive of Affinities, a website devoted to the collection and display of architectural b sides. His recent design work includes a proposal for a dog park in downtown Los Angeles and the renovation of an Airstream trailer into a mobile retail store that travels the Pacific Coast Highway.

Angela Deuber Architect

Angela Deuber is a Swiss architect educated at ETH Zurich. Her practice is based in Chur, Grisons. She has taught at the ETH Zurich and at Lucerne University. Her office has produced a number of significant buildings and projects including the House on the Outer Hebrides, Scotland, UK in 2013; 2009–2013, School building in Thal, Canton St. Gallen, 2009–2012 Conversion of a late medieval House in Stuls, Grisons. The willful architectural character and very particular qualities of her first built works and projects aroused a considerable commendation. Her architecture possesses a strong material and tectonic identity and exhibits a clear commitment to the constructive conscience.

Aranda\Lasch and Terrol Dew Johnson

Aranda\Lasch is a New York and Tucson based design studio established in 2003 by Benjamin Aranda and Chris Lasch. Aranda\Lasch designs buildings, installations, and furniture. Their recognitions include the United States Artists Award, Young Architects Award, Design Vanguard Award, AD Innovators, and the Architectural League Emerging Voices Award. Their early projects are the subject of the book, Tooling. Aranda\Lasch has exhibited internationally in galleries, museums, design fairs, and biennials. Their work is part of the permanent collection of the MoMA in New York.

Terrol Dew Johnson is a community leader, nationally recognized advocate for Native communities as well as a renowned artist and weaver. Johnson co-founded Tohono O'odham Community Action (TOCA), a grassroots community organization dedicated to creating positive programs based in the O'odham Himdag – the Desert People's Way. In 1999 Johnson was named one of "America's top ten young community leaders" by the Do Something Foundation and in 2002 he received the Ford Foundation's Leadership for a Changing World Award. As an artist, Johnson is recognized as one of the top Native American basketweavers in the U.S. He has won top honors at such shows as Santa Fe Indian Market, O'odham Tash, the Heard Museum Fair and the Southwest Indian Art Fair. His work is in the permanent collections of museums including the Smithsonian Institution's National Museum of the American Indian and the Heard Museum.

Archi-Union Architects

Archi-Union Architects was founded by Philip F. Yuan in 2003. Their practice is focused on the integration of Chinese traditional culture and digital technology including computational design, robotic fabrication, and architectural industrialization. There are currently over 70 designers in the office. Recent projects include Linear House-Jiujiantang in Shanghai, Lanxi Curtilage in Chengdu, Taisheng Garden, Jade Museum, Shangart Gallery on the West Bund, Fab-Union, Chi She, Hefei Bashang Street Mixed-use Project, Shanghai Stomatological Hospital, Songjiang Art Campus, Aux Campus (Shanghai) etc.

Archi-Union has been actively involved in the relevant academic activities and exhibitions including the Hong Kong Biennale, Shanghai Biennale, Milan Triennial.

architecten de vylder vinck taillieu

architecten de vylder vinck taillieu—a dvvt—is the name under which Jan De Vylder, Inge Vinck, and Jo Taillieu share their united view on what architecture can possibly be. The point of departure for a dvvt is to embrace "making" in its broadest sense. It is only through an understanding of how to build something that architecture can play out its critical potential. As a response to what is expected of architecture today, a dvvt instead focuses on the construction of a banal and everyday reality, in which it finds opportunities to greatly surpass that which is expected. Through their practice, a dvvt demonstrates how a critical attitude is not just a gesture, but, rather, a perspective on architecture to go beyond all requirements. This critical perspective is based on a sense of social responsibility as architects. The responsibility of the architect is to transcend given expectations and give architecture a chance at cultural production. The skillfulness of the architect—craftsmanship and critical insight—is crucial here. The skilled architect is able to build an everyday reality founded on cultural sustainability, safeguarding architecture from becoming a mere solution—the métier as the key to the future.

Atelier Manferdini

Elena Manferdini, principal and owner of Atelier Manferdini, has over fifteen years of professional experience in architecture, art, design, and education. Atelier Manferdini has completed art and architectural projects in the US, Europe and Asia. Notable among the firm's projects are the Pavilion for the Museum of Contemporary Art in Los Angeles, Bianca, a three storey boat in Japan, and a series of interior design renovations in Los Angeles.

Elena Manferdini received a Graham Award for architecture, the 2013 ACADIA Innovative Research Award of Excellence, and she was selected as recipient for the Educator of the Year presidential award given by the AIA Los Angeles. In 2011 she was one of the recipients of the prestigious annual grants from the United States Artists (USA) in the category of architecture and design.

Elena currently teaches at the Southern California Institute of Architecture (SCI-Arc) where she is the Graduate Programs Chair.

AWP Office for Territorial Reconfiguration

AWP is an award winning interdisciplinary office for architectural and territorial reconfiguration. Based in Paris and London the office develops projects internationally working on a wide variety of programmes; from architecture, landscape design, strategic planning, and urbanism ranging from major large scale public projects to temporary installations both in France and internationally. AWP was awarded the French Ministry of Culture's Prize for Best Young Architects in 2006, and the French Ministry of Transport, Housing and Ecology's PJU urban planning award 2010. AWP is currently working on the strategic masterplan plan for the development of urban space in Paris' La Défense business district, and designing an iconic 800 m long public space just below the Grande Arche de la Défense, as well as a series of follies and buildings. The three partners have exhibited their work, lectured at architectural venues worldwide, and taught at Columbia, Cornell and Carleton Universities, the Berlage, UVa among other institutions.

Bak Gordon Architects

Bak Gordon Architects is an architectural office based in Lisbon, Portugal founded by architect Ricardo Bak Gordon in 2002. The studio has developed projects of different scales, programs, and typologies in Portugal and abroad. In all designs, Bak Gordon explores—with rigor and precision—a vision that is simultaneously poetic and technical, as well as carefully related to site and public space. Currently, the studio has a team of 10 architects. Their main work themes are housing and urban planning as well as cultural, industrial, educational, and sporting facilities. The studio participates in national and international competitions. Their work has been shown in exhibitions in Portugal, Europe, Asia, Central America, and South America. They have been published in prestigious editions of the specialty publications worldwide. Ricardo Bak Gordon is a lecturer and visiting professor at several international universities and institutions.

Barbas Lopes Arquitectos

Barbas Lopes Arquitectos established their practice in 2006. They have designed and realized projects from public and private buildings, single-family housing, exhibition designs, and interiors. The practice is also engaged in collaborations with architects such as Peter Märkli and Gonçalo Byrne. Their work was nominated for Icon Awards 2012, Designs of the Year 2013 and Mies van der Rohe 2013. Patrícia Barbas graduated in Architecture at FAUTL, Lisbon. The firm has collaborated with Aires Mateus, Gonçalo Byrne, and João Pedro Falcão de Campos. Patrícia was the project coordinator for Promontório Architects in Salvador da Bahia, Brazil, during 2005 and 2006. She was also a member of FAD Awards 2016.

Barkow Leibinger

Barkow Leibinger is an American German architectural practice, founded in 1993, based in Berlin and New York. The office has internationally realized buildings of a wide-range of scales and types including building for workplace (industry, office, and master-planning), culture, housing, events, exhibitions, and installations in the public realm. Their discursive research-based approach to architecture and design allows the work to respond to advancing knowledge and technology, locating the practice as an international leader in digital and analogue fabrication techniques. This skill set expands to include new materials and applications that drive the practice forward as a continuously evolving activity. This focus revolves around a commitment to academic teaching, research, and the practice itself: each are autonomous work areas that simultaneously inform each other beneficially. This is an approach that distinguishes each project as distinct in relationship to client and architect dialogue, location, aesthetic, and purpose.

Barozzi Veiga

Barozzi Veiga is an architectural office devoted to architecture and urbanism, founded in 2004 in Barcelona by Fabrizio Barozzi and Alberto Veiga. Barozzi / Veiga has won numerous prizes in national and international competitions, among them the refurbishment of the Palace Santa Clara in Úbeda, the Auditorium of Águilas, the Headquarter for the D.O. Ribera del Duero in Roa, the Philharmonic Hall in Szczecin, the Cantonal Museum of Fine Arts in Lausanne, the extension of the Cantonal Museum of Fine Arts in Chur, the Music School in Brunico, the Tanzhaus in Zürich, and the housing projects in Bergamo and Badalona. The work of Barozzi / Veiga has been presented in different exhibitions and published in a wide range of specialized literature. Barozzi / Veiga has won many international awards and citations for design excellence, among them the European Union Prize for Contemporary Architecture – Mies van der Rohe Award 2015.

baukuh

baukuh produces architecture. Designs are independent of personal taste. No member of baukuh is ever individually responsible for any single project, each of which s the product of the office as a whole. Working without a hierarchical structure or a stylistic dogma, baukuh produces architecture out of a rational and explicit design process. This process is based on a critical understanding of the architecture of the past. The knowledge encoded in the architecture of the past is public, and starting from this public knowledge, any architectural problem can be solved.

baukuh was founded in 2004 and is now composed by Paolo Carpi, Silvia Lupi, Vittorio Pizzigoni Giacomo Summa, Pier Paolo Tamburelli and Andrea Zanderigo. baukuh is based in Milan and Genoa. baukuh recently completed the House of Memory in Milan (2015) and is currently involved in the realization of several public commissions throughout Europe.

Besler & Sons LLC

Erin Besler and Ian Besler are co-founders of Besler & Sons, LLC, a Los Angeles-based practice that works to expand the definition of architecture through active participation with amateur creators, construction trades, and design software. They work to create new audiences and opportunities for social engagement. Their work has been published in Log, Pidgin, Future Anterior, Project, San Rocco, and Perspecta. Their work has been exhibited internationally. They were finalists for MoMA PS1's Young Architects Program. They participated in the Chicago Architecture Biennial and the Shenzhen and Hong Kong Bi-City Biennale of Architecture/Urbanism.

BLESS

BLESS is a fashion/design studio created in 1997 by Ines Kaag—based in Berlin—and Desiree Heiss—in Paris. The two designers escape from any calibrated definition of fashion. They are faithful to their initial concept: dividing and combining creation between fashion, art, design, and architecture. They engage an independent work method, which often implements collaborations and interactions with friends, customers, and other contributors. Their creations are born from true personal needs: aiming for simplicity and comfort throughout daily life while aspiring for more visionary horizons. Their products, as well as their distribution systems, do not fit into any pre-established category; BLESS passes, without transition, from one area to another: from highly functional forms to conceptual propositions on the verge of abstraction. An unlimited, fluid and contemporary conception, BLESS does not promote any style—BLESS fits every style.

Brandlhuber+ and Christopher Roth
Brandlhuber+ is a collaborative architecture practice based in Berlin. It was founded by Arno Brandlhuber in 2006. He works as an architect and urban planner. Aside from his building practice—including Haus Brunnenstrasse 9 (Berlin, 2009) and Antivilla (Krampnitz, 2014)—he is researching the spatial production of the Berlin Republic, including numerous exhibitions and publications, aiming to examine the interplay of Berlin's history, legislation, and the built environment.

Together with Christopher Roth, he is currently working on the film project titled *Legislating Architecture*.

Christopher Roth works as an artist and director. His practice may be best understood as a proactive intellectual scholarship combining the factual and fictitious with both analytic and poetic qualities. Roth's work seeks to understand how information, words, pictures, and ideas are received, travel, and are mediated at a constantly accelerating pace. His work has been included in several exhibitions and congresses around the world.

BUREAU SPECTACULAR
BUREAU SPECTACULAR (BS) is an operation of architectural affairs founded and led by Jimenez Lai since 2008. It is located in Los Angeles. The body of work of BS is widely exhibited and published around the world, including *White Elephant* which is in the collection of the Museum of Modern Art in New York. In 2014, BS designed the Taiwan Pavilion at the 14th Venice Architecture Biennale.

Caruso St John and Thomas Demand
Since its foundation in 1990, Caruso St John has been pursuing an architecture that is rooted in place. The practice resists the thin-skinned abstraction that characterizes much global architecture in favor of buildings that are perceived slowly over time and that have an emotional content. Its work is enriched by an on-going dialogue with the European city and with history — that of architecture, art, and culture more widely.

The practice rose to prominence with the acclaimed New Art Gallery Walsall, completed in 2000. Many cultural sector commissions have followed, including the Millbank Project for Tate Britain, a suite of commercial galleries for Gagosian, and Damien Hirst's Newport Street Gallery in London for which the practice was awarded the 2016 RIBA Stirling Prize. The practice has offices in London and Zurich, and now works on a wide range of projects, both public and commercial.

Thomas Demand studied with the sculptor Fritz Schwegler, who encouraged him to explore the expressive possibilities of architectural models at the Kunstakademie Düsseldorf, where Bernd and Hilla Becher had recently taught photographers such as Andreas Gursky, Thomas Struth, and Candida Höfer. Like those artists, Demand makes mural-scale photographs, but instead of finding his subject matter in landscapes, buildings, and crowds, he uses paper and cardboard to reconstruct scenes he finds in images taken from various media sources. Once he has photographed his re-created environments—always devoid of figures but often displaying evidence of recent human activity—Demand destroys his models, further complicating the relationship between reproduction and original that his photography investigates.

Demand has been the subject of one-person exhibitions at The Museum of Modern Art, New York, and the Neue Nationalgalerie, Berlin, and he has represented Germany at the Venice Biennale and the Bienal de São Paulo. Demand lives and works in Berlin.

Charlap Hyman & Herrero
Charlap Hyman & Herrero began in 2014 as the chance collaboration of two friends from the Rhode Island School of Design who found themselves working on the same project: a house for which Charlap Hyman was commissioned as interior designer and Herrero was project architect with the firm SO–IL. The idea for the firm grew out of the spirit of storytelling—designing a space, from macro to micro, that interacts with history through reference in order to craft a narrative.

The varied nature of the principals' skill sets has allowed them to pursue projects of different scopes and typologies, from set designs to stores to houses. Charlap Hyman & Herrero's approach, however, is uniform. With gesamtkunstwerk (the total work of art) at the core of their objective, they aim to create spaces that become worlds unto themselves. In every project, Charlap Hyman & Herrero endeavors to consider divergent art forms and the experience of multiple senses.

Charles Waldheim
Charles Waldheim is a Canadian-American architect and urbanist. Waldheim's research examines the relations between landscape, ecology, and contemporary urbanism. He is author, editor, or co-editor of numerous books on these subjects, and his writing has been published and translated internationally. Waldheim is John E. Irving Professor at Harvard University's Graduate School of Design where he directs the School's Office for Urbanization. Waldheim is recipient of the Rome Prize Fellowship from the American Academy in Rome; the Visiting Scholar Research Fellowship at the Study Centre of the Canadian Centre for Architecture; the Cullinan Chair at Rice University; and the Sanders Fellowship at the University of Michigan.

Christ & Gantenbein
After internationally acclaimed projects in London, Mexico, and China, Christ & Gantenbein continues to cement its reputation with museum concepts such as the renovations and extensions to the Kunstmuseum in Basel (2016), the Swiss National Museum in Zurich (2016), as well as the Wallraf-Richartz-Museum in Cologne (ongoing). Housing schemes in Paris and Switzerland, as well as the Lindt Chocolate Competence Centre in Switzerland are, among others, currently on the drawing board. Five associates and 35 architects staff the practice established in 1998. Through the years, Christ & Gantenbein have equally committed to academic activities: most recent lectureships were at the ETH Zurich (2010–2015) and the Harvard GSD (2015–2016). In 2016, the studio was also invited to contribute the results of its work and research to the 15th edition of the Venice Biennale as well as the 4th Lisbon Architecture Triennial.

Christian Kerez
Christian Kerez was born in 1962 in Maracaibo, Venezuela and educated at the Swiss Federal Institute of Technology Zurich. After extensive published work in the field of architectural photography, he opened his own architectural office in Zurich, Switzerland in 1993. Christian Kerez has been appointed as a visiting professor in design and architecture at the Swiss Federal Institute of Technology Zurich since 2001, as assistant professor since 2003 and as full professor for design and architecture since 2009. In 2012–13 he led the Kenzo Tange Chair at Harvard University, Cambridge. He is currently working on different programs in various scales in France, Bahrain, the Czech Republic, Brazil and China.

Daniel Everett
Daniel Everett is an artist and professor working across a range of media including photography, video, sculpture, and installation. He received his MFA from The School of The Art Institute of Chicago in 2009. Daniel currently teaches at Brigham Young University as an assistant professor of New Genres. His work has been exhibited widely in group exhibitions throughout Europe and North America including recent group exhibitions at L'Atelier Néerlandais in Paris, East Wing Gallery in Dubai, and Luis Adelantado in Mexico City. He has had solo exhibitions at the Museum of Contemporary Art in Chicago (2010) and at the Utah Museum of Fine Arts in Salt Lake City (2012). Recent publications include two monographs published by Études—*Throughout the Universe in Perpetuity* (2015) and *Standard Edition* (2012)—as well as features in *Blind Spot* (2013), *Foam Talent* (2014), *Granta* (2014), and *Mousse* (2015).

David Schalliol
David Schalliol is academically and artistically interested in issues of social stratification and meaning in the social and physical worlds. His writing and photographs have appeared in such publications as Social Science Research, Places, and The New York Times, as well as in numerous exhibitions, including the inaugural Belfast Photo Festival and the Museum of Contemporary Photography's Midwest Photographers Project. Schalliol contributed to *Highrise: Out My Window*, an interactive documentary that won the 2011 International Digital Emmy for Non-Fiction. His book, *Isolated Building Studies*, was published by Utakatado in 2014. Currently an assistant professor of sociology at St. Olaf College, David worked with the John S. and James L. Knight Foundation and the Chicago Community Trust to increase journalistic coverage of underserved communities. He earned his PhD in the Department of Sociology at The University of Chicago.

Dellekamp Arquitectos
Dellekamp Arquitectos is a Mexican architecture practice dedicated to the development and supervision of architectural projects, regardless of scale or program type, with a rigorous research methodology. They aim to find unique solutions to the specific conditions of each project to maximize its intended budget, image, use, context, and spirit. The coordination and collaboration with various disciplines such as engineering, graphic design, industrial design, environmental engineering, and landscape architecture makes up a significant part of their activities, adding value to this team of specialists focused on the accomplishment of integral solutions. Simultaneously, Dellekamp Arquitectos is involved in ongoing architectural research, a laboratory of ideas that foster the building activities. In this way, they are constantly a part of the academic and teaching realms as well as research studies, lectures, publications, biennales, and exhibitions.

Design With Company (Dw/Co)
Design With Company (Dw/Co) is the Chicago-based architectural collaborative of Stewart Hicks and Allison Newmeyer. Dw/Co seeks to transform the world through textual and visual narratives, speculative urban scenarios, installations, and small-scale interactive constructions. Hicks is currently an assistant professor in Architecture at the University of Illinois at Chicago and previously served as the Hyde Chair of Excellence at the University of Nebraska-Lincoln. Newmeyer is a visiting assistant professor at the University of Illinois at Chicago and has recently taught at the University of Wisconsin, Milwaukee as well as the Illinois Institute of Technology, Chicago. The practice was recently included in the 2015 Chicago Architectural Biennial. They completed construction on a pavilion as part of Design Miami 2015, another in Vancouver Canada, and a temporary outdoor theater at the Ragdale Artist Colony.

Diego Arraigada Arquitectos
Diego Arraigada graduated from the Faculty of Architecture at the National University of Rosario with a degree in Architecture in 1999 and from the School of Architecture at the University of California Los Angeles with a Master of Architecture degree in 2003. In 2005, he established his professional office in Rosario, Argentina.
He is a professor at the Torcuato Di Tella University in Argentina. He was awarded the Arquitectonica Foundation Prize in 1999, a Fulbright scholarship in 2001, the Silver Medal at the XII International Architecture Buenos Aires Biennale in 2009, and the National Prize for Technological Innovation in Architecture in 2015. In 2011, he was selected to represent Argentina in the II Latin-American Architecture Biennale in Pamplona, Spain and in 2014 he was selected for a solo exhibition at LIGA Espacio para Arquitectura, Mexico DF. In 2016, he was nominated for the Mies Crown Hall Americas Prize for Emerging Architecture, Chicago.

Dogma
Dogma was founded in 2002 and is led by Pier Vittorio Aureli and Martino Tattara. From the beginning of its activities, Dogma has worked on the relationship between architecture and the city by focusing on urban design and large-scale projects. Parallel to their design work, the members of Dogma have intensely engaged with teaching, writing, and research: activities that have been an integral part of the office's engagement with architecture. For the past few years, Dogma has developed through multiple projects and studies on the transformation of domestic space. The work of the office has been widely published and exhibited. In 2006, Dogma has won the first Iakov Chernikhov Prize for the best emerging architectural practice. In 2013, on the occasion of the exhibition *Dogma: 11 Projects in London*, the first monograph on the work of the office was published by AA Publications.

Dominique Perrault Architecture
Praemium imperial award winner (Japan), the french architect and urban planner, Dominique Perrault, is a professor and director of the Underground Architecture Laboratory (SUB) at the Ecole Polytechnique Fédérale de Lausanne in Switzerland. He is also the founder of DPAx, a multidisciplinary research platform exploring architecture from a wider perspective, and DPA Lab, a laboratory of research and innovation developing processes that reinvent the vocabulary of architecture. Along with the Bibliothèque Nationale de France, his main projects to date include the olympic velodrome and swimming pool in Berlin, the extension of the Court of Justice of the European Union in Luxembourg, the Olympic Tennis Stadium in Madrid, the EWHA Woman's University in Seoul and the Fukoku Tower in Osaka. In recent years, Dominique Perrault inaugurated the tallest tower of Austria in Vienna, the DC Tower 1, and led various heritage rehabilitation projects, including the new public entry pavilion for the Château de Versailles. Current studies and urban research projects include the Olympic Village – Paris 2024 and the "Mission Ile de la Cité," an urban study commissioned by the president of the French Republic that reflects upon the future of the thriving, historical center of Paris from now until 2040.

Ensamble Studio
Ensamble Studio is a cross-functional team established in 2000 and led by architects Antón García-Abril and Débora Mesa. Balancing education, research, and practice, the office explores innovative approaches to architectural and urban spaces and the technologies that build them. Among the studio's most relevant completed works are Hemeroscopium House and Reader's House in Madrid (Spain), Music Studies Center and SGAE Central Office in Santiago de Compostela (Spain), The Truffle in Costa da Morte (Spain), Telcel Theater in Mexico City, and—more recently—Cyclopean House in Brookline (USA) and Structures of Landscape for Tippet Rise Art Center in Montana (USA). Their work is extensively published in both printed and digital media and has been exhibited and awarded internationally. Beside their professional career, both principals keep a very active research and academic agenda as directors of the POPlab (Prototypes of Prefabrication Research Laboratory) at the Massachusetts Institute of Technology (M.I.T.), that they founded in 2012.

Éric Lapierre
Éric Lapierre is an architect and theoretician of architecture. He is the founder and principal of Éric Lapierre Experience (ELEx), a Paris based organization that coordinates both practice and writing. ELEx buildings are recognized on national and international level through many awards and publications. Éric Lapierre teaches design and theory of architecture at École Nationale Supérieure d'Architecture in Marne-la-Vallée Paris Est, and in École Polytechnique Fédérale de Lausanne (EPFL), and has been guest teacher at Accademia di Architettura di Mendrisio, Université de Montréal (UdM), Université du Québec à Montréal (UQAM), and KU Leuven in Ghent. Among other books, Éric Lapierre has edited Identification d'une ville – Architectures de Paris, 2002; Guide d'architecture de Paris 1900–2008, 2008; Le Point du Jour A Concrete Architecture, 2011; Architecture Of The Real, 2004.

fala atelier
Fala is a naïve architecture practice based in Porto led by Filipe Magalhães, Ana Luisa Soares, and Ahmed Belkhodja. Established in 2013, the atelier works with methodic optimism on a wide range of projects—from territories to birdhouses.

Filip Dujardin
Filip Dujardin studied History of Art at the University of Ghent, with a specialization in architecture, before studying photography at the Academy of Ghent. After training as a technical assistant for Magnum-photographer Carl De Keyzer, he started a professional collaboration with Frederik Vercruysse. In 2007 he established himself as an independent photographer for private and public clients, in the fields of architecture, interior and product design. In 2008 he presented *Fictions*, his first series of independent artworks.

Fiona Connor and Erin Besler
Fiona Connor is a New Zealander born in 1981, currently living and practicing her art in Los Angeles. She received a degree in Fine Arts and History from the University of Auckland, and she earned her Masters in Fine Arts at California Institute of the Arts. Her installations are held by the Auckland City Art Gallery, The Dowse Gallery, the Te Papa in Wellington, the Christchurch Art Gallery, and the Hammer Museum in Los Angeles. Connor's artistic career has displayed a consistent attraction to working in a collaborative way and fluidly between curating, facilitating and object making. An example being the Newspaper Reading Club founded in 2011, and the conversion of her own Los Angeles apartment over 12 months into a gallery titled Laurel Doody in 2016. Connor is now initiating the Varese Group: a loose collective of her associates, mentors, and fellow artists will meet annually in an old house in Marzio, Northern Italy over the next five years for a month starting May, 2017.

Erin Besler was born in Chicago, Illinois in 1982. She is a co-founder of the Los Angeles based practice Besler & Sons. Erin is currently faculty at UCLA in the Department of Architecture and Urban Design where she was the 2013–2014 Teaching Fellow. She holds a Bachelor of Arts from Yale University and a Master of Architecture with distinction from the Southern California Institute of Architecture. Recently she was awarded the Architectural League of New York Young Architects Prize.

First Office
Anna Neimark and Andrew Atwood are founders of First Office in downtown Los Angeles. Built projects include a collaboration on the Pinterest office headquarters in San Francisco, a temporary screening room at the MAK Center for Art and Architecture in Los Angeles, and some small houses. Their texts have been published widely in *Log*, *Perspecta*, *Project*, and *Future Anterior*. Their texts have also been compiled in a Graham Foundation book *Nine Essays*, published with Treatise Press in 2015. That same year, First Office received the Architect's Newspaper Best of Young Architects prize and became a finalist in MoMA PS1's Young Architects Program. Neimark is on the faculty at SCI-Arc. Her work focuses on prehistoric stone formations—called dolmens—and other rude stone monuments. Atwood is Assistant Professor at UC Berkeley. His interests center on techniques of representation as historical and conceptual instruments, specifically in the production of architecture and architectural pedagogy.

formlessfinder
formlessfinder was founded by Garrett Ricciardi and Julian Rose in 2010. The studio was selected as a finalist for the MOMA PS1 Young Architects Program in 2011 and received the 2012 AIA NY New Practices award. Formlessfinder's design work, ranging from residential additions to public pavilions, has been exhibited at institutions such as the Museum of Modern Art in New York, the MAXXI in Rome, the Storefront for Art and Architecture, and Design Miami. They have been featured in publications including *Architecture Record*, *Domus*, *Surface*, *Metropolis*, and *W magazine*. Ricciardi and Rose have lectured on their work at The Cooper Union, Princeton University, University of Chicago, and other universities. They published their *Formless Manifesto* with Lars Muller in 2014. Formlessfinder's recent clients include Design Miami, Museum of Art and Design (NY), Museum of Modern Art (NY), AIA NY Center for Art and Architecture, and Blue Hill Restaurant.

Fosbury Architecture
Fosbury Architecture is a collective of architectural research and design based in Milan and welcomes young architects of different cultures and ambition.

The Fosbury Flop is an undisciplined proposal, but the result of a careful reading. The attitude of the collective is to transform the major limitations of the context (both physical and cultural) in a starting point: playing with innocence within the rules, but afford to react to the existing, to discuss what is being proposed and to expand (or reduce) the field of investigation and its ambitions. To subvert the order of things from the inside, but to propose questions beyond the project.

Fosbury Architecture received awards in several international competitions in Tallin (2013), Porto (2013), Bologna (2014) and Milan (2015). Fosbury Architecture oversaw the research project, *Potlatch* about the role of architects under 30. *Potlatch* currently counts 150 participants from 24 different countries, it has been published in numerous platforms and exhibited at Adhocracy Athens (2015). Fosbury Architecture has edited *Rroark!*, an independent free press initially printed in Milan. Fosbury Architecture recently participated to *Migrant Garden, Untouchable Landscape* [2015] a travelling exhibition which involves 40 selected architecture studios from across the world.

Francois Perrin
Francois Perrin lives and works in Los Angeles, California. He was born in Paris, France, where he earned his professional degree in Architecture. He has completed several residential, commercial and exhibition designs. Concerned with site specificity, his work is always unique to the immediate environmental context and addresses issues of local and sustainable systems. His projects have been featured in *Artforum*, *Domus*, *New York Times*, *Los Angeles Times*, *Wallpaper*, *Sunset*, *Dwell*, and *The Architect's Newspaper*. In addition to his work as a designer, he is also an educator and curator. He has organized several exhibitions including *Dialogues* and *Yves Klein-Air Architecture* at the MAK Center for Art and Architecture and Architectones in several locations. Perrin has taught at UCLA, Art Center College of Design, Cal Poly Pomona, Woodbury University, and Sci-Arc and has lectured on his work internationally including the Jan Van Eyck Akademie, MAK Vienna, Columbia University, USC, UCLA, Universite de Montreal and Ecole Speciale d'Architecture.

Frida Escobedo
Frida Escobedo is principal and founder of an architecture and design studio based in Mexico City. The projects produced at the studio operate within a theoretical framework that addresses time not as a historical calibration but rather a social operation. This expanded temporal reading stems from Henri Bergson's notion of 'social time,' and is materialized in such conceptual works as the *El Eco Pavilion* (2010), *Split Subject* (2013), and *Civic Stage*, presented at the 2013 Lisbon Architecture Triennial. By these measures of practice and thought, social time unfolds across multiple subjects, at multiple speeds and modes of duration.

Frida Escobedo has taught at Columbia University's Graduate School of Architecture, Planning and Preservation; Harvard Graduate School of Design; and the Architectural Association, London. She is the recipient of the 2014 BIAU Prize, the 2016 Architectural Review Emerging Architecture Award, and most recently, the 2017 Architectural League Emerging Voices Award.

Gerard & Kelly
Brennan Gerard & Ryan Kelly have collaborated since 2003. Their installations and performances use choreography, writing, video, and sculpture to address questions of sexuality, memory and the formation of queer consciousness. Their work has been been exhibited internationally at Palais de Tokyo, Paris; Guggenheim Museum, New York; New Museum, New York; Hammer Museum, Los Angeles; and The Kitchen, New York; among other institutions.

Modern Living, an ongoing project exploring queer space, was recently presented by The Glass House, New Canaan, Connecticut, and the MAK Center for Art and Architecture at the Schindler House, Los Angeles, in association with Art Production Fund.

Gerard & Kelly completed the Whitney Museum Independent Study Program in 2010, and received their MFAs in 2013 from the UCLA Department of Art. They have received numerous recognitions for their work, including the 2014 Juried Award from The Bessies as well as grants from the National Dance Project (2015), Art Matters (2014), and the Graham Foundation (2014).

Go Hasegawa
Go Hasegawa is a Japanese architect based in Tokyo. Hasegawa graduated with a Master of Engineering from the Tokyo Institute of Technology in 2002, after which he worked at Taira Nishizawa Architects before establishing Go Hasegawa & Associates in 2005. He has taught as a visiting professor at the Tokyo Institute of Technology, the Academy of Architecture of Mendrisio, Oslo School of Architecture and Design, the University of California in Los Angeles, and, currently, the Harvard University Graduate School of Design. He has received a number of awards—including the 2008 Shinkenchiku Prize and the 2014 AR Design Vanguard—and has made many publications such as *Go Hasegawa Works* (TOTO Publishing, 2012), *Go Hasegawa Conversations with European Architects* (LIXIL Publishing, 2015), and *a+u* in January 2017 as the recent monograph. In 2015, he received his PhD in Engineering from the Tokyo Institute of Technology.

HHF Architects
HHF Architects was founded in 2003 by Tilo Herlach, Simon Hartmann, and Simon Frommenwiler. They have realized numerous projects in Switzerland, Germany, China, France, Mexico, and the U.S. The scope of work ranges from urbanism and large-scale construction to public pavilions and interior design.

From the beginning, HHF was looking for collaborations with other architects and artists to widen its view on projects and enrich the quality of specific proposals. In addition to building, teaching is an important activity for HHF. The principals have taught at numerous international universities such as MIT in Cambridge, UIA in Mexico City, the University of Innsbruck, the University of Karlsruhe, the ENSA Strasbourg, and many others.

HHF was invited to the 13th and 14th Venice Architecture Biennale and has been honored with numerous national and international awards including the Wallpaper Design Award, the German Häuser des Jahres award, the Berlin Architecture Award, and the Swiss Architectural Award.

Iñigo Manglano-Ovalle
Iñigo Manglano-Ovalle is a conceptual artist working across media to create works that are formally seductive, technologically sophisticated, and conceptually rigorous. He is engaged in an investigation of how certain extraordinary forces and systems—both natural and man-made—perpetually reshape our world and challenge our notions of the political and the cultural. He has received numerous awards including the United States Artists Guthman Fellowship 2011, Guggenheim Memorial Foundation Fellowship 2009, John D. and Catherine T. MacArthur Foundation Award 2001, and a fellowship from the National Endowment for the Arts 1995. He has presented major projects at international and U.S. institutions, including most recently: SITE Santa Fe, New Mexico 2014, 2012; Christopher Grimes Gallery, Santa Monica 2015, 2012; Ernst Schering Foundation, Berlin 2013; The Art Institute of Chicago 2011; The Power Plant, Toronto 2011; Massachusetts Museum of Contemporary Art 2009; and Documenta XII, Kassel 2007. He is professor and chair of Art Theory & Practice at Northwestern University.

J.MAYER.H Architects and Philip Ursprung

In 1996, Jürgen Mayer H. founded J.MAYER.H Architects which focuses on the intersection of architecture, communication, and innovative technology. J.MAYER.H has a wide array of completed national and international projects including Metropol Parasol; the redevelopment of the Plaza de la Encarnación in Seville, Spain; the Court of Justice in Hasselt, Belgium; and Pavilion KA300, built in celebration of Karlsruhe's 300th jubilee. He has completed several public and infrastructure projects in Georgia including the Queen Tamar Airport, Mestia; the border checkpoint in Sarpi; and three highway rest stops in Gori and Lochini. Upcoming projects include a parking garage façade in Miami, Florida; the FOM University and the residential high-rise; Rhein740 in Düsseldorf; and VOLT, a new retail and experience complex in the heart of Berlin. From urban planning schemes and buildings to installation work and objects with new materials, the relationship between the human body, technology, and nature form the background for a new production of space.

Philip Ursprung is Professor of the History of Art and Architecture and designated Dean of the Department of Architecture at ETH Zurich. He earned his PhD in Art History at Freie Universität Berlin after studying in Geneva, Vienna and Berlin. He has taught at the Hochschule der Künste Berlin, the GSAPP of Columbia University, the Barcelona Institute of Architecture, and the University of Zürich. He is Principal Investigator of the research project Tourism and Urbanization at Future Cities Laboratory of Singapore ETH Centre, Singapore. He is editor of *Herzog & de Meuron: Natural History* (CCA Montreal and *Baden: Lars Müller*, 2002) and *Caruso St John: Almost Everything* (Barcelona: Poligrafa, 2009). His most recent books are *Allan Kaprow, Robert Smithson, and the Limits to Art* (Berkeley: University of California Press, 2013), *Brexas y conexiones* (Barcelona: Puente Editores, 2016) and *Der Wert der Oberfläche* (Zürich: gta Verlag, 2017).

James Welling

James Welling was born in 1951 in Hartford, Connecticut. He studied at Carnegie Mellon University and the University of Pittsburgh and received his B.F.A. and M.F.A. from the California Institute of the Arts in Valencia, California. Since 2005, his work has been represented by David Zwirner. In 2015, James Welling: Choreograph marked his sixth solo show at the gallery in New York. In 2014, Welling was a recipient of the Infinity Award given by the International Center of Photography, New York. In 2016, he received the Julius Shulman Institute Excellence in Photography Award from Woodbury University, California. From 1995 to 2016, he was Area Head of Photography at UCLA. He is presently a Visiting Professor of Photography at Princeton University.

Welling's work is held in major museum collections, including the Centre Georges Pompidou, Paris; Hammer Museum, Los Angeles; Kunstmuseum Wolfsburg, Germany; Los Angeles County Museum of Art; The Metropolitan Museum of Art, New York; Museum of Contemporary Art Chicago; Museum of Contemporary Art, Los Angeles; Museum of Fine Arts, Boston; The Museum of Modern Art, New York; Solomon R. Guggenheim Museum, New York; Tokyo Metropolitan Museum of Photography; Vancouver Art Gallery; Wadsworth Atheneum Museum of Art, Hartford, Connecticut; and the Whitney Museum of American Art, New York.

Jesús Vassallo

Jesús Vassallo is a Spanish architect and writer. He is currently an assistant professor at Rice University. His work interrogates the problem of realism in architecture through the production of design and scholarship. He is the author of *Seamless: Digital Collage and Dirty Realism in Contemporary Architecture* (Park Books, 2016) and is currently finishing a second manuscript titled *Epics in the Everyday*. His articles have been published internationally in magazines such as *AA Files*, *2G*, *Log*, *Harvard Design Magazine*, *Future Anterior*, *Domus*, *Arquitectura Viva*, and *Arkitektur DK*. Since 2011, he is also an editor of *Circo Magazine*.

Jorge Otero-Pailos

Jorge Otero-Pailos works at the intersection of art, architecture, and preservation. He is Director and Professor of Historic Preservation at Columbia University's Graduate School of Architecture in New York. His work has been commissioned and exhibited by major museums, foundations, and biennials, notably: Artangel, Venice Art Biennial, Victoria and Albert Museum, Louis Vuitton Museum La Galerie, Thyssen-Bornemisza Art Contemporary, and the Yerba Buena Center for the Arts. He is the founder and editor of the journal *Future Anterior*, co-editor of *Experimental Preservation* (2016), author of *Architecture's Historical Turn* (2010), and contributor to scholarly journals and books including the *Oxford Encyclopedia of Aesthetics* and Rem Koolhaas' *Preservation Is Overtaking Us* (2014). He is a member of the Academy of Arts and Sciences of Puerto Rico, the Academy of Science and Culture of Ibero-America. He has received awards from major art, architecture, and preservation organizations including a 2012 UNESCO Eminent Professional Award, the American Institute of Architects, the Kress Foundation, the Graham Foundation, the Fitch Foundation, and the Canadian Center for Architecture.

June14 Meyer-Grohbrügge&Chermayeff

The studio is a collaborative practice between Johanna Meyer-Grohbrügge from Germany and Sam Chermayeff from New York. The two met at SANAA in Tokyo where they worked from 2005 to 2010. Their new venture, June14 Meyer-Grohbrügge&Chermayeff, begins with a desire to make things, places, and atmospheres for people. Their office and work aims to have people relate to architecture, for architecture to relate to people, and for people to relate to themselves. June14 searches for an understanding of different ways of living and working in the contemporary world. The work stems from a belief that architecture can make things happen and that things can happen to architecture. The office is an exchange with its users. It is open to new ideas. On a practical level, the principals have experience with a wide range of projects from small gardens and bespoke furniture to office towers. The office's intention is to expand that range while maintaining a dynamic understanding of the human scale. The office is based in Berlin and New York.

junya ishigami+associates

Born in Kanagawa, Japan, Junya Ishigami graduated from Tokyo University of the Arts with an MFA in Architecture in 2000 and joined Kazuyo Sejima & Associates. In 2004, he founded junya.ishigami + associates. The firm gained considerable international recognition following the completion of the Kanagawa Institute of Technology's KAIT Workshop in 2008 and has won several awards, including the Bauwelt Prize (2009), the Architectural Institute of Japan Prize (2009), and the Golden Lion for Best Project of the 12th International Architecture Exhibition of the Venice Biennale (2010). Ongoing projects include the reconstruction of the Russian Polytechnic Museum in Moscow, as well as the first prize-winning projects Park Groot Vijversburg in the Netherlands, Port of Kinmen Passenger Service Center in Taiwan, and Cloud Arch in Australia. In 2014 Ishigami was the Kenzo Tange Design Critic at the Harvard Graduate School of Design, and in 2015 he was a visiting professor at the Princeton University School of Architecture.

Karamuk * Kuo

Karamuk * Kuo was established in 2010 by Jeannette Kuo and Uenal Karamuk who bring their international background and diverse building experiences to their design process. Foregrounding the relationship of space and program, each project is approached with the optimism that architecture is the translation of fresh ideas into reality.

The office works on projects of a range of scales—from spatial installations and exhibitions to complex multi-family housing projects—and is always looking for new creative opportunities. In addition, both partners are committed to intellectual pursuits in design research and have been teaching since 2006 at various universities in the U.S. and Switzerland. Jeannette is currently Assistant Professor in Practice at Harvard University's Graduate School of Design.

Keith Krumwiede

Keith Krumwiede is Associate Professor of Architecture in the College of Architecture and Design at the New Jersey Institute of Technology, where he directs the graduate program in architecture. Krumwiede has written about the sub-networks and porous enclaves of Los Angeles, the almost viral annexations pattern of Texas cities, and the sophisticated and sinister practices of homebuilders. Recent essays include "The Bauhaus Tweets" in *Log 22: The Absurd* and "(A)Typical Plan(s)" in *Perspecta 43: Taboo*. Prior to teaching at NJIT, he taught at Otis College of Art and Design in Los Angeles; Konstfack University College of Arts, Crafts and Design in Stockholm; Rice University in Houston; and Yale University, where he was awarded the King-Lui Wu Award for Distinguished Teaching. In 2009, Professor Krumwiede was one of the first recipients of a research grant from The Hines Research Fund for Advanced Sustainability in Architectural Design at Yale University for his work on high density, high performance wood housing in the United States.

Kéré Architecture

Francis Kéré is a German-trained architect from the small, West African town of Gando in Burkina Faso. Parallel to his studies, he founded the Kéré Foundation (formerly Schulbausteine für Gando e.V.) to fund the construction of the Gando Primary School, which earned the prestigious Aga Khan Award in 2001. Kéré continues to reinvest knowledge back into Burkina Faso and sites across four different continents. He has developed innovative construction strategies that combine traditional materials and building techniques with modern engineering methods. Since founding Kéré Architecture in 2005, his work has earned numerous prestigious awards such as the Global Award for Sustainable Architecture, BSI Swiss Architectural Award, Marcus Prize, Global Holcim Gold Award, and Schelling Architecture Award. Kéré was granted the honor of chartered membership of the Royal Institute of British Architects (RIBA) in 2009 and honorary fellowship of the American Institute of Architects (FAIA) in 2012. He has held professorships at the Harvard Graduate School of Design and the Swiss Accademia di Architettura di Mendrisio.

Kuehn Malvezzi
Simona Malvezzi, Wilfried Kuehn, and Johannes Kuehn founded Kuehn Malvezzi in Berlin in 2001. Public spaces and exhibitions are the main focus of their work. They realized the architectural design for Documenta 11 and the Julia Stoschek Collection in Dusseldorf, which was nominated for the Mies van der Rohe Award. The firm has designed the reorganization of a number of art collections and dealt with sensitive preservation issues for listed buildings such as the Museum Belvedere in Vienna and the Berggruen Collection in Berlin. Kuehn Malvezzi won the international competition for the inter-religious House of One in Berlin in 2012 and for the Insectarium in Montreal in 2014. In 2017, they will complete a new venue for the Moderne Galerie at the Saarlandmuseum. Their projects have been shown in the 10th, 13th, and 14th Architecture Biennale in Venice, the Manifesta 7 in Trento, and the inaugural Chicago Architecture Biennial.

LAN with Franck Boutté Consultants and produced by Pavillon de l'Arsenal Paris
LAN (Local Architecture Network) was created by Benoît Jallon and Umberto Napolitano in 2002, with the idea of exploring architecture as an area of activity at the intersection of several disciplines. This attitude has developed into a methodology enabling LAN to explore new territories and forge a vision encompassing social, urban, functional and formal questions. LAN's projects seek to find elegant, contemporary answers to creative and pragmatic concerns. The firm's projects give shape to this universe at different scales and through very diverse programs.
    LAN is in charge of the extension and renovation of the Grand Palais in Paris, the construction of the Maillon Theater in Strasbourg, and the development and coordination of new neighborhoods in Bordeaux and Nantes.

Created in 2007 by Franck Boutté, engineer and architect, Franck Boutté Consultants is comprised of about thirty engineers, architects and urban planners, often with hybrid profiles, working in Paris, but also Bordeaux and Nantes. Covering a broad spectrum of disciplines and skills—bioclimatism and passive strategies, comfort, environment, health, optimization of resources, energy, water, skin design, natural ventilation, modeling and simulation, renewable energies, carbon and LCA approach, French and foreign environmental certifications—Franck Boutté Consultants operates at all scales, from material to territory.

Created in 1988, Pavillon de l'Arsenal, Center of information, documentation and exhibition of Town planning and Architecture of Paris

and Parisian metropolis, is a unique place where the arrangement of the city and its architectural realizations are put within the reach of all.
    The main activities of the Pavillon de l'Arsenal are to exhibit Parisian and metropolitan architecture and urban-planning; to give visitors the most accurate documentation possible; to publish reference books on topics affecting the day-to-day life of Parisians and to provide a forum for the individuals and authorities involved in shaping the city. The Pavillon de l'Arsenal aims to allow a large public to understand the evolution of Paris and its projects. In order to preserve the balance of the Parisian cityscape, today's planners must use an urbanism centered on proximity issues involving dialogue and concerted actions.

Luisa Lambri
Luisa Lambri is an artist who currently lives in Milan. Her work has been included in the Venice Art Biennale in 1999 and 2003, and in the Venice Architecture Biennale in 2004 and 2010. Solo exhibitions include the Menil Collection, Houston; the Baltimore Museum of Art; the Hammer Museum of Art in Los Angeles; the Isabella Stewart Gardner Museum, Boston. Lambri's work has been included in thematic exhibitions at the Carnegie Museum of Art, Pittsburgh; the Museum of Contemporary Art, Chicago; the Solomon R. Guggenheim Museum, New York; the Museum of Contemporary Art, Los Angeles; the Los Angeles County Museum of Art; the J. Paul Getty Museum, Los Angeles; the Wexner Center for the Arts, Columbus; the Aldrich Contemporary Art Museum, Ridgefield; the Tamayo Museum, Mexico City; the Museum of Modern Art, Sao Paulo; Tate Liverpool; and the Henry Moore Institute, Leeds, among others.

Lütjens Padmanabhan Architekten
Lütjens Padmanabhan Architekten was established by Oliver Lütjens and Thomas Padmanabhan in 2007. The recent work of the practice focuses on housing in the residential districts surrounding the cities of Zürich, Basel and Munich. Despite their love for a more refined, urbane architecture, Oliver Lütjens and Thomas Padmanabhan have light-heartedly embraced the fact that most of their commissions are set in the mundane anonymity of suburbia. Their interest in complex architectural expression has distanced the practice from the craft-oriented mainstream of Swiss architecture. Their current projects explore the impossible task of reconciling the autonomy of the exterior facade with the typological uncertainty of interior spaces and loose urban contexts.
    After teaching assignments at ETH Zürich and TU Munich Oliver Lütjens and Thomas Padmanbhan are currently teaching as guest professors at EPF Lausanne.

Machine Project
Mark Allen is an artist, educator and curator based in Los Angeles. He is the founder and executive director of Machine Project, a place for artists to do fun experiments, together with the public, in ways that influence culture. Machine Project supports collaborative and interdisciplinary artistic practices that broaden the audience for innovative, experimental contemporary art and remove traditional barriers to participation. Under his direction Machine has produced shows with the Los Angeles County Museum of Art, The Hammer Museum at UCLA, the Museum

of Contemporary Art in Denver, the Walker Museum in Minneapolis and the Tang Teaching Museum in Saratoga Springs, New York. He has produced over 1000 events in Los Angeles at the Machine Project storefront space.

Made In
François Charbonnet and Patrick Heiz are co-founders of the architecture studio Made In, based in Geneva, Switzerland. After graduating from the ETH Zurich, they collaborated with Herzog & de Meuron and OMA before setting up their own office in 2003. In addition to their practice, they are frequent lecturers and have been visiting professors at the EPF Lausanne (2010–2011), the ETH Zurich (2011–2013), and the Accademia di Archittetura, Mendrisio (2014–2015).

MAIO
MAIO is an architectural office based in Barcelona examining spatial systems that allow theoretical and practical positions to converge. The practice has developed a wide range of projects and scales: from furniture or exhibition design to housing blocks or urban planning. MAIO was founded in 2012 by Maria Charneco, Alfredo Lérida, Guillermo López, and Anna Puigjaner. They combine professional activities with academic, research, and editorial projects. They have been in charge of the magazine *Quaderns d'Arquitectura i Urbanisme* (2011–2016) and teach at Barcelona School of Architecture – UPC. MAIO has lectured at institutions such as MET Museum, GSAPP, Yale University, Berkeley University, FAU Lisboa, and Brussels UCL-LOCI. MAIO's works have been published in international magazines such as *Domus*, *A10*, *Monocle*, *Frame*, and *Detail* among others. They have exhibited at Biennale di Venezia, MOMA, and at Art Institute of Chicago. They have received awards including the FAD Award and the Harvard University Wheelwright Prize.

Marianne Mueller
Marianne Mueller is a Zurich-based artist working mostly with photography, video, installation, and books. She collects observations of quotidian environments that she recontextualizes in her works, often in reaction to the specific site of an exhibition. She is a professor at the Zurich University of the Arts. Her publications include *The Flock* (2004), *The Proper Ornaments* (2008), and *Stairs Etc.* (2014).

Marshall Brown
Marshall Brown is a licensed architect, principal of Marshall Brown Projects, and an associate professor at the IIT College of Architecture. Brown is a Graham Foundation grantee and recently exhibited at the 2016 Venice Architecture Biennale. He has also exhibited at the Arts Club of Chicago, the Museum of Contemporary Art Detroit, and Western Exhibitions. In 2016, he appeared in the PBS documentary *Ten Towns that Changed America*. His projects and essays have appeared in several books and journals including Metropolis, Crain's, Architectural Record, The New York Daily News, Art Papers, and The Believer. Brown has lectured at the Cranbrook Academy of Art, University of Michigan, Northwestern University, Harvard, the Frank Lloyd Wright School of Architecture, and, most recently, at Princeton University with a lecture titled *The Architecture of Creative Miscegenation*.

335

MG&Co.
Noëmi Mollet and Reto Geiser are the founding partners of the Houston based collaborative design practice MG&Co., which develops spatial strategies in a range of scales from the book to the house. Both were trained as architects at ETH Zurich, where Geiser also received a PhD from the Institute for the History and Theory of Architecture (gta). He has taught in the United States and in Europe, and is currently the Gus Wortham Assistant Professor at the Rice University School of Architecture. Oscillating between theory and practice and taking on the different roles of designers, scholars, curators, editors, and publishers has allowed MG&Co. to explore the boundaries between design and research and to negotiate the productive intersections between architecture, installation, and typography. Their work has been recognized by the Swiss Federal Office of Culture, the German Architecture Museum, Stiftung Buchkunst, and the American Institute of Graphic Arts.

Monadnock
Monadnock is a Rotterdam-based practice producing architecture. Monadnock designs, researches, writes, and produces discourse in the fields of architecture, urbanism, interior, and staging, shifting in scale between the space of the city and the street to the scale of the interior. Monadnock was found in 2006 by Job Floris and Sandor Naus. Both founders were trained as interior and furniture designers during their studies at the Academy of Fine Arts St. Joost in Breda (NL) and subsequently graduated from the Academy for Architecture and Urbanism in Rotterdam and Tilburg. Monadnock received international attention for realizing tailor-made buildings, many of which are public. These include a beach pavilion on the River Maas, a huge installation called *Make No Little Plans*, and a landmark—or viewing tower—for the municipality of Nieuw Bergen (NL). Currently, Monadnock is involved in projects on several scales, including a new visitors' centre for De Hoge Veluwe National Park (NL), a private tower residence, and two substantial housing projects.

MOS
MOS is a New York-based architecture studio founded by principals Hilary Sample and Michael Meredith in 2005. An internationally recognized architecture practice, MOS was the recipient of the 2015 Cooper Hewitt, Smithsonian Design Museum National Design Award in Architecture and the 2010 American Academy of Arts and Letters Architecture Award. Individual works have similarly received numerous awards and distinctions, most notably: the 2015 Global Holcim Award for sustainable construction for Community Center No. 3 (Lali Gurans Orphanage); the 2014 accession of the firm's modular, off-grid House No. 5 (Museum of Outdoor Arts Element House) into the MoMA, Architecture and Design Collection; and the acquisition of House No. 3 (Lot No. 6 / Ordos) into the permanent collection of The Art Institute of Chicago. Recent work includes: Store No. 2 (Chamber) in Chelsea, NYC; House No. 10, currently under-construction; School No. 2, a competition proposal for the Institute for Advanced Study Commons Building; and Housing No. 4 at the Dequindre Cut, Detroit. Recent and forthcoming publications include *MOS: Selected Works* (2016), *An Unfinished Encyclopedia of Scale Figures Without Architecture* (forthcoming), and an *a+u* monograph (forthcoming).

Norman Kelley
Norman Kelley is an architecture and design collaborative founded by Carrie Norman and Thomas Kelley. The practice was established in 2012 and is operated jointly between New York City and Chicago. Carrie Norman (B.Arch University of Virginia, M.Arch Princeton University) is a licensed architect and an adjunct assistant professor at Columbia University GSAPP and the New Jersey Institute of Technology. Thomas Kelley (B.Arch University of Virginia, M.Arch Princeton University) is a fellow of the American Academy in Rome and an assistant professor at the University of Illinois at Chicago's School of Architecture. Together, their work reexamines architecture's relationship to vision and prompts its observers to look closely. Their design work is currently represented by Volume Gallery in Chicago.

Nuno Brandão Costa and André Cepeda
Nuno Brandão Costa is a Portuguese architect and educator who practices and teaches in Porto. Nuno's work was included in the Portuguese representation of the 8th Venice Biennale International Exhibition, the São Paulo Architecture Biennale, Portugal Now at Cornell University in New York, Tradition is Innovation in Tokyo, and the Milan Architecture Triennale. He was a nominee for the Mies van der Rohe Award and for the BSI–Swiss Architectural Award. He was awarded the Secil Prize and the Vale da Gândara Prize. He was a guest teacher at ETSA in Universidad de Navarra, in Taller Barozzi at the University of Girona, and at the EHL Campus Lausanne.

André Cepeda lives and works in Porto, Portugal, and has exhibited his work in several galleries, museums and art institutions, as: The Faulconer Gallery, Grinnell, Iowa, USA; Museo de Arte Contemporánea de Vigo; Haus der Photographie, Hamburg; Kasseler Fotoforum, Kassel; Galerie Invaliden 1, Berlin; Standard/deluxe, Lausanne; The Mews-Projeto Espaço, London; Galleri Image, Aarhus; Wohnungsfrage-Haus der Kulturen der Welt, Berlin; Museu Oscar Niemeyer, Rio de Janeiro; MASP- Museu de Arte de São Paulo; Serralves Contemporary Art Museum, Porto; CGAC-Centro Galego de Arte Contemporánea, Santiago de Compostela, Galicia; Calouste Gulbenkian Foundation, Lisbon; Le Bal, Paris.
In 2012 he was artist in residence at the FAAP, São Paulo and in 2016 he was artist in residency at the Residency Unlimited, in Brooklyn NY. André gives a one week workshop every year at the Photography School CEPV, Vevey, Switzerland and is work is represented by Cristina Guerra Contemporary Art in Lisbon, Galeria Pedro Oliveira in Porto and Benrubi Gallery in New York.

OFFICE Kersten Geers David Van Severen with Peter Wächtler and Michaël Van den Abeele
OFFICE Kersten Geers David Van Severen is one of the most interesting and uncompromising young architectural practices at work today. It is renowned for its idiosyncratic architecture, in which utopian and unrealized projects are also customary. It does not invent the architecture, but reflects and considers what architecture can signify and be today, reducing the discipline to its bareness and essence. Their architectonic ideas start from geometrical corrections and rather rigid classifications, in order to

measure the world as it presents itself to us and to allow life to unfold in all its complexities. OFFICE Kersten Geers David Van Severen was founded in 2002 by Kersten Geers and David Van Severen.

Peter Wächtler has recently had solo exhibitions at Schinkel Pavillon, Berlin (2017), M HKA, Antwerp (2017), Chisenhale Gallery, London (2016), Renassaince Society, Chicago (2016), Reena Spaulings, New York (2014), Westfälischer Kunstverein, Munster (2014), and dépendance, Brussels (2013). His work has been featured in numerous international group exhibitions, including *The Absent Museum*, WIELS, Brussels (2017), *L'Almanach 16*, Le Consortium, Dijon (2016), *2015 Triennial: Surround Audience* at the New Museum, New York (2015), the Liverpool Biennial (2014), La Biennale de Lyon 2013, and *Pride Goes Before a Fall – Beware of a Holy Whore* at Artists Space, New York (2013). The SOTOSO project was an artist-run apartment exhibition coordinated by Peter Wächtler and Hans-Christian Lotz (2011–2014) A book of his texts, *Come On*, was published in 2013 by Sternberg Press.

Michaël Van den Abeele is a Brussels based artist with a practice that combines painting, furniture pieces and the writing of lyrical essays. He is equally a member of the Brussels based exhibition-space Etablissement d'en face. Recent exhibitions include *The Squater* at Gaudel de Stampa, Paris, France; *P P P Punctual* at Galerie Levy Delval, Brussels, Belgium, *Relax* at Galerie Trampoline Antwerp, Belgium, and *Opacity Please* at the Museum Leuven, Belgium. He recently published *Forked Apologies* with FOREST publications.

Pascal Flammer
Pascal Flammer works and lives in Zurich. He opened his office in 2005. He received the Swiss Art Award, the Weissenhof Architecture Award, and the Best Family House Award. He has taught at the Accademia di Architettura di Mendrisio, the GSD at Harvard University, the Sandberg Instituut in Amsterdam, and the ETH in Zurich.

Paul Andersen and Paul Preissner
Paul Andersen and Paul Preissner are Chicago-based architects who first worked together on a pair of barns in Denver's primary urban park for the Biennial of the Americas. Ordinarily, they run separate offices that invest in formal and informal work, with associations with pop and alternative cultures. Their collaborative work combines their different interests and results in thoughtful, and sometimes polemical, speculative and built projects. Their collaborative title is Paul and Paul, and their work has been published in the *Chicago Tribune*, *Domus*, *Architectural Record*, *PLOT*, and numerous other national and international publications. The office was recognized with a Chicago AIA Honor Award for its pavilion for the Biennial of the Americas (2013).

Pezo von Ellrichshausen
Pezo von Ellrichshausen is an art and architecture studio founded in 2002 by Mauricio Pezo and Sofia von Ellrichshausen. They live and work in the southern Chilean city of Concepción and teach regularly at the IIT in Chicago. Their work has been distinguished with several international awards, edited in monographic publications and widely exhibited, among other venues, at the Venice Biennale, the Royal Academy of Arts in London and at the MoMA in New York.

Philipp Schaerer
Philipp Schaerer is a visual artist and architect. He graduated from the ETH Lausanne. His work is at the intersection between architecture, photography, and graphic design. Philipp worked from 2000 to 2006 as an architect and knowledge manager for Herzog & de Meuron. During this time he created many well-known architectural illustrations for the studio that substantially influenced the visual language of today's established architectural visualizations. Until 2008, he was responsible for the Postgraduate Studies in CAAD at the Chair of Prof. Dr. Ludger Hovestadt at the ETH Zurich. Since 2008, he has been a lecturer at several universities and—since 2014—a visiting professor at the ETH Lausanne. His work has been widely published and exhibited and is represented in several public and private collections such as the collection of the MoMA, the ZKM Center for Art and Media Technology, and the Fotomuseum Winterthur. Philipp Schaerer lives and works in Zurich and Steffisburg, Switzerland.

Philippe Rahm architectes
Philippe Rahm is a Swiss architect, principal in the office of Philippe Rahm architectes, based in Paris, France. His work, which extends the field of architecture from the physiological to the meteorological, has received an international audience in the context of sustainability. He began teaching architecture design at the GSD, Harvard University, USA, in Fall 2014. In 2002, Mr. Rahm was chosen to represent Switzerland at the 8th Architecture Biennale in Venice, and was one of the 25 Manifesto's Architects of Aaron Betsky's 2008 Architectural Venice Biennale. He is nominee in 2009 for the Ordos Prize in China and in 2010 and 2008 for the International Chernikov Prize in Moscow where he was ranked in the top ten.

PIOVENEFABI and Giovanna Silva
PIOVENEFABI is an office based in Milan, which works in national and international context in the fields of architecture, urban research and design. Founded in 2012 by Ambra Fabi and Giovanni Piovene, the office work has been exhibited in the following venues: Trienal de Arquitectura de Lisboa (2013 and 2016), Rotterdam Biennale (2014), Chicago Architecture Biennial (2015), Campo (Rome, 2016) and Frac Orleans (2017). The office will co-curate the next Lisbon Architecture Triennale in 2019, together with Eric Lapierre, Sebastien Marot, Mariabruna Fabrizi and Fosco Lucarelli.

Giovanna Silva is an Italian photographer, based in Milano. She holds a Master of Science in Architecture from Politecnico di Milano and a Master in Cultural Anthropology, Ethnology, Ethnolinguistics from Università Ca' Foscari, Venezia. She has always used photography for editorial purposes, first in magazines and later on in her publications. She established her own publishing house, Humboldt Books, so that she could also work with other photographers as an editor. She sees photographs as an instrument to build narration; using them to tell stories often accompanied by texts.

Point Supreme
Point Supreme was founded by Greek architects Konstantinos Pantazis and Marianna Rentzou, after they studied and worked in Athens, London, Rotterdam, Brussels, and Tokyo. Their urban projects have been exhibited at the 2012 Venice Architecture Biennale. The office has won the first prize at Europan 10 for a social housing and masterplan in Trondheim, Norway, and they recently built a public space in Tel Aviv.
In 2012, Point Supreme was included by LIFO newspaper among the 20 most influential personalities in Greece.

PRODUCTORA
PRODUCTORA is a Mexico City based Architecture Office. Integrated by the architects Abel Perles, Carlos Bedoya, Victor Jaime and Wonne Ickx. PRODUCTORA's work is distinguished by its interest in precise geometry, legible projects, clear gestures, and the search for timeless buildings in their own material and programmatic resolutions. Currently, the office is working on several projects in Mexico and abroad, from residential to public and corporate buildings. Its work has been present in Architectural Biennials and museums of different countries around the world. It has been awarded by the Architectural League NY with the Young Architects Forum in 2007 and the Emerging Voices in 2013. PRODUCTORA also collaborates frequently with local and international artists and curators. In 2011, PRODUCTORA along with curator and art critic Ruth Estevez, founded 'LIGA, Space for Architecture', a platform that promotes young and emerging Latin-American architecture.

REAL Foundation
REAL is an architectural and cultural institute founded by Jack Self. Its activities include events, exhibitions, publications, design, and architecture. It promotes social equality and examines conditions of ownership, capital, and labour. REAL publishes *Real Review* and previously curated the British Pavilion at the 2016 Venice Biennale.

SADAR+VUGA
SADAR+VUGA was founded by Jurij Sadar and Boštjan Vuga in Ljubljana in 1996. Over nearly two decades it has focused on open, innovative, and integral architectural design and urban planning. The office has been driven by a quest for quality. They carry a strong belief that forward-leaping architectural production contributes to our well-being, and generates a sensitive and responsive development of the physical context we live in—broadening our imagination and stimulating our senses.
Their portfolio of built work ranges from innovative town planning to public space sculpture, from interactive new public buildings to interventions within older existing structures. Their client base reflects their diversity of built and project experience: ranging from Municipal Councils and Central Government to encompass national and private arts bodies and multinationals to the best developers in Slovenia and abroad.

Sam Jacob Studio
Sam Jacob is principal of Sam Jacob Studio for architecture and design. His work spans scales and disciplines ranging from master planning and urban design through architecture, design, and art projects. Previously, Sam was a founding director of FAT Architecture where he was involved in many internationally acclaimed projects including the BBC drama production village in Cardiff, the Heerlijkheid Hoogvliet park and cultural center in Rotterdam, and the curation of the British Pavilion at the 2014 Venice Biennale. He has exhibited at leading galleries and museums including the Victoria & Albert Museum in London, the MAK in Vienna. Sam is also a contributing editor for *Icon magazine* and a columnist for both *Art Review* and *Dezeen*. He is a regular participant in talks and events for institutions such as MoMA, the Southbank Centre, and the Soane Museum.
Jacob is Professor of Architecture at the University of Illinois at Chicago, a visiting professor at the Yale School of Architecture, and Director of Night School at the Architectural Association

SAMI-arquitectos
SAMI-arquitectos was established in 2005 by Inês Vieira da Silva and Miguel Vieira. Its projects are informed by a sensitive approach to place and a careful reading of history and tradition in a quiet but eloquent dialogue between space, material, and place. The practice has won recognition from architectural critics and numerous national and international awards, among them the BSI Swiss Architectural Award 2016 in which they were finalists, the European Award Architectural Heritage AADIPA (2015), the X BIAU and IX BIAU Award (2014, 2016), the Tektónica/OA National Architecture Prize (2009), and second prize for the National Prize of Architecture in Wood 2011 Award.

Sauter von Moos
Sauter von Moos is an architecture studio established in Basel, Switzerland, in 2010, by Florian Sauter and Charlotte von Moos. The studio engages in work on all scales, both in theory and practice. Amongst their best-known projects are the House with a Tree (Basel, 2013) that received the Swiss Architecture Award in 2015, the competition entry for a Natural History Museum and City Archive (Basel, 2015) and several pivotal exhibition contributions (e.g. *Books for Architects*, gta Exhibitions, 2015). Besides their practical activities, both partners have been engaged in teaching and research, amongst others at ETH Zurich, the Accademia di Architettura in Mendrisio and Harvard GSD. As co-editors and authors they have published a series of books including *Earth Water Air Fire* (Actar, 2014) and *achtung: die Landschaft* (Lars Müller Publishers, 2015), while *Painting the Sky Black: Louis Kahn and the Architectonization of Nature* (de Gruyter Open) is forthcoming this year.

Scott Fortino
Scott Fortino developed his approach to photography out of experiences directly related to his position as a Chicago police officer. This work led to the publication of his monograph, Institutional, which depicted seemingly impersonal architectural spaces while revealing the embedded evidence of personal use. He received his MFA from the University of Illinois at Chicago and a BA from Columbia College Chicago. He has had solo exhibitions in Chicago at the Museum of Contemporary Art and the Museum of Contemporary Photography. His work is in the collections of the Art Institute of Chicago, Milwaukee Art Museum, Worcester Art Museum and the Museum of Contemporary Photography, and numerous public and private collections. He lives and works in Chicago.

Sergison Bates
Established in 1996, Sergison Bates architects have earned a reputation as one of the UK's leading architectural practices by successfully engaging with all dimensions of architectural and urban design. The main office in London is

international in outlook and staff composition, and in 2010 a second office was opened in Zürich. Both offices are currently involved in a wide range of international projects ranging from urban planning to regeneration, public buildings, housing and private houses.

Sergison Bates' projects are informed by a sensitive approach to place, the experiential potential of materials and construction and a concern for the environmental, social and economic aspects of sustainability. They aspire to create a design-led architecture that is contemporary and rooted in its context, at all scales, and are committed to a research-based approach, supported by the partners' academic work.

The practice has won recognition from architectural critics and numerous national and international awards—among them the Erich Schelling Prize and Heinrich Tessenow Gold Medal.

Serie Architects
Christopher Lee is the co-founder and principal of Serie Architects and Associate Professor in Practice at Harvard University's Graduate School of Design. His research, writings, and teaching on the embedded intelligence and cultural values of building types underpin the work of Serie. With offices in London, Mumbai, Singapore, and Beijing, the practice has gained a reputation for designing distinctive buildings in the public realm. The work of Serie is known for its organizational intelligence, elegance, and contextual engagement and has been recognized through many prestigious awards, including the BD Young Architect of the Year Award, Architectural Record Design Vanguard, World Architecture Festival Award, and the Leading European Architects Review. Serie is currently working on a string of high-profile, civic and cultural buildings including the new Singapore State Courts Complex; the new School of Design & Environment; the National University of Singapore; the International Institute of Human Settlement, India; and the Jameel Art Centre.

Shingo Masuda + Katsuhisa Otsubo Architects
Shingo Masuda + Katsuhisa Otsubo Architects is a Tokyo-based architecture firm. The firm's work has won numerous architectural prizes including runner-up in the AR Emerging Architecture Awards from Architectural Review in 2011 and winner of the AR Emerging Architecture Awards from Architectural Review in 2014. They were selected to be part of the team for the Japanese Pavilion of the Venice Biennale 2016 where they received special mention. Their works have been published across the world, in publications including *Japan Architect*, *Global Architecture*, and *Architecture Review*. Masuda graduated with a bachelor of arts in architecture from Musashino Art University, and has been a lecturer and critic in the department of architecture at the Musashino Art University since 2010 and was the Baird Visiting Critic at Cornell University in 2015. Otsubo graduated with a bachelor of arts in architecture from Tokyo University of Fine Art and Music.

SO-IL and Ana Prvački
In her videos, services, concoctions and drawings, Ana Prvački uses a gently pedagogical and comedic approach in an attempt to reconcile etiquette and erotics. She aims for a conceptual practice with a low carbon footprint. Florian Idenburg is founder of SO-IL, an architecture firm in New York.

Stan Allen Architect
Stan Allen Architect has realized buildings and urban projects in the United States, Latin America, and Asia. Responding to the complexity of the modern city in creative ways, Stan Allen has developed a catalog of innovative design strategies, in particular looking at field theory, landscape architecture, and ecology as models to revitalize the practice of architecture. In 2016, he was one of twelve architects representing the United States in *The Architectural Imagination*, the American Pavilion at the Venice Biennale. In addition to this urban-scale work, we have recently completed a number of studios and houses for artists and collectors in the Hudson River Valley. These two complementary scales will be documented in *Four Projects: A Stan Allen Sourcebook* to be published in 2017 by ORO Publishers.

Studio Anne Holtrop
Anne Holtrop practices architecture between Amsterdam and Bahrain. His work ranges from models to temporary spaces and buildings. In 2015, the first two major buildings—the Museum Fort Vechten and the National Pavilion of the Kingdom of Bahrain—were completed. In 2016, Anne Holtrop co-curated and designed the Bahrain Pavilion at the Venice Architecture Biennial: *Places of Production, Aluminium*. The studio is currently working on the conservation and new additions of fourteen historic buildings in Muharraq and Manama including the redevelopment of the public streets and squares of the Sheikh Ebrahim Center. He is currently guest professor at the Accademia di Architettura di Mendrisio in Switzerland. For his practice, Anne has been awarded several grants from the Mondrian Fund. For his practice he has been awarded several grants from the Mondrian Fund, as well as receiving the Charlotte Kohler Prize for Architecture from the Prins Bernhard Cultuurfonds in 2007. Holtrop won the prestigious Iakov Chernikhov International Prize 2014. The 2G monograph series dedicated its seventy-third issue to Studio Anne Holtrop.

Studio Gang
Founded by MacArthur Fellow Jeanne Gang, Studio Gang is an architecture and urban design practice with offices in Chicago and New York. We work as a collective of more than 90 architects, designers, and planners. We collaborate closely with our clients, expert consultants, and specialists from a range of fields to design and realize innovative projects at multiple scales: architecture, urbanism, interiors, and exhibitions. We use design as a medium to connect people socially, experientially, and intellectually.

Studio Mumbai
Founded by Bijoy Jain, Studio Mumbai works with a human infrastructure of skilled artisans, technicians, and draftsmen who design and build the work directly. This group shares an environment created from an iterative process where ideas are explored through large-scale mock-ups, models, material studies, sketches, and drawings. Through careful consideration of place and practice, projects draw on traditional skills, local building techniques, materials, and an ingenuity arising from limited resources.

Bijoy Jain was born in Mumbai in 1965 and received his M. Arch from Washington University in 1990. He worked in Los

Angeles and London between 1989 and 1995, returning to India in 1995 to found his practice. The work of Studio Mumbai has been presented at the XII Venice Biennale and the Victoria & Albert Museum. In 2014, the University of Hasselt, Belgium bestowed an honorary doctorate on Bijoy Jain. He has taught in Copenhagen, at Yale, and in Mendrisio.

Sylvia Lavin
Sylvia Lavin is a critic, historian and curator whose work explores the limits of architecture across a wide spectrum of historical periods. She is Professor, Director of PhD Programs and former Chair of the Department of Architecture and Urban Design at UCLA and has taught at Princeton, Harvard, and Columbia among other schools. She is a is a frequent contributor to journals such as Artforum, Perspecta and Log and among her books are *Form Follows Libido: Architecture and Richard Neutra in a Psychoanalytic Culture, Kissing Architecture and Flash in the Pan.* Curated exhibitions include *Everything Loose Will Land: Art and Architecture in Los Angeles in the 1970s, The New Creativity* and *The Artless Drawing.* She has been recognized by many grants and awards, most recently from the American Academy of Arts and Letters, the Getty Research Institute and the Graham Foundation. She is currently working on *The Duck and The Document: True Stories of Postmodern Procedures*, an exhibition that originated at the Princeton School of Architecture Gallery as Salvage, will be opening at the SCI-Arc Gallery in 2017 and in an expanded form at the Canadian Center for Architecture in 2018.

T + E + A + M
T + E + A + M is an architecture practice led by Thom Moran, Ellie Abrons, Adam Fure, and Meredith Miller. Their work focuses on materiality, image, and digital environments. Current projects include a full-scale installation that tests an experimental approach to material reuse and a temporary pavilion that makes concrete the immaterial aspects of digital production. T + E + A + M has exhibited at the 2016 Venice Biennale, Storefront for Art and Architecture in New York, Museum of Contemporary Art Detroit, and Current Space Gallery in Baltimore.

Tatiana Bilbao Estudio
Tatiana Bilbao tries to understand, through the work of her multicultural and multidisciplinary office, the place that surrounds us in order to translate its rigid codes into architecture. Her projects strive to regenerate spaces to humanize them as a reaction to global capitalism, opening up niches for cultural and economic development. Her work includes a botanical garden, a master plan and open chapel for a pilgrimage route, a biotechnological center for a tech institution, a house built with US$5,000, and a funeral home. Bilbao was the recipient of the Kunstpreis Berlin in 2012 and the Global Award for Sustainable Architecture in 2013 and was named an Emerging Voice by the Architectural League of New York in 2009. Her work is part of the collection of the Centre George Pompidou in Paris, France, and the Heinz Architectural Center at the Carnegie Museum of Art. She is currently a visiting professor at the Yale School of Architecture and has been published in *a+u*, *Domus*, and the *New York Times*, among others.

Tham & Videgård Arkitekter
Tham & Videgård Arkitekter is based in Stockholm, Sweden and directed by co-founders and chief architects, Bolle Tham and Martin Videgård. Founded in 1999, the practice has won several national and international architecture awards and has attracted attention for its experimental and innovative projects. Major completed works include the New School of Architecture at the Royal Institute of Technology (KTH) in Stockholm, the Kalmar Museum of Art, the Moderna Museet Malmö (the Swedish Museum of Modern Art), the Västra Kajen housing, the Archipelago house, the House Lagnö, the Creek House, and the Mirrorcube for the Tree Hotel in Harads.

Tham and Videgård teach and lecture in Sweden and abroad. From 2014 to 2015, they were invited to be guest professors at the Peter Behrens School of Architecture in Düsseldorf, Germany. Recent exhibitions include the Venice Architecture Biennale; the Louisiana Museum of Modern Art in Denmark; the Victoria & Albert Museum in London, UK; and a monographic exhibition at La Galerie d'Architecture in Paris.

The Empire
The Empire is an architecture and planning office founded in 2013 by Ludovico Centis. The office's wide-ranging activity involves design, teaching, research, and writing. The Empire's research focuses on the ways in which individuals and institutions, as well as desires and power, shape cities and landscapes.

Ludovico Centis is an architect, and co-founder and editor of the architecture magazine San Rocco. He was a partner at the architectural office Salottobuono from 2007 to 2012. He has lectured and taught in Italian and international universities such as IUAV (Venice), the Politecnico (Milan), the A.A. School of Architecture (London), Cornell University (Ithaca, NY), and Princeton University (Princeton, NJ). Centis has been the 2013 through 2014 Peter Reyner Banham Fellow at the University at Buffalo-SUNY and was a participant in the CLUI Wendover Residence Program in 2015.

The Living
The Living combines research and practice, exploring new ideas through prototyping. Focusing on the intersection of biology, computation, and design, the firm has articulated three frameworks for harnessing living organisms for architecture: bio-computing, bio-sensing, and bio-manufacturing. The Living has won many design prizes, including the Emerging Voices Award from the Architectural League, the New Practices Award from the AIA New York, the Young Architects Program Award from the Museum of Modern Art and MoMA PS1, and a Holcim Sustainability Award. Clients include the City of New York, Seoul Municipal Government, Google, Nike, 3M, Airbus, BMW, Miami Science Museum, and Björk. Recent projects include the Princeton Embodied Computation Lab (a new building for research on next-generation design and construction technologies), Pier 35 EcoPark (a 200-foot-long floating pier in the East River that changes color according to water quality), and Hy-Fi (a branching tower for MoMA PS1 made of a new type of biodegradable brick).

The LADG (Los Angeles Design Group)
Andrew Holder is an assistant professor at the Harvard Graduate School of Design and co-principal of The LADG.

Claus Benjamin Freyinger is co-principal and founding member of The LADG.

Thomas Baecker Bettina Kraus
Thomas Baecker Bettina Kraus was founded in Berlin in 2013. With a diverse team, the founding partners—Bettina Kraus and Thomas Baecker—work on both architectural and urban design issues as well as product design. Each task is approached independent of scale and instead measured according to creative, economic, ecological and socio-cultural parameters. Every project is fundamentally based on conceptual, rational, and intuitive thought processes. While navigating through the issues of functionality, context and technical feasibility of any given project, the work itself begins to develop its own formal and intellectual dimensions. A dialogue with the client then leads to the emergence of a custom-made solution with a specific spatial figure and materiality.

Toshiko Mori Architect
Toshiko Mori Architect(TMA) is known for over thirty years of innovative and influential work in a diverse body of projects that have received numerous design awards. Mori's intelligent approach to ecologically sensitive siting strategies, historical context, and innovative use of materials reflects a creative integration of design and technology. Her designs demonstrate a thoughtful sensitivity to detail and involve extensive research into the site conditions and surrounding context.

Toshiko Mori Architect has worked on a broad range of programs including urban, civic, institutional, cultural, residential, museum and exhibition design. Architectural Digest listed TMA three times amongst their biennial AD100 and the firm's artists' residency and cultural center in rural Senegal was awarded the 2017 AIA Institute Honor Award. TMA also recently completed the Center for Maine Contemporary Art, the Novartis Institutes for BioMedical Research and was selected to design the Watson Institute for International & Public Affairs at Brown University.

The firm continues to engage in an architecture of material exploration, technological invention and theoretical provocation.

UrbanLab
UrbanLab is an architecture and urban design office founded by Sarah Dunn and Martin Felsen. The office's realized projects range in scale from small houses to urban districts. UrbanLab's recent book titled Bowling speculates on ways to realign architecture and infrastructure with dwindling natural resources. The firm was awarded the American Institute of Architects College of Fellows Latrobe Prize, the History Channel's "City of the Future" competition prize, and many design awards from the American Institute of Architects. UrbanLab's work has been published and exhibited widely, including in the 2010 and the 2012 Venice Biennale and the 2015 Chicago Architecture Biennial. The office's work is in the permanent collection of the Art Institute of Chicago. Dunn is an associate professor at the University of Illinois at Chicago, and Felsen is an associate professor at the Illinois Institute of Technology.

Urbanus
Founded in 1999, under the leadership of partners Xiaodu Liu, Yan Meng and Hui Wang, Urbanus is recognized as one of the most influential architectural practices in China. Urbanus has its offices in Beijing and Shenzhen, two most complicated contemporary metropolitan laboratories in China. Many Urbanus works have become new focal points of urban life. Having been exhibited and published worldwide, Urbanus projects have received numerous prominent design awards. The partners are regularly invited to lecture at renowned universities, academic institutions, and served as jurors for international competitions. Urbanus research department (UPRD) focuses on the contemporary urban China to conduct a series of research projects including creative city development, post-urban village development, typologies for hyperdensity and historical renewal. The works of Urbanus have drawn international attention due to its sensitivity to urban historical and social structure, integration of potential resources of space and society, and effectiveness in responding to complicated urban situations.

Veronika Kellndorfer
Veronika Kellndorfer is a Berlin based artist whose work focuses on the representation of modernity through photography and installation. Her most recent solo shows examine the legacy of Lina Bo Bardi and Tropical Modernism in Brazil. These include *Casa de Vidro* at the Nasjonalmuseet Art and Architecture, Oslo, Norway; *Tropical Modernism: Lina BoBardi* at Christopher Grimes Gallery; Santa Monica; and *Cinematic Framing, Casa de Vidro*, Instituto Lina Bo Bardi, São Paulo. She has been a fellow, most recently, at the IKKM, Bauhaus University Weimar and held residencies at Villa Kamogawa, Kyoto, Villa Massimo in Rome and Villa Aurora, Los Angeles.

WELCOMEPROJECTS
WELCOMEPROJECTS is a practice of discursive sensibilities focused on the production of real things in the world along with all the incumbent, critical fictions needed for their survival. They design projects large (buildings, houses, interiors), medium (installations, films, furniture) and small (handbags, games, wagons) imbuing each with curiosity and playful seriousness. WELCOMEPROJECTS is directed by Laurel Consuelo Broughton, a designer and academic in Los Angeles.

WORKac
Amale Andraos and Dan Wood founded the architecture firm WORKac in 2003 and have achieved international recognition for projects that reinvent the relationship between urban and natural environments. They are committed to sustainability and go beyond its technical requirements by thinking more broadly about the relationship between buildings and nature. The firm is known for embracing reinvention and collaboration across disciplines. They strive to develop intelligent and shared infrastructures and a more careful integration between architecture, landscape, and ecological systems. WORKac recently completed the first two Edible Schoolyards in Brooklyn and Harlem and re-imagined the future of work for Wieden+Kennedy in Manhattan. In Libreville, Gabon, the firm is building a new 2,000 square-foot Conference Center for the African Union. WORKac recently completed a residential

conversion of a historic New York cast-iron building. They will soon complete a public library in Queens and a facade for a parking garage in Miami.

Zago Architecture
Zago Architecture brings open-ended, creative inquiry to disciplinary concerns in architecture. Noted for its prescient articulation of emerging sensibilities, the practice weds quasi-autonomous aesthetic studies to the art of making buildings and cities. In doing so, Zago Architecture reaffirms the substantial and productive link amongst art, architecture, and urbanism.

ZAO/standardarchitecture
Founded by Zhang Ke in 2001, ZAO/standardarchitecture is a leading new generation of design firm engaged in practices of planning, architecture, landscape, and product design. Based on a wide range of realized buildings and landscapes in the past ten years, the studio has emerged as the most critical and realistic practice among the youngest generation of Chinese architects and designers.

Consciously distancing themselves from many of the other "typical" young generation architects who are swallowed by a trend of noise making, the office remains detached in a time of media frenzy and their focus is consistently positioned on the realization of urban visions and ideas. Although ZAO/standardarchitecture's built works often take exceptionally provocative visual results, their buildings and landscapes are always rooted in the historic and cultural settings with a degree of intellectual debate.

This catalogue and exhibition came together in record time due to the expertise and hard work of many committed and inspired collaborators. Sarah Hearne, led our editorial efforts in Los Angeles, keeping us on schedule while always advancing the conceptual framework of the project. Letizia Garzoli was also indispensable, leading the collaborative exhibition design and production with our participants, and offering help whenever and however we needed it. Younha Kim and Juan De Robles supported the exhibition design development through each phase. And finally, we must thank all of the participants and the writers who contributed to this catalogue; their outstanding work and belief in the questions we posed as part of *Make New History* made this endeavor possible.

Every biennial requires the optimism and conviction of many dedicated individuals. We want to thank Mayor Rahm Emanuel for his steadfast vision and support for the biennial program in Chicago. Together with the mayor, the board of the Chicago Architecture Biennial have worked tirelessly to help us reach our goals and in particular we want to extend special thanks to Jack Guthman. Sarah Herda offered her wisdom and encouragement at every crucial juncture, and we are deeply grateful for her trust in us to follow in her footsteps. Executive Director Todd Palmer was a key partner for us on both the content and logistics front. Manager of Production Rachel Kaplan was the glue that kept everything together and moving forward, from concept to fabrication. At the Cultural Center, we want to thank Mark Kelly, Commissioner of the City of Chicago's Department of Cultural Affairs and Special Events and his predecessor Michelle T. Boone, who both believed in the potential of this program and offered their creativity and their professional staff to help us realize this exhibition. And to our audience, we thank you for coming. We hope you enjoy the show and the conversations that the work will inspire.

Sharon Johnston & Mark Lee
Artistic Directors
2017 Chicago Architecture Biennial

This publication accompanies the 2017 Chicago Architecture Biennial, on view from September 16, 2017, through January 7, 2018, at the Chicago Cultural Center, the Chicago Water Tower, and the Garfield Park Conservatory in Chicago.

Editors: Mark Lee, Sharon Johnston, Sarah Hearne, and Letizia Garzoli
Catalogue design: Zak Group
Copy editors: Eli Pulsinelli and Christie Hayden
Project manager: Stephanie Emerson

Distribution: Lars Müller Publishers
Zurich, Switzerland
www.lars-mueller-publishers.com

Printed in Germany

ISBN 978-3-03778-535-5